LINGUISTIC CHANGE
AND GENERATIVE THEORY

Linguistic Change and Generative Theory

Essays from the
UCLA Conference on Historical Linguistics
in the Perspective of Transformational
Theory   February 1969

Edited by
Robert P. Stockwell
University of California, Los Angeles
and
Ronald K. S. Macaulay
Pitzer College, Claremont

Indiana University Press
Bloomington and London

Published in Canada by Fitzhenry & Whiteside Limited, Don Mills,
    Ontario
Library of Congress catalog card number: 70-180483
ISBN: 0-253-33440-3
Manufactured in the United States of America

Contents

Acknowledgment

The conference from which these essays were selected for publication was sponsored and funded in its entirety out of the academic budget of the Department of Linguistics of the University of California, Los Angeles, with the approval of the Dean of the Humanities Division. The editors wish to express their appreciation to the Department and to the Administration for their support of the conference, and to the nearly one hundred participants, who contributed so much to its success. The participants were affiliated with the various branches of the University of California, in particular San Diego and Berkeley, and with the following other universities: California State College at Dominguez Hills, Columbia University, Harvard University, Indiana University, Massachusetts Institute of Technology, Ohio State University, Pitzer College, Rockefeller University, Stanford University, University of Chicago, University of Hawaii, University of Michigan, University of Texas, University of Washington.

Introduction

The papers in this volume were presented at the UCLA Conference on Historical Linguistics in the Perspective of Transformational Theory, February 1969. All but two deal with phonology. Although they are not equally concerned with linguistic change there is a common theme running through them—the need to remedy the excessive formalism in "classical generative phonology" as exemplified in Chapters 1-8 of *The Sound Pattern of English* by Noam Chomsky and Morris Halle.

The publication in 1968 of this long-awaited volume marked the end of one period in generative phonology and the beginning of another. The earlier period was characterized by a Saussurean separation of synchronic and diachronic description; in the later approach such a dichotomy has appeared increasingly impractical. Although both periods are represented in *SPE* it is the earlier approach which predominates until the last chapter. In Chapter 8 Chomsky and Halle state their basic methodological approach for the greater part of the book:

> First we develop a system of formal devices for expressing rules and a set of general conditions on how these rules are organized and how they apply. We postulate that only grammars meeting these conditions are "entertained as hypotheses" by the child who must acquire knowledge of a language. Secondly, we determine a procedure of evaluation that selects the highest valued of a set of hypotheses of the appropriate form, each of which meets a condition of compatibility with the primary linguistic data. [p. 331]

Then they add a word of caution on the idealization involved in this approach:

We have been describing acquisition of language as if it were an instantaneous process. Obviously, this is not true. A more realistic model of
language acquisition would consider the order in which primary linguistic
data are used by the child and the effects of preliminary "hypotheses" developed in the earlier stages of learning on the interpretation of new,
often more complex, data. To us it appears that this more realistic study
is much too complex to be undertaken in any meaningful way today and
that it will be far more fruitful to investigate in detail, as a first approximation, the idealized model outlined earlier, leaving refinements to a time
when this idealization is better understood. The correctness of this guess,
of course, will have to be judged by the long-range effectiveness of a research program of this sort, as compared with alternatives that might be
imagined. In the meantime, this idealization must be kept in mind when
we think about the problem of the "psychological reality" of the postulated mental structures. [p. 331]

It is clear, however, that the idealized model of language acquisition
as an instantaneous process is less likely to be "fruitful" in diachronic linguistics since it excludes many possible explanations of
linguistic change. It is therefore necessary in studying linguistic
change to investigate somewhat less idealized approaches to the
writing of grammar.

In Chapter 9 of *SPE* Chomsky and Halle acknowledge the limitations of the earlier approach:

The entire discussion of phonology in this book suffers from a fundamental
theoretical inadequacy. Although we do not know how to remedy it fully,
we feel that the outlines of a solution can be sketched, at least in part. The
problem is that our approach to features, to rules, and to evaluation has
been overly formal. [p. 400]

Their proposed solution to this excessive formalism is the system
of marking conventions and linking rules. In a sense, all the phonological papers in this volume are attempts to refine or improve on
Chapter 9 of *SPE*. In particular, they are concerned with evaluative
criteria that are not purely formal.

In quite different ways, Bach and Harms, Schane, and Labov all
present evidence of the dangers of abbreviatory conventions for
combining rules. If they are correct, then the evaluation metric cannot be a simple matter of counting symbols. Vennemann's argument that it is the *weight* of the marked features rather than the
sum of such features that should count as a measure of complexity

has similar implications. It is therefore necessary to look for other than formal criteria in evaluative procedures.

One possibility is to replace marking conventions with a hierarchy of features. Foley and Vennemann present evidence in this direction from historically attested changes and Zwicky other evidence from allegro speech. Obviously, this is something which could be explored further in experimental situations as well as in comparative studies of the development of children's phonological systems. Jakobson's pioneering work in this area is now thirty years old, so there is justification for a re-examination of his conclusions in the light of the evidence that has accumulated since then.

A second possibility is to take a closer look at the evidence from phonetics. The relationship between phonology and phonetics has always been an uneasy one, for an obvious reason: The phonetician is likely to remind the phonologist that his idealizations are leading him rather a long way from the data of real speech. Labov's use of spectrographic evidence shows how impressionistic subjective judgments of vowel height may miss the point. The use of "naturalness" as a criterion demands that our knowledge of the phonetic facts be as accurate as possible. However, it is also important that the phonetician study speech in "natural" situations as well as in the laboratory, since stylistic variation may affect the results. Zwicky's study of allegro variants, for example, needs to be followed up by the collection of evidence on the actual use of such variants. This is particularly important since the speaker's intuitions are likely to be more accurate in reporting his formal speech than is the case with his informal speech.

A third area to be explored is the range of dialect variation that can exist within one language. Bailey's implicational scales show how dialect characteristics may be grouped into internally consistent sets. However, there is great need for more accurate information on dialect variation. Too often discussion of dialect differences is based on relatively crude distinctions or on subjective impressionistic judgments. Labov's work in New York City has demonstrated the feasibility of collecting accurate and representative data. We need comparable data for other dialects of English. Only then will it be possible to consider seriously the differences between dialects that can be explained by rule ordering or by distinct underlying lexical representations. It may also be useful to investigate possible cases of unidirectional intelligibility in which the speaker of dialect A can easily understand the speaker of dialect B but not vice versa. Obviously, there are great problems in conducting empirical tests of such a situation, but the results might have important implications for a theory of naturalness.

There are no doubt many other ways in which naturalness could be investigated, but the main point to emphasize is that we need objective empirical support to supplement and correct the linguist's intuitions in this respect. In practice, this means taking a less idealized view of linguistic competence and being prepared to admit a wider range of data.

The study of natural rules and hierarchies is important if we are to understand one of the primary forces in linguistic change, namely, simplification. However, if all changes were of this kind languages would be a good deal more homogeneous than they actually are. Clearly, there are opposing forces which counteract this tendency. In Vennemann's terms, in addition to rules which decrease complexity there are rules which increase it. It is only in terms of the conflict of opposing forces that the dynamics of linguistic change can be understood. As Lakoff points out in her paper, the "drift" towards analyticity in Indo-European is paralleled by the contrary tendency in other language families. It would thus be wrong to assume that Lakoff's metacondition for "drift" in Indo-European ("segmentalize whenever possible") is a linguistic universal. However, it could belong to a set of universal metaconditions, any one of which may at a given time exert a powerful influence on linguistic change.

Bever and Langendoen claim that the conflict which produces linguistic change is "the historical competition between what makes a language easy to understand and what makes it easy to learn." While many people will be reluctant to accept Bever and Langendoen's view that a language with a greater variety of inflectional endings than modern English, especially with many irregularities, must be more difficult to learn, the possibility that such a claim could be correct is of great importance for a theory of linguistic change. We need empirical studies of "what makes a language easy to understand" as well as of "what makes a language easy to learn." Such questions will not be simple to investigate, since preconceptions of the relative complexity of linguistic structures may be quite wrong. One source of useful information will be the evidence from the order in which children learn to use certain linguistic constructions and the kind of "incorrect hypotheses" which they set up on their way to the adult norms.

We cannot conclude that the conference presented the sense of unity that the preceding summary of the problems that were faced might suggest. The participants shared a common theoretical orientation, and a common concern with the historical development of languages. At the end, many seemed to share also a sense of despair that perhaps transformational theory had less to contribute than we had imagined. But the worth of the work represented in these essays gives us reason to believe that the sense of despair was the result of sheer exhaustion after two hard days of endless discussion rather than from lack of accomplishment and promise. Lest the preceding summary give a wrong impression of unity, however, we present a brief summation of the major import of each paper, as we understand it, to enable the reader to select more readily the essays of greatest concern to his interests.

Bach and Harms's paper revolves around the attempt to find "tighter constraints on phonological systems" than were found in "classical generative phonology" (e.g., *The Sound Pattern of English*, Chapters 1-8). After illustrating how historical evidence may support the use of such abbreviatory notations as alpha-variables, they tackle the problem of the *plausibility* of phonological rules. In brief, their argument is that innovations should be "plausible rules," but that the simplification that occurs in transmission may lead to "crazy rules," i.e., rules which fail to satisfy the criterion of "plausibility":

> Thus, languages have rules which are plausible or which can be derived from plausible rules by a sequence of steps involving (among other things) simplification, but in the process rules can become highly implausible.

The most important part of this argument is that if strict "plausibility conditions" are set up for simplification then it is impossible to see how languages get "crazy rules."

Bach and Harms's point is clearly of great importance for a theory of linguistic change, since it would mean that two distinct processes are at work: innovation and simplification. This in itself is not new, but the notion that simplification can lead to "crazy rules" raises the question as to what psychological reality such rules could have. If it should turn out that "crazy rules" operate only where there is an idiosyncratic residue of certain historical changes, then it may be wrong to claim that such rules represent an essential part of any single native speaker's linguistic competence. In other words, there may be minor regularities observable in the *langue* which are unsystematically represented in the competences of native speakers. Another way of putting it is to question the validity of having underlying representations and phonological rules for processes which are no longer productive for the native speaker. The existence of "crazy rules" in the grammar may be more a reflection of the ingenuity of the linguist than of the actual linguistic system.

Bailey's paper focuses on the need for a notation to represent the fact that the native speaker can usually understand other dialects than the one he normally speaks. Bailey uses implicational scales to group together blocks of rules in which the presence or absence of one rule implies the presence or absence of certain other rules, and he shows how such blocks of rules characterize dialects and their relation to each other. Bailey is thus aiming at a "panlectal" grammar, that is, a grammar which can account for all the dialects in a language, rather than concentrating on a single dialect which is claimed to be representative of the whole language. Clearly, no theory of linguistic change can have any empirical support unless it starts from the assumption that "a language" is at least as complex as the situation Bailey describes. Moreover, since one of the possible causes of linguistic change is borrowing from another dialect, implicational scales of the kind Bailey sets up may help to explain the possibilities and direction of borrowing.

Bever and Langendoen's paper confronts the question of how a well-defined system (or at least a highly stable one), such as the syntactic rules which characterize the competence of a fluent speaker of a language, can change. The Chomsky-Halle hypothesis of change in phonology, with late rules added which bring about restructuring through simplification, has no clear analog in syntactic change: A possible analog might be the addition of conditions on a transformational rule which become so cumbersome that it causes the rule to change. But Bever and Langengoen's hypothesis is a rather different one, arising from the view that there are strategies of perception—strategies that enable the speaker/hearer to put his competence to use. Their hypothesis is that these strategies may come into conflict with the rules of the competence model in such a way as to change those rules. In particular, when some set of signals utilizable by the perceptual strategies are eliminated from the language (for any reason: e.g., the loss of Old English inflections either because the noun inflection system became cumbersome with many small and irregular classes or because purely phonetic processes were at work), new perceptual strategies must arise which take advantage of different devices in the surface structure for the reconstruction of the deep structure and semantic interpretation. These strategies are relatively intolerant of ambiguities of a certain type: what Hockett has called "garden-path" ambiguities, as in

*The secretary discouraged the man wanted to see the boss.

where, lacking an accusative marker on *man* and lacking a relative pronoun introducing the clause *(who) wanted to see the boss,* there would be hesitation in the strategy that assigns the phrase *the man* to the relationship of object of *discourage* or subject of *wanted.* Such hesitation appears not to be easily tolerable, and if there is no obvious strategy to eliminate it, then the structures from which it arises must be modified. In the development of this hypothesis, Bever and Langendoen provide a rich analysis of the history of English relative clauses, which may well provide the beginning of new and more insightful research into historical syntax. And it should perhaps not go unremarked that the "strategies" they propose bear a close family resemblance to the kinds of analysis that were called "signals grammar" in the early 1950s.

The theory of markedness, or what is natural and unnatural in phonological systems, appears repeatedly in these papers. James Foley presented the most far-reaching, and the most vulnerable, set of proposals in this direction at the conference, but in these proceedings his contribution is represented only in summary form because his presentation was frankly programmatic and not yet fully buttressed with detailed argumentation and exemplification. He believes that "historical changes . . . occur in groups definable by meta-rules." The nonphonetic distinctive features that he uses for the characterization of these changes are motivated by the same considerations that motivated notions of markedness (naturalness): Some changes simply strike us intuitively as more natural than others, and cry out for explanation. Whether one accepts, as a basis for further investigation, the particular proposals that Foley puts forward is irrelevant to the conviction that Foley is seeking "explanation" in some more basic sense than the standard works on historical change. His ideas are stimulating and controversial.

William Labov deals with the progress of a sound change through the lexicon, from the earliest stage, when the only manifestations of the sound change are in certain environments and under certain conditions, until the final stage, when the change is complete in all contexts, apart from sporadic exceptions. For the first stage Labov uses the notion of a "variable rule," which predicts the situations in which an optional rule is most likely to apply. This is an attempt to show that "free variation" is not a random process but is subject to certain constraints, which can be expressed in the formal notation of a variable rule. In his accounts of the centralization of /ay/ and /aw/ on Martha's Vineyard and the raising of "short a" in New York City, Labov is able to illustrate how the constraints on the rule are gradually removed until the original variable rule finally becomes a categorical rule. However, perhaps the most important part of Labov's paper is his account of the raising of "short a" before front nasals. Among older speakers the nasal environment inhibits raising, whereas for younger speakers the presence of a following nasal accelerates the raising. Labov shows how an alpha-switching rule can reflect this change but he claims that such a notation distorts the nature of the sound change by representing it as a discrete change instead of the continuous movement in one direction, as the spectrographic evidence seems to indicate.

Labov is thus arguing against the use of complex schema for combining separate rules if this is done solely on the grounds that "the same" processes are at work:

> But the structural economy thus achieved is not all gain. The parallels
> are not exact in most cases, and in such gross rule schema we find more

and more vagueness as to detail, which moves us farther and farther away
from the articulatory, acoustic, and distributional facts in which explanation may lie. The paradox is that the deeper we exercise our talent for
linguistically significant generalization, the more we lose the formal detail
on which linguistic generalizations are based.

Labov is thus also arguing against "unnatural" or "crazy" rules and
illustrating the kind of empirical evidence that may help to identify
such rules. It is important to realize, however, that Labov is not
claiming that there are no discrete sound changes, but in this particular case the data suggest that it would be a mistake to represent
the change as discrete in spite of the fact that it is possible to describe the situation by means of an alpha-switching rule.

Robin Lakoff's paper considers a number of syntactic and morphological changes which have occurred widely and repeatedly in
Indo-European languages as manifestations of a single general principle of change: "If there is a choice between a rule and a lexical
item to produce a surface structure containing independent segments, as opposed to one containing morphologically bound forms,
pick the former." She takes this as a metacondition on change, perhaps not expressible formally, but nonetheless influential within a
specifiable range of languages in a specifiable period of time. The
challenge of her paper is to find a way to represent such a condition,
if it is real. And if it is not real, then, as she says, "all the Indo-
European languages have been subject to an overwhelming series
of coincidences." Her paper is thus part of the trend in linguistics
today to seek out and confirm the broadest and deepest kinds of
universals, universals which clearly exist and for which we have no
satisfactory explanations yet.

Sanford Schane is concerned not so much with "crazy rules" as
with "unnatural rules," e.g., the nasalization of final vowels in a
dialect of German. He shows that in this particular situation an apparently unnatural rule may be the result of a sequence of natural
rules, in the example cited the nasalization being caused by a final
nasal consonant which is subsequently deleted. The question Schane
then raises is how we can categorize "natural rules." He gives three
examples of general processes or categories of natural rules: assimilation, preferred syllable structure, and maximum differentiation.
As Schane points out, it is not enough to state that such processes

are at work; it is also necessary to have a precise statement of the conditions under which these processes can take place. Schane conjectures that assimilative processes may be largely due to the physiological properties of the articulatory mechanism, whereas dissimilation is more likely to be a consequence of perceptual strategies, i.e., psychological in origin. He also suggests that linguistic change may come about through conflict between the naturalness condition on segments in lexical representations and the uniqueness criterion which requires a single underlying representation for each lexical morpheme. His argument runs as follows: Because natural phonological rules guarantee that derived structures will conform to naturalness conditions, they may have the effect of violating the uniqueness condition on morphemes. Perceptual strategies may then cause restructuring of the underlying representation in order to restore the uniqueness condition. Although Schane's remarks on linguistic change are put forward tentatively, they draw attention to a problem generally ignored by the other participants at the conference, namely the motivation for a particular underlying representation and the effects of a change in such a representation. Finally, Schane goes on to suggest an evaluation metric in which the metatheory favors natural rules because they apply generally whereas less natural rules require restrictions placed on them. His conclusion: "Natural rules, which are context-free rules, are universal; unnatural rules, which are context-sensitive rules, are language-specific."

Theo Vennemann's paper proposes and elaborates extensive revisions in the theory of markedness, and its relevance to historical sound change. He argues that previous work has underestimated the possibilities inherent in the markedness notation, and develops a theory of marking in which there are two levels of representation, "a descriptive level, on which features are specified for what they are materially, independent of the context in which they occur, and an interpretative level, on which such material specifications are characterized as more or less predictable (more or less natural) in their . . . contexts." Within this framework he explains "a number of . . . apparently unrelated consonant changes as consequences of a single change" of a type that increases the complexity of all affected segments. The paper presents a wealth of detailed evidence for this view and appears to represent a substantive and permanent enrichment of the Chomsky-Halle markedness conventions (Chapter 9 of *SPE*).

Arnold Zwicky, rather than dealing directly with some aspect of historical change as most of the other authors do, is concerned with "some aspects of English phonology which supply evidence about the content of grammatical theory and thus, derivatively, about linguistic change." In particular, he is concerned with the view that there are hierarchies among the segments of phonological systems, that one such hierarchy is the sequence "vowels, glides, [r], [l], [n], [m], [ŋ], fricatives, stops," and that evidence for such a hierarchy is to be found in the variants that are produced by the rules of allegro speech. He presents evidence concerning the nature and functioning of such rules as a prolegomenon to work in historical linguistics that remains to be done.

May 1970   Robert P. Stockwell
                                University of California, Los Angeles

                                Ronald K. S. Macaulay
                                Pitzer College, Claremont

1.

How Do Languages Get Crazy Rules?

Emmon Bach and Robert T. Harms,
University of Texas

It has been proposed that one of the major internal forces in linguistic change is rule simplification (Bach 1968, Harms 1966, Kiparsky 1965, 1968). This hypothesis is a corollary to the more general hypothesis that the language learner acquires his language by constructing the simplest grammar compatible with the data presented him. If the data were equally complete for every learner and if grammar construction were completely determinate, the language would never change (assuming no external influences). But the data made available to the learner or noticed by him is, as we all know, highly fragmentary and skewed. Hence, other things being equal, the new grammar will be simpler (more general) than the original grammar. Since one way in which one grammar may be simpler than another is in the form of a particular rule, we would expect rule simplification to occur with more than random frequency. Of course other things never are equal and many other forces impinge on the development of a language.

Two kinds of empirical support could be sought for such conjectures. On the one hand, we can look to studies of language acquisition, and we could even devise simple experiments to test the hypothesis. Let us teach a group of children an invented language, which contains the rule "make vowels lax before /p/ and /t/ but not before /k/" (where these are the only voiceless stops in the language). Now let us systematically exclude from the sentences

taught the children all items containing postvocalic /k/. Our prediction will be that the children's language will contain the rule
"make vowels lax before voiceless stops."

Second, we can look to historical change to see if, in fact, rule
simplifications have taken place. If we find many examples of
simplification and no examples of complication, then our hypothesis is confirmed. We can also make predictions about the direction
of spread for adjacent dialects that show differences in the form of
a rule. Suppose that Dialect A has a rule R, and Dialect B a rule
R', which is in the obvious sense a counterpart to R but not as
simple. The hypothesis about simplification implies that the rule
was transmitted (if it was transmitted at all and not independently
developed) from Dialect B to Dialect A. This then is a factual consequence of the hypothesis and we can look for independent evidence to see if it is correct. We can actually observe the process of
rule transmission (see various results reported by Labov, e.g., 1965),
and it behooves us to examine afresh the evidence about the chronology and geographical diffusion of well-known changes like the
High German consonant shift.

Notions like simplification are not, as we are periodically re-
minded, given to us somehow in advance of linguistic investigation.
The evaluation metric with its associated set of notational conventions represents a hypothesis about language, subject to falsi-
fication or confirmation. Moreover, as Paul Kiparsky 1968 has
neatly demonstrated, the study of linguistic change provides an
important testing ground for hypotheses about the nature of grammars. Let us consider a new example of the way in which infer-
ences about linguistic theory can be drawn from historical change.

The logic of the argument is as follows: We are interested in a
notational convention made available by a particular formulation
of the evaluation metric. We need to know whether the convention
represents linguistically significant generalizations, such as are incorporated into a real grammar in someone's head. We find a particular historical change where at Stage II a rule exists which is related to a rule at Stage I in exactly the way expressed by the
convention in question. On the assumption that language change
proceeds by simplification of rules, that is, by incorporating linguistically significant generalizations, we conclude that the hypoth-

esis is confirmed in some small measure. We find a further confirmation of the linguistic reality of the convention in the occurrence of a later change in which exactly the rule schema in question is lost.

We choose for an example the Greek letter variable convention for abbreviating pairs of rules related in the well-known way (in this instance for expressing agreement in feature specifications). The reason for our choice is that it is this convention which will figure crucially in our later argument about the role of phonetic plausibility in sound change. (Part of the following is alluded to briefly in Bach 1968.) The facts involved are summarized as follows. In the history of German a rather remarkable sequence of changes occurred:

$$\text{I. } a > e \ / \ \_i$$
$$\text{II. } a > o \ / \ \_u$$
$$\text{III. } \begin{aligned} e &> a \ / \ \_i \\ o &> a \ / \ \_u \end{aligned}$$

The explanation of these parallel changes in the German diphthongs, where a sound change was precisely reversed, provides a particularly striking confirmation of the view of historical change as change in grammars (and in particular, grammars provided by a specific set of assumptions made in generative phonology).

In the eighth century in Old High German a rule was added which changed *ai* into *ei*. The following evidence justifies the claim that the rule remained part of the synchronic grammar of Old High German and was not just a change in underlying representation. In Ablaut classes II–V the form of the first and third singular preterit indicative shows a replacement of the nuclear vowel of the stem (a front vowel) by *a*. Thus we have

	Base form	Pret. sg. 1/3 ind.
II.	fleug-	flaug
III.	rinn-	ran
	werf-	warf
IV.	stel-	stal
V.	geb-	gab

In Class I we have (after the change of *ai* to *ei*)

rīt-   reit

We posit an underlying representation for *rīt-* as *reit-*. There is independent support for this representation in the other forms, where the underlying nuclear vowel *e* is deleted to give *ritum* like *flugum* (from *fleug-*). The independence of the rule changing *ai* to *ei* (as against an addition to the rule giving the preterit singular form) is shown by the fact that we would need such a rule anyway at some level to account for the fact that after the change we have *ei* in all cases. That is, the rule applies not only to diphthongs derived by the Ablaut rule but to underlying diphthongs as well. Thus we posit

$$\text{Rule O'}: \begin{bmatrix} V \\ +\text{low} \end{bmatrix} \rightarrow \begin{bmatrix} -\text{back} \\ -\text{low} \end{bmatrix} / - \begin{bmatrix} +\text{high} \\ -\text{back} \\ -\text{cons} \end{bmatrix}$$

Slightly later (toward the end of the eighth century, completed by about 850) we find that forms like the preterit of *fleogan* assume the form *floug* (and again all *au* become *ou*). Evidently the rule has been extended in just the way expressed by changing the specification [-back] to [α back]:

$$\text{Rule O}: \begin{bmatrix} V \\ +\text{low} \end{bmatrix} \rightarrow \begin{bmatrix} \alpha\ \text{back} \\ -\text{low} \end{bmatrix} / - \begin{bmatrix} +\text{high} \\ \alpha\ \text{back} \\ -\text{cons} \end{bmatrix}$$

Language history is full of examples of this kind of generalization (for the OHG facts see the relevant sections of Braune/Mitzka 1963). Thus we have rather strong historical support for the hypothesis that the alpha notation expresses linguistically significant generalizations.

Rule O remains operative throughout the MHG period. But, as we have noted, in the period between then and the modern language the diphthongs revert to their original form. Thus, just as with the laxing rule of English, which was used by Kiparsky 1968 as support for the brace notation, we find strong confirmation of the linguistic (i.e., psychological) reality of the rule schema incorporating the abbreviatory convention in question. Without the alpha notation we would have two completely disconnected changes happening twice in the history of the language. Without the notion of linguistic change as rule addition, simplification, and loss we would have no explanation for the initial change and the reversion of the forms to their original form. Incidentally, this sequence of changes is an especially bad case for versions of autonomous phonemics with an invariance condition. Throughout the period in question there are *o* and *e* phonemes to which the first members of the diphthongs *ou* and *ei* must be assigned. If sound change must be stated in terms of autonomous phonemes, then we have two mysterious facts to explain: first, a very unnatural shift (lowering and centralizing of both *o* and *e* before high vowels); second, the fact that this implausible shift is an exact reversal of a change that the language has just undergone.

So far we have done nothing more than consider a paradigm case for the role of simplification as generalization in sound change, and we have illustrated the way in which historical evidence can be brought to bear on questions of synchronic theory. Such arguments are cogent to the extent that we can place them in the context of relatively specific hypotheses about theoretical constructs like "rule," "evaluation metric," "alpha-variable," and the like. This discussion as well as those referred to above have been carried out largely under the assumptions of what might be called classical generative phonology (as represented in Chapters 1-8 of Chomsky and Halle 1968). A number of linguists have begun to emphasize the serious limitations in this account of phonological theory. The main criticism has been directed at the lack of substantive assumptions about the content of rules, the particular generalizations that are available for the human (as opposed to the dolphin) communicator and so on. Under the headings of "markedness," "naturalness," or "archetypal rules" linguists have begun to search for tighter constraints on phonological systems and rules.[1] Such discussions frequently take the following form: Linguistic theory should define a class of possible grammars. Under Theory X it is possible to construct a grammar with such and such a rule. We agree that the rule is inadmissible. Therefore Theory X is wrong.[2] Or as a variation: Theory Y does not distinguish between two rules in terms of cost, naturalness, expectedness, and the like. We agree that there is a difference which should somehow be reflected in the evaluation measure (to be tested in the usual highly indirect way). Therefore, Theory Y is inadequate.

We can illustrate this point by looking again at the OHG rules O′ and O. Given only the formal measure available in classical theory, Rule Z would be an equiprobable simplification:

$$\text{Rule Z:} \begin{bmatrix} V \\ +\text{low} \end{bmatrix} \rightarrow \begin{bmatrix} \alpha\ \text{back} \\ -\text{low} \end{bmatrix} \Bigg/ - \begin{bmatrix} +\text{high} \\ -\text{back} \\ \alpha\ \text{cons} \end{bmatrix}$$

that is, $a > e$ before i, and $a > o$ before palatals, palatalized dentals, and labial consonants.

In order to preserve neutrality toward specific revisions we refer to these various attempts to remedy such defects in phonological theory as attempts to come to terms with the requirement of phonological *plausibility* (whether in underlying systems or in rules—we shall be concerned mainly with the latter). We are fully in agreement with the intent of such revisions. In the rest of this paper, however, we shall argue against one particular way in which some linguists have suggested bringing plausibility considerations into linguistic theory.

What we are concerned with is the suggestion that plausibility constraints should be reflected directly in the evaluation metric.[3] Our argument is based on the fact that such an attempt runs into insuperable difficulties when we try to understand historical changes of the sort just considered. Further, we shall suggest that plausibility and simplicity play quite different roles in language change, the former bearing largely on innovation, the latter on transmission. The central fact that needs to be explained is that although some rather strong plausibility conditions seem to play a crucial part in determining what rules a language can initiate, these same conditions do not seem to bear any relation to changes that take place in rules.

Thus, languages have rules which are plausible or which can be derived from plausible rules by a sequence of steps involving (among other things) simplification, but in the process rules can become highly implausible. In short, languages have crazy rules. This fact is inexplicable if simplification is constrained too much by plausibility conditions.

First we would like to establish that we are not just setting up a straw opponent. Unfortunately, although there is a great deal in the air and even some in print about the general considerations we have just sketched, there is relatively little in the way of specific proposals toward the position we are attacking. At the very least, then, we can hope to raise some questions and perhaps make some negative suggestions about future work.

We can, however, cite a few examples. In Chapter 9 of *The Sound Pattern of English*, Chomsky and Halle introduce the notion of linking. Two mechanisms for blocking the application of linking rules are also suggested, both connected with questions of rule simplification.

Suppose a language has a rule fronting high vowels in some environment. According to linking theory the result will be an unrounded front vowel unless the rule is complicated by a specification for rounding. Thus the phonological rule P will change *u* to *i* by linking:

$$\text{Rule P:} \quad [+\text{high}] \rightarrow [-\text{back}]$$

In order to preserve rounding for vowels like *ü*, which might result from such a rule, it will be necessary to complicate the rule:

$$\text{Rule P}': \begin{bmatrix} +\text{high} \\ +\text{round} \end{bmatrix} \rightarrow \begin{bmatrix} -\text{back} \\ +\text{round} \end{bmatrix}$$

At first blush, this seems to be an attractive idea. We can now interpret certain sound changes as simplifications of rules like P'. So, for instance, Ancient Greek *υ* is usually interpreted as a front rounded vowel. This vowel later becomes unrounded to *ι*. Obviously, this is exactly the change from P' to P.[4]

On second thought, however, certain embarrassments arise. Note first that in order to overcome a certain technical defect in the proposal of Chomsky and Halle for blocking linkage we have had to introduce a specification of the nonoptimal feature "+round" in both the structural change and structural analysis parts of the rule. A rule like (56) in Chomsky and Halle 1968: 433:

$$[+\text{high}] \rightarrow \begin{bmatrix} -\text{back} \\ +\text{round} \end{bmatrix} \text{ / in certain contexts}$$

will have the unwanted effect of changing not only the *u* to *ü*, as desired, but also *i* to *ü*, unless we add [+round] to the structural analysis, as we have done. But now we have a unique kind of rule in phonological theory, namely, one in which we are forced to mention a feature specification which is unchanged by the rule in both the analysis and the change parts.[5] What is particularly objectionable is that the notation suggests that such a rule has exactly the same status with respect to a simplicity metric as a rule like the following:

$$\text{Rule Q:} \begin{bmatrix} +\text{high} \\ +\text{round} \end{bmatrix} \rightarrow \begin{bmatrix} -\text{back} \\ -\text{tense} \end{bmatrix}$$

that is, *u, ū > ü,* whereby two features select the natural class [u ū] and two features are altered by application of the rule.

A second, somewhat weaker, argument against the proposed blocking device and the concomitant idea that ordinary simplification of such a rule leads to changes like the one in Modern Greek is that three possible changes could actually take place with respect to a rule like P'. Besides P we could also have had P″

$$\text{Rule P″:} \ [+\text{high}] \rightarrow \begin{bmatrix} -\text{back} \\ +\text{round} \end{bmatrix}$$

Now P″ suggests a highly unlikely development (we know of no language that has only *ü* in the high vowel range, and we know of no cases of such a change even when some other vowels come to fill the *i* and *u* places by other rules). (A rule P‴ produced by deletion of "+round" in the change would automatically merge with P.) There could be even wilder results from P', say a rule fronting all rounded vowels, or rounding all high vowels, but these are troubles shared by all accounts of simplification, as with Rule Z above. The basic trouble here is that the format of Rule P' suggests that it differs from Rule P by two independent properties, whereas all of us would probably agree that it really differs in only one—its behavior with respect to linking or some similar device for specifying values of features connected to the new specifications in the rule.

Third, the proposed explanation of the change from P' to P by simplification and linking provides no way to account for the fact that in every case that we know of, rules such as P are not automatically accompanied by the further shift of [ü] to [i] suggested by linking. Where we have documentary evidence we find that this further shift occurs later, and rather significantly, it generally occurs by context-free rule; for example, Greek, Estonian, and Swiss German and Yiddish dialects (in Estonian only the first /ü/ of the stem is excepted). To take another example, the [r] which develops from /z/ by rhotacism in Germanic is distinguished in Runic Norse from original /r/. Thus, the moving force behind such changes seems to be a tendency to decrease the markedness of lexical items rather than a tendency toward natural rules. Note that the interpretation of later shifts like $ü > i$ as the result of rule addition as opposed to a linking convention leads to testable predictions. By linking theory we should expect a development such as rule (a) u → ü to rule (b) u → i to result in a differentiation of rule-derived segments and underlying representations: If a language has an [ü] from an underlying /ü/ and an [ü] derived by a rule like an Umlaut rule, then the change from a system with rule (a) to one with rule (b) will result in a split of the relevant segments into [ü] (from lexical /ü/) and [i] (from /u/ via rule (b)). The fact that we have no instances of this split is strong evidence against the linking explanation.

By linking we should also expect the unrounding of front vowels, say *ü ö* to *i e,* to occur as a single historical process. Yet, even in the case of English fronting, the only case cited in support of unrounding by linking (see below), the shift [ö] > [e] was historically prior to [ü] > [i].

We encounter similar difficulties in the all-or-none condition posited by Chomsky and Halle 1968:43 as a second hypothesis about blocking of linking: "A linking rule applies either to all or to none of the segments formed by a given rule." We have here a rather different connection between the evaluation metric and marking theory. In the cases just considered rule simplification leads to linking and the creation of less highly marked segments. But by the all-or-none principle rule simplification is supposed to lead to blocking and the creation of more highly marked segments. This result in itself might lead us to suspect that the attempt to incorporate notions of rule plausibility directly into the evaluation metric is misconceived. But we can cite direct evidence against the all-or-none principle.

From the all-or-none principle and the simplification hypothesis we can derive the prediction that generalization of a rule from segments that are linked by a particular convention to segments that are not will lead to a rather drastic change. Suppose for instance that there is a rule which spirantizes p or t (or both). By linking we will get f and s. If the rule is extended to include k, linking will be blocked and the results will now be ϕ, θ, and x, that is $f, s > \phi, \theta$. Note further that if the generalization is in the opposite direction, we must predict that the marked labial and dental spirants will be the direct result and that f and s will only arise by later addition of rules. The High German Sound Shift is a typical example of a rule that was spread by generalization. Needless to say there is not a shred of evidence that either of these results took place.

As a matter of fact the HG sound shift provides some particularly telling evidence against the attempt to use linking to explain changes from marked to unmarked segments. At the beginning of the OHG period the shifted segments remain distinct not only from the results of the Germanic sound shift but also from the inherited /s/ of Indo-European. That is, we have the voiceless obstruents: /p^f t^s k $f_1 \theta$ h f_2 s_2 x s_1/ (for Franconian dialects, no particular claims about underlying forms or assignment to phonemes is implied). Of these /$f_1 \theta$ h/ and /$f_2 s_2$ x/ result from the first and second sound shifts, respectively. There is quite firm evidence for the distinctness of these segments. Ultimately in German we get a system in which some of these distinctions are wiped out. In particular, /$f_1 f_2$/, /$s_1 s_2$/, /h x/ merge in varying ways, respectively, and /θ/ disappears completely. If we had records for only the first and last stages of this development we would probably consider it to be a particularly clear instance of the way in which linking operates to reduce the number of highly marked segments. But although the development as a whole is strong evidence that historical change tends toward this goal, we can show by direct documentary evidence that in case after case linking plays not the slightest role. For instance, /θ/ disappears as a result of merger with /d/, and we can follow the course of this merger as a generalization of a conditioned sound change (i.e., rule addition). The merger of /$s_1 s_2$/ is the result not of a change in the segment produced by a rule but a change in the underlying IE /s_1/. Transcriptions of Slavic materials in Bavaria show that the IE /s_1/ was in the [š] range, while the shifted segment was [s]. Obviously, if change of a rule to incorporate linking is to be invoked to explain a change from marked to less marked segments, it must be the segments resulting from the rule that change and not, as here, the underlying segments.[6]

The only real evidence given in any detail by Chomsky and Halle to support the all-or-none principle is the difference between English fronting and German Umlaut. Since the English fronting rule does not affect the low vowels, while the German Umlaut rule does, the linking convention for rounding operates in the first but not the second case. Hence, we have English alternations like *mouse/mice*, but German ones like *Hut/Hüte*. But this "explanation" is only possible if we are willing to swallow a completely unsupported assumption about German Umlaut. As noted (in Chomsky and Halle 1968:433, fn. 19) the result of the Umlaut rule in German for /a/ is not a low front vowel, but /e/. The simplest formulation of the facts is to incorporate the specification [-low] in the structural change of the German rule. But now the all-or-none principle should affect the fronted vowels in exactly the same way in German as in English. There are many German dialects in which the results of the Umlaut rule are front unrounded vowels, but there is absolutely no connection between this fact and the treatment of low vowels. Note further that in Old English (when the Umlaut rule affected all vowels just as in German, but retained a low front long /æ/) the derounding of the front vowels was already in operation. The all-or-none principle has no more explanatory force for this example than for the facts of the HG Sound Shift.

In fact, a moderate sampling of changes in various languages which might bear on the correctness of the principle leads to the conclusion that whatever might have been explained by the principle must be explained in some other way. Note that in each case where the principle fails we are forced either to posit extra rules or to complicate the rule in question. It would seem that the burden of justification for such rules or complications must fall on those who want to maintain the principle that necessitates them.

In the Japanese dialect of Nagoya /oi/ and /ui/ go to [ö] and [ü], respectively (Wenck 1954:154). Since the low vowel is not affected we should expect linking to produce unrounded vowels. In Spanish, voiced stops are spirantized after vowels. Since the rule affects all three stops, the principle correctly predicts that bilabial and interdental spirants will remain as such. In Amharic, there is a similar rule which affects only /b/ (as in *Addis Ababa*); the result is not [v] but a bilabial spirant. In both the first and second Sound Shifts of German /p/ goes to /f/ against the prediction. In Japanese, initial /p/ goes to a bilabial spirant, again against the prediction.

Let us reiterate that we are not arguing against marking theory as such, or the general intent of putting more substance into phonological theory. What we are arguing against is the particular way in which linking theory has been used to build plausibility directly into the evaluation metric.[7]

We have shown that the mechanisms of linking and its associated blocking devices lead to great difficulties when we try to understand historical change. Aside from the arguments against the particular devices discussed, however, we can make a more general argument against all such attempts. If simplification is the major force in internal language change, and if plausibility enters directly into the evaluation metric, then rules should in general tend to become more plausible. But rule change does not seem to lead to more plausible rules; therefore we must conclude that one of the premises is false. Since there seems to be a lot of evidence in favor of the first premise, there must be something drastically wrong with the second. Let us now examine two cases which support this reasoning. In each case we exhibit a relatively implausible rule claimed to exist in a language, and then seek an explanation for its presence as a result of rule simplification which goes its way, blind to plausibility constraints.

Basic to the argument, of course, is the assumption that the rules in question are present in the languages. It will not do to argue that the rules are incorrect because they are implausible. If we allow ourselves to construct an ad hoc sequence of plausible rules with appropriate changes in underlying forms just to avoid apparently unnatural rules, we will completely trivialize any hypothesis about plausibility constraints in phonology. Moreover, in the two situations we shall consider, it appears that we could construct such ad hoc plausible rules only at the cost of introducing other unmotivated and just as unnatural rules. To take a simple hypothetical example, suppose we find a language in which underlying /tu/ and /ti/ are realized phonetically as [č256u] and [ti], respectively—clearly an unexpected and implausible result. A much more plausible rule would be one taking /t/ to [č] before /i/. But we can only do this by positing an interchange between /i/ and /u/. Now, the worst case will be one in which we have some independent motivation for the original assignments of the phones to underlying vowels, say paradigms like the following:

Form a	Form b
aku	aki
apu	api
aču	ati

In this instance, we will have to posit a rule interchanging /i/ and /u/ exactly after /t/, and then change just these vowels back to their underlying forms in just the context where they have done their well-behaved phonological job. At best there will be no evidence for the underlying character of the vowels, and we will have to have an implausible context-free interchange of vowels.[8]

There is a well-known alternation in Japanese between dental stops, affricates, and spirants. The synchronic evidence for the phonological rules is very good, having to do with quite regular paradigmatic changes in verbs, and a widespread voicing of initial segments in compounds. We can illustrate by citing possible syllable types (letting *a* represent not only itself but the other non-high vowels *e* and *o* as well):

ta	či	cu
da	ǰi	
sa	ši	su
za		zu

Note the neutralization of the voiced obstruents /z/ and /d/. We can formulate a rule to account for these phonetic results as follows:

$$\text{Rule J:} \begin{bmatrix} -\text{sonorant} \\ +\text{coronal} \\ <+\text{voice}> \end{bmatrix} \rightarrow \begin{bmatrix} +\text{delrel} \\ +\text{strident} \\ \alpha \text{ anterior} \\ <\alpha \text{ continuant}> \end{bmatrix} / - \begin{bmatrix} V \\ +\text{high} \\ \alpha \text{ back} \end{bmatrix}$$

Under any feature system that we can think of the rule exhibits interconnections that do not seem to have any particular phonetic or phonological plausibility. The appearance of /t d s/ as [č ǰ š] before /i/ is a result that can be matched by rules in many languages. But the affrication of /t/ before /u/ is not. A change of [dᶻ] to [z] seems quite plausible (and can again be matched in many languages), but a change of [ž] to [ǰ] does not. Finally, the neutralization of the voiced segments in favor of an affricate before /i/ but a continuant before /u/ seems highly haphazard.

We suggest that this rule is to be explained as a series of simplifications and amalgamations of more plausible rules. Assume that some dialect adds a quite plausible rule palatalizing the dentals before /i/:

$$\text{Rule J1:} \begin{bmatrix} -\text{sonorant} \\ +\text{coronal} \end{bmatrix} \rightarrow \begin{bmatrix} +\text{delrel} \\ +\text{strident} \\ -\text{anterior} \end{bmatrix} / - \begin{bmatrix} V \\ +\text{high} \\ -\text{back} \end{bmatrix}$$

Now suppose that the rule was generalized in some dialects by alpha-generalization over anterior and back:

$$\text{Rule J2:} \begin{bmatrix} -\text{sonorant} \\ +\text{coronal} \end{bmatrix} \rightarrow \begin{bmatrix} +\text{delrel} \\ +\text{strident} \\ \alpha \text{ anterior} \end{bmatrix} / - \begin{bmatrix} V \\ +\text{high} \\ \alpha \text{ back} \end{bmatrix}$$

We would now have the alternations that would occur if we filled in the missing members of the table above:

ta	či	cu
da	ǰi	dᶻu
sa	ši	su
za	ži	zu

This is the state of affairs that appears to have existed in the seventeenth century and which is fixed in the *kana*-orthography (on this whole question, see Wenck 1959: 351-78). It is also the situation in the present-day Tosa dialect (Wenck 1954: 170). (Note that there are also dialects that apparently generalized J1 in a different way, by deletion of "+high," thus palatalizing before all front vowels.[9])

Now all that we need to explain is the neutralization of the voiced segments in the peculiar way noted. Once again we can posit the addition of a very plausible rule in some dialects, taking [dᶻ] to [z]:

$$\text{Rule J3:} \begin{bmatrix} -\text{sonorant} \\ +\text{strident} \\ +\text{voice} \\ +\text{anterior} \end{bmatrix} \rightarrow [+\text{continuant}]$$

We suppose that this rule was also generalized:

$$\text{Rule J4:} \begin{bmatrix} -\text{sonorant} \\ +\text{strident} \\ +\text{voice} \\ \alpha \text{ anterior} \end{bmatrix} \rightarrow [\alpha \text{ continuant}]$$

This gives exactly the change needed: [ǰ] and [z] collapse to [ǰ];
[dᶻ] and [z] to [z]. Now we have two rules dealing in large part
with the same sets of features and involved in related paradigms:

mata-	mači-	macu
hanasa-	hanaši	hanasu
cuyo ~	zuyo	
šima ~	ǰima	

They must all be collapsed into the unholy Rule J.

Note that the hypothesis about linking provides no way to get
beyond the first rule, which would presumably be something like
this:

$$\text{Rule F:} \begin{bmatrix} -\text{sonorant} \\ +\text{coronal} \end{bmatrix} \rightarrow [+\text{high}] \ / \ - \begin{bmatrix} V \\ +\text{high} \\ -\text{back} \end{bmatrix}$$

Various linking conventions would then have the same effect as our
Rule J. But now there is no way to proceed to explain the affrication of dentals before high back vowels. (Note that deletion of
"–back" would lead to [č] here as well.) This example illustrates
the major defect of the linking proposals. It makes no sense to talk
about the generalization of a linking convention. The germ of truth
contained in linking theory must be captured by a theory about
changes in *rules*. Only if we actually end up with a rule like J1 can
we use the explanatory power of rule simplification to account for
the changes posited above.

The objection will no doubt be raised that Rule J is an artifact,
that we have illegitimately lumped together into one schema three

disparate rules, say Palatalization (ti > či), Affrication (tu > cu), and Neutralization of Voiced Stridents. There are three answers to this objection. The first is that such a solution would fail to capture the generalization that the three rules affect the same natural class of obstruents. The second is that splitting the rule in three fails to account for the fact that the distribution of the rules in Japanese dialects is not independent (the last rule, of course, depends on the other two). There are dialects with Palatalization, and dialects with both Palatalization and Affrication, but as far as we know none with just Affrication (*ti > ci) (Wenck 1954: 139-77) except as a result of the special development noted below. The third answer is that no dialect shows a separation of the putative rules by some other rule, and in the two cases we found that involve apparent reordering, the reordering takes place around all three. On Hachijō-jima (Wenck 1954: 152), initial /r/ becomes [d] and the resulting segment undergoes all the results of Rule J. We must assume that the rule was either introduced directly before Rule J or reordered. Many Japanese dialects have low-level rules which tend to minimize the difference between /i/ and /u/ (normally only weakly rounded) after spirants and affricates, including the spirant allophones of h from underlying /p/. In some, the rule has apparently been reinterpreted as a rule backing /i/ after dentals and reordered before Rule J, so that we have a complete collapse of syllables with stridents followed by high vowels (in favor of the forms found in other dialects before /u/: [cï, sï, žï]).

The Russian Oboyan dialect is known for its strange rule which dissimilates pretonic nonhigh vowels after palatalized consonants: They become [i] if the following stressed vowel is low, and [a] if the stressed vowel is not low (discussed in Harms 1968):

$$\text{Rule R: } \begin{bmatrix} V \\ -\text{high} \end{bmatrix} \rightarrow \begin{bmatrix} \alpha \text{ high} \\ -\alpha \text{ low} \\ -\alpha \text{ back} \end{bmatrix} / C' \underline{\quad} C_0 \begin{bmatrix} V \\ +\text{stress} \\ \alpha \text{ low} \end{bmatrix}$$

Thus, at the stage in a derivation at which Rule R applies the following changes take place:

$$[e \ \epsilon \ o \ \mathfrak{o} \ a] \rightarrow \begin{cases} i \text{ when } [\epsilon \ \mathfrak{o} \ a] \text{ follow} \\ a \text{ when some other vowel follows} \end{cases}$$

A partial explanation for this unlikely set of changes is suggested by the subrule expansions of R:

$$
\text{R-a} \begin{bmatrix} V \\ -\text{high} \end{bmatrix} \rightarrow \begin{bmatrix} +\text{high} \\ -\text{low} \\ -\text{back} \end{bmatrix} / C' \underline{\quad} C_0 \begin{bmatrix} V \\ +\text{stress} \\ +\text{low} \end{bmatrix}
$$

$$
\text{R-b} \begin{bmatrix} V \\ -\text{high} \end{bmatrix} \rightarrow \begin{bmatrix} -\text{high} \\ +\text{low} \\ +\text{back} \end{bmatrix} / C' \underline{\quad} C_0 \begin{bmatrix} V \\ +\text{stress} \\ -\text{low} \end{bmatrix}
$$

Expansion a is considerably more reasonable than expansion b. In fact, expansion b can be explained as an alpha-variable extension of an earlier rule equal to R-a.

Yet, even taking R-a as the source for rule R is not entirely satisfactory. It is perfectly natural for an unstressed vowel to become [i] following a palatalized consonant, but it is difficult to understand that this happens only when the following vowel is low.

The history of two of the above Oboyan low vowels shows that they were originally high lax vowels, corresponding to IE */i u/, and deeper synchronic analysis shows that even in the modern Russian dialects they are best treated as underlying high vowels (cf. Lightner 1965). In so-called strong position they become low; in weak positions they are lost (e.g., Rus. [rɔt] < /rutu/ "mouth," [rta] < /ruta/ "mouth (gen.)"). If we now restate rule R-a in terms of [ɛ ɔ] as underlying high vowels and consider the rule not to apply before [a], the "low stressed vowel" of the environment is now replaced by "high lax stressed vowel," and the result is a significant shift in the direction of greater plausibility. The rule now becomes an instance of phonetically motivated assimilation: (a) nonbackness is determined by the preceding consonant and (b) highness is determined by the position between palatalized consonant and high vowel. After the shift of /i u/ to low vowels the transfer of this rule could also be based on the alternation before stressed [ɛ ɔ], and the most general phonetically based rule would specify the environment as "low stressed vowel," thus pulling in [a] as well. Once the environment is generalized to include [a], there is little point in trying to state it in terms of underlying high vowels and it becomes dissimilatory. It is this process of dissimilation which is generalized to give the modern Oboyan rule.

In the original rule, in addition to being high and front, the vowel affected was also made tense, thus [ī], the primary source of modern Russian [i]. Otherwise it would be subject to the same lowering and deletion rules as lax [i]. The reason that the change originally occurred only before the *lax* high vowels may be related to their status as reduced vowels in Slavic and the vowel-lengthening type of stress which developed in Russian. The stress-induced quantity was thus shifted to the pretonic vowel, which became tense. We note, however, that in general Russian pretonic vowels are less strongly reduced than the other unstressed vowels.

The case for the Oboyan example rests in part on the assumption that certain types of dissimilation generally involve adjustments of a primarily prosodic nature, such as Grassmann's Law or backness dissimilation of high vowels after homorganic glides.

In conclusion, the fact that languages have plausible rules is, in our opinion, the result of strong naturalness constraints on the initiation of phonetic rules. These constraints are essentially diachronic and should not be incorporated into the simplicity metric. Although little is known of the nature of these constraints, we find the notion of archetypal rule as developed in Foley 1968 an attractive basis for their formulation. The apparent historical striving toward more optimal segments is most likely to find explanation as a consequence of some kind of marking theory, although attempts to build marking into rule economy (linking) seem ill-founded.

The existence of implausible rules can be shown to result in large part from the transmission and simplification of plausible rules. There are obviously substantive constraints on the kinds of simplification that can take place, such as limitations on the features which can be related by Greek letter variables. We do not consider simplifications like those leading to Rule Z or Rule P″ to be possible. Yet these constraints must be much weaker than those restricting rule initiation, perhaps identical with the universal conditions needed to distinguish permissible from impermissible uses of diacritics suggested by Chomsky and Halle 1968: 170, fn. 7.

NOTES

1. Among the linguists who have been discussing these questions are Chomsky and Halle 1968, Cairns 1969, Lightner 1968, Foley 1968, and Stampe (in several papers and lectures).

2. Such arguments involve a tacit and probably unwarranted assumption that the class of possible grammars for natural languages is derivable from theories of linguistic competence alone. In fact, theories about competence might provide a class of grammars from which the class of possible actual grammars is selected by other theories about language acquisition, performance, neurophysiology, etc.

3. Note the following typical passages:

Chomsky and Halle 1968: 427: "To give a general solution to the problem in these terms, we would have to extend the theory of rule plausibility so that it would automatically provide a 'simplest interpretation' for each possible case."

Foley 1968: 6: "More generally, I make the requirement that every putative first order rule [i.e., rule in an individual grammar EB RTH] must be an interpretation of a second order rule."

Lightner 1968: 199: "If assimilation is a natural and favored process in the physical realization of utterances, it seems correct to say that a natural and favored way of writing abstract phonological rules is in terms of assimilation."

4. Note that the linking explanation presupposes the existence of a rule fronting /u/ in Ancient Greek. We assume such a rule for the sake of the argument without attempting to support it. If there is no synchronic evidence for such a rule at the time when the further change to *i* is supposed to have taken place, then the linking explanation for the further development obviously has no basis whatsoever.

5. One could circumvent this objection by adding "+back" in place of "+round" on the left. Obviously this is just a trick, possible only on the assumption, unstated above, that the language has no high back unrounded vowels. Under the type of linking suggested by Postal 1968, "+round" on the right would be replaced by "M round." In any case the following arguments apply equally to these suggestions.

6. There is no evidence that either of the *f* sounds was bilabial. The exact nature of the difference is unknown. The development of the velar spirant is somewhat different. In medieval German /h/ and /x/ came to be positional variants of one phoneme.

7. It might be suggested that linking should be constrained so as to distinguish between systems in which certain contrasts exist at the systematic phonemic level and those in which they are non-distinctive. (Compare also Postal 1968: 185: "It seems then that here a difference between two different kinds of [*u* Voice] may be showing up. [*u* Voice] appears to behave one way in a

context X__Y if there is a contrast in X__Y, but another way if there is not.")
For example, in a language with an underlying system /i ü u/ and Rule P, the
change u (> ü) > i/__ü is clearly unnatural. Equally unlikely is the motivation
for the linking-motivated shift ü (from underlying /u/)> i while systematic
/ü/ remains unaffected. Neither of these types of change is known from historical change. The evidence presented above, however, appears to justify the
stronger conclusion that linking is not a property of synchronic grammars. The
phenomena which seem to favor linking are generally illusory, resulting from
constraints on rule initiation and a tendency toward less highly marked lexical
representations.

8. The procedure of our hypothetical example is abundantly illustrated in
Foley 1968. For example, to account for Javanese alternation of the type (1a)
p— (1b) m— and (2a) b— (2b) mb— considerations of rule plausibility
(in terms of archetypal rules) lead Foley to posit underlying forms /mb−/ and
/mp−/ for (1b) and (2b), respectively. Two phonological rules then operate
on:

	/mb−/	/mp−/
(1) assimilating the stop by one feature	mm−	mb−
(2) reducing the geminate cluster	m−	mb−

Foley does not discuss the fact that this solution also entails rules of question-
able naturalness which simultaneously voice initial voiceless stops and devoice
initial voiced stops.

9. A different explanation for the development of J2 might be given, as an
amalgamation of two rules, one a palatalization rule, and the other a deaffrication rule, and there is even an interpretation of the history of the Japanese
dental obstruents which would favor this explanation. Against it we can put
the fact noted that there are no dialects with only an affrication (or deaffrication rule). In any event, should the latter explanation prove to be correct, it
will simply change the details of our argument without affecting its conclusion: that simplification can lead to unnatural rules.

REFERENCES

Bach, Emmon. 1968. Two proposals concerning the simplicity metric in phonology. *Glossa* 2:128-49.

Braune, Wilhelm. 1963. *Althochdeutsche Grammatik,* 11th ed., Walther
Mitzka, ed. Tübingen: Niemeyer.

Cairns, Charles E. 1969. Markedness, neutralization, and universal redundancy
rules. *Language* 45: 863-85.

Chomsky, Noam, and Morris Halle. 1968. *The Sound Pattern of English.* New
York: Harper and Row.

Foley, James. 1968. Morphophonological investigations II. Dittoed.

Harms, Robert T. 1966. Review of Terho Itkonen, *Proto-Finnic Final Consonants. Language* 42: 825-31.

——. 1968. Review of I. Vahros and M. Kahla, eds., *Lingua viget. The Slavic and East European Journal* 12: 111-14.

Kiparsky, Paul. 1965. Phonological change. Unpublished M.I.T. dissertation.

——. 1968. Linguistic universals and linguistic change. *Universals in Linguistic Theory*, Emmon Bach and Robert T. Harms, eds., pp. 170-202. New York: Holt, Rinehart and Winston.

Labov, William. 1965. On the mechanism of linguistic change. *Report of the Sixteenth Annual Round Table Meeting on Linguistics and Language Studies*, pp. 91-114. Washington, D.C.: Georgetown University Press.

Lightner, Theodore M. 1965. Segmental phonology of Modern Standard Russian. Unpublished M.I.T. dissertation.

——. 1968. An analysis of *akan'e* and *ikan'e* in Modern Russian using the notion of markedness. *Studies Presented to Professor Roman Jakobson by His Students*, Charles E. Gribble, ed., pp. 188-200. Cambridge, Mass.: Slavica Publishers.

Postal, Paul M. 1968. *Aspects of Phonological Theory*. New York: Harper and Row.

Wenck, Günther. 1954. *Japanische Phonetik: I*. Wiesbaden: Harrassowitz.

——. 1959. *Japanische Phonetik: IV*. Wiesbaden: Harrassowitz.

2.

The Integration of Linguistic Theory: Internal Reconstruction and the Comparative Method in Descriptive Analysis

Charles-James N. Bailey,
University of Hawaii

The fact that children can understand, and on occasion imitate, a good deal more of their native language than they can usually produce suggests that investigating linguistic *competence* in terms of what a speaker usually produces wrongly limits the scope of competence investigations to a fraction of what is actually known about one's native language. Current generative theory should therefore be adapted to a new emphasis on communicating by extending the scope of the data admitted to include everything that lies within the child's hearing competence. An adequate theory would have to go well beyond the current static models based on idiolects to provide a psychologically plausible way of organizing the complex data known to the child, who understands his grandparents (who may be from different locales), his schoolmates of different ethnic and economic classes, announcers on the communication media, etc.—not to speak of the different styles he himself produces.

There is no reason to suppose that the child stores or organizes in his competence those variables due to age and temporal differences which he is exposed to in a different fashion from the organizational principles of the class, regional, and stylistic variables which are known to him and are in his competence. Once we recognize this fact, the incorporation of temporal and regional variables, along with class and stylistic variables, into our theory of competence is only a matter of course. But it puts us—structuralist and transformationalist alike—at odds with both the agreements and disagreements of modern linguistic theory with Saussure's concept of *langue*. Rejecting the at-present axiomatic Saussurian dichotomy between diachronic and static (synchronic) modes of analysis becomes as obvious as does the acceptance of Saussure's social view of *langue*—entailing the rejection of the currently accepted idiolectal basis of synchronic analysis. Thus the separation of descriptive analysis from historical linguistics and from dialectology are both abandoned, and the tools of these analyses are put at the disposal of synchronic studies. The result is an integrated theory of linguistics which a scholar can use in the afternoon when engaged in historical investigation as well as in the forenoon when working on descriptive analysis. The current schizophrenia is no longer necessary.

Among the tools of diachronic investigation which the dynamic theory of polylectal analysis will require to organize the variation are: (1) The method of internal reconstruction already applied so successfully to synchronic analysis by Chomsky and Halle (e.g., 1968: 148-50, 233); (2) the comparative method. The subtlety of the task requires additional tools discussed below. What needs to be emphasized at this juncture is that patterned variation will no longer have to be relegated to performance or consigned to some other well-known scrap heap. The polylectal approach, being subtle and complex, will be able to handle the over-simplified homogeneous situation. But there is no reason to suppose, conversely, that theories adequate for the freak, desert-island homogeneity could ever suffice for the complex diversity normally encountered in the data.

Lacking such a comprehensive theory of descriptive analysis, a linguist must suppose that children and adults handle the lectal[2] variety which they are observed to handle quite competently (1) by guess-work, in the face of evidence like that amassed by Labov 1966 (cf. Greenberg 1969: 107-10); or (2) with a multiplicity of internalized grammars individually formulated for each variety of the native language known to the language-user. To state these hypotheses is to refute them. A more credible hypothesis, and one more worthy of testing, is the claim that children constantly re-

vise a single internal grammar of their native language until they
arrive at one which will handle the observed variety, asymptotically approaching a panlectal grammar through the incorporation of a
sufficient number of diverse, non-leveled variant types (see below).

Even if Saussure's view of *langue* were adopted, a description of
synchronic variation patterns would require bringing time into the
picture. For rule changes leading to neutralizations and wholly new
rules are known to spread by the borrowing of isolated semantactic
idioms or pronunciations of individual words (as is evident from
past dialectology and current studies by sociolinguists); these spread
in waves, and linguistic waves (like those in physics) have to be
specified by means of a temporal parameter. Waves specifying
linguistic relationships also require the specification of an abstract
space in lock-step with time. The extent of the real geographical or
sociological space is not important, since the abstract relationships
survive the disturbances of real space, migration, and the like, as I
shall show later in a study of the extraordinarily complex developments of English //ī ū//.[3]

In this connection it is also important to note that rule changes
of the sort being described could never occur in a homogeneous
grammar. For after a pronunciation of *dawn* like *don* had been
borrowed, for example, all that would result would be a relexifica-
tion in such a grammar. Without the retention of the older forms
in a different style or in a different class lect known to a speaker
long enough for a rule change to be generalized, such a generalization could not occur. Only a polylectal grammar is adequate for
historical linguistics (Weinreich, Labov, and Herzog 1968).

The static theory of a homogeneous grammar common to structur-
alism and transformationalism (cf. Becker 1967: 7) has two widely
divergent sources: (1) the nominalist-empiricist-positivist view that
only individual entities are real; and (2) the rationalist-idealist view
of fluctuation in phenomena as depriving them of full reality. In
view of Labov's (1963, 1966) findings, Chomsky's (1965: 3-4)
claim that "no cogent reason for modifying it [*scil.*, the primary
concern of linguistic theory with completely homogeneous speech]
has been offered" is now untenable.

Once the underlying lexicon and rules of the grammar have been
formulated by internal reconstruction and the comparative method,

the grammar being proposed here organizes the variety of outputs by means of principles that take advantage of the following psychologically plausible and empirically testable notions: (1) Rules are formulated in their least general forms, since knowledge of such formulations entails knowledge of more general formulations (having fewer features). (2) Rules are listed in their marked applicational order,[4] since it is possible from this listing to predict and know the only unmarked order of the rule into which it may be reordered (Kiparsky 1968) in another lect.[5] (3) The rules (or forms of them) not common to all lects can be organized in a psychologically convincing manner by listing all, or nearly all of them, in an implicational order—a principle I was led to as a result of reading DeCamp's important paper of 1968.[6] (4) Some variations are formulable with weighted rules of the type proposed by Labov 1969 and Fasold 1970. Note that for speakers not cognizant of certain lects of their native language, lexical redundancy rules (not psychologically internalized) would be required to convert the maximal distinctions of the panlectal lexicon to their lexicon. (For intonation in a polylectal grammar, see Bailey 1970.)

It should be feasible for psycholinguists to test the predictions entailed by the foregoing claims: (1) whether more generalized variants of a rule are more easily understood by a person whose production utilizes a less general formulation, or whether the converse is true; (2) whether the output of the unmarked ordering of a rule is more easily understood by a person whose production has it in a marked applicational order, or whether the converse is true; (3) whether the presence of a rule lower on an implicational scale results in a more easily understood variety of speech for a person for whom the rule is present and implied by another rule feature higher up on such a scale, or whether the converse is true; (4) whether the absence of a rule results in a lect that is less easily understood by a speaker whose production not only lacks the rule in question but also another rule higher up on the same implicational scale.

Heretofore *dialects* have been regarded as mutually intelligible forms of a language delimited by a bundled group of isoglosses. How valid the criterion of mutual intelligibility could be is implicit in the above; related lects are probably always less intel-

ligible in one direction than in the other. A conceivable, but highly
unlikely, exception would be lects differentiated *only* by rules not
implicationally related, like the English late rules that (1) change
//t// to [d] intervocalically and that (2) change /ɚ/ (from //r//) to
[ə] when not followed by a vowel (in which case it may be desyl-
labified or it may remain). As for the significance of bundled isoglosses, it may be profitable to consider Figs. 1 and 2, where feature A implies B, and B implies C, but not the converse. It is clear

Fig. I   Fig. 2

that, from the point of view of what is linguistically relevant,
the patterns of both figures are identical, and the bundling exhibited at the top of Fig. 2 is without synchronic significance.

To put the matter concisely, (systematic) idiolects do not exist
(Labov 1966), and dialects are equally fictitious; everyone always
speaks what traditional dialectologists labeled a *transitional dialect*
(Weinreich, Labov, and Herzog 1968: 184). Investigations under
way (to be reported on in greater detail in later articles) of different languages, but especially English, afford evidence that is consonant with the view that the lects of a language, except social lects
identifiable only by members of a given speech community, *can be
uniquely designated by points on an implicational scale of the sort
described above.* Such points would represent the presence or absence of a given rule of the language (in a particular isolect). Certain
conclusions emerging from my polylectal investigation of English
phonology will be mentioned at the end of this paper.

But first a word is in order concerning the problem of defining
the limits of a linguistic *system* (embracing lectal *subsystems*).
It is clear that if there are no constraints on what rules are to be regarded as natural language rules, any two subsystems are trivially
unifiable in some ad hoc manner into a single system, and the concept *system* becomes vacuous. What the limits of a system are is
perhaps the most serious problem facing linguistic theory at the

present time. In actual attempts to construct polylectal phonologies, I have encountered the question of whether certain phenomena were to be formulated as separate rules or as variable outputs of a single rule (cf. Labov 1969). Even if, as seems likely, it turns out that the notion of a system is simply a matter of degree (i.e., the percentage of idiom-particular rules in the listing of all the rules, including those common to all the lects involved[7]), it would still be necessary to know what the universal naturalness constraints on rules are. This is a matter of concern to other participants in the present meeting. I myself am strongly of the opinion that much is to be learned from the traits common to pidginized speech and from the polylectal reductions seen in Slavish, Middle Arabic, and Punti—reduced forms of Slavic, Arabic, and Chinese used to communicate among speakers of different lects of these languages, and varying according to the constituency of speakers involved at a given time.

It should be stressed that despite differences in the data that are admissible in synchronic and diachronic investigations, and despite the different aims of the two studies, their theory and basic methodology are not different. It is of course true that differences in aim will require different evaluations of isolated phenomena (relics).[8] But the fact that historical linguistics admits past data unknown to a child acquiring a later stage of a language and synchronic analysis may not, should no more be construed as requiring a methodological difference between the two disciplines than the fact that synchronic analyses of Samoan and Hindi employ different data. And the same leveling out observed in historical investigation may logically be assumed to occur in polylectal synchronic descriptions. The addition of more and more language families after the data from a few critical (unleveled) languages have been incorporated into reconstructions of Proto-Indo-European supplies only details here and there to the overall picture. Similarly, it may be presumed (as claimed above) that after a child has been well exposed to a few critical (unleveled) lects he formulates an internal grammar which is fairly close to a panlectal grammar of his native language and which is modified only in details through exposure to further variants.

I should now like to summarize briefly the results of a polylectal analysis of English phonology embracing some 115 rules, which seems to be of sufficient scope to warrant drawing a few tentative conclusions from the admittedly only approximate statistics. As far as I could determine, something in the neighborhood of 63 rules are identical for all the lects included: all the standard lects of American, British Received Pronunciation, and some data of Scots, northern English, Cockney, and a few nonstandard American lects well known to me or well described in the literature. Many other rules differ among the lects only in the generality of their formulations. Some twelve or thirteen rules are either wholly present or absent in a substantial number of the lects; about three are absent in only one lect, and fifteen are present in only one or two (very unleveled) lects. It is clear that most lectal differences depend on the degree of generality of rules which are more or less common to English.

About thirty differences in rule-reordering were found. Only two or three served both to differentiate lects and to account for exceptional lexical items within given lects (the exceptional words having the unmarked applicational ordering). More than twenty reorderings differentiated lects, and more than five served only to account for exceptional lexical items. Investigations subsequent to the time this paper was read have turned up many more reorderings in the last function. It has been found that a rule can skip over as many as twenty-six intervening rules to get into the unmarked order. One would like to know from psycholinguists whether the larger number of rules skipped over results in a greater decrease in intelligibility toward speech having the older, marked ordering. In one probable case, the change to the unmarked order resulted in a new marked order with respect to other rules.

It transpired that there are lectal blocs of rules with their own subordinate implicational interrelations. For speakers whose lects do not have the rules in such blocs it is likely that any one of them can function in place of the entire bloc within the implicational ordering of the rules for English as a whole. This means that the number of implications any speaker would have to retain in his head would be much less than the total number affecting those rules not common to English as a whole. Northern States English, which has few if any rules peculiar to itself and is therefore the most leveled lect of English, is probably more intelligible to other lects than they are to each other or to it. The opposite conclusion would hold for Southern States English, which has the largest number of rules peculiar to it.

Very few rules neither imply nor are implied by others (see above). These rules happen to generate some of the phenomena most noticeable to nonlinguists. Since the phenomena in question are often those taken most notice of by dialect geographers, it is not a point in favor of traditional dialectology that its research has concentrated on these superficial (very late-rule) and unrevealing phenomena, which normally vary even within a given "dialect" (e.g., the "r-less" rules in American English or the $//t// \rightarrow$ [d] rule in London, etc.).[9] The number of intrinsically ordered implications in English is trivial by anyone's standards.[10] ·

NOTES

1. The views in this paper were adumbrated to a certain extent in Stockwell 1959 and even more so in Bailey 1968. Through conversation and correspondence, I am indebted and grateful to many linguists, too numerous to list here, for help in focusing on the claims presented in this writing. But I should like to mention that ideas of Gary J. Parker and Larry Martin are included here and that I have had helpful discussion and correspondence with William Labov, Fred Householder, George Grace, W. P. Lehmann, and Donald Becker. They are of course not necessarily to be associated with my views.

2. For reasons that will appear below, I avoid the term *dialect(al)*. Varieties of a language distinguished solely by a rule designating an isogloss may be referred to with G. B. Milner's term, *isolect* (Albert Schütz, personal communication). A more general term covering one or more isolects (or a given portion of an implicational scale of the sort discussed below) is *lect*; this term was conceived independently by A. A. Afendras and by me.

3. Studies of New York City English by Labov, and my own investigations of the developments of $//\bar{\imath}\ \bar{u}//$, show that front-vowel changes precede in time identical back-vowel changes. It will soon be possible to demonstrate also that vowel changes in labial environments progressively antedate such vowel changes in progressively more retracted environments.

4. Since giving the present paper, it has occurred to me that the reason I have found only one marked ordering of rules in the various lects of a language must be the limitation that newly acquired rules can be added (in a marked ordering) only at the end of the others. Nothing prevents a simultaneous re-ordering to the unmarked order (cf. Chafe 1968). Stampe's (1969) concept of unmarked ordering provides an explanation for another observation I have made. I have never found a rule reordered to a merely less marked ordering, but only to the maximally unmarked one. And it seems that rules move backward, not forward, in order to produce a new unmarked applicational order.

5. Cf. Saporta 1965 and Vasiliu 1966 for important studies of dialectal differentiation through rule reordering.

6. Cf. Elliott, Legum, and Thompson 1969 for a lucid implicational analysis of syntactic data; I have repeated this test several times with comparable results—except for non-native speakers.

7. Since giving this talk, I have come to believe that the boundary of a system will be a discrete break with no ambiguous fuzziness, and that a variety of a language can move outside its original system only when a social cleavage exists such that children hear their parents speaking another language; e.g., English children hearing Francophone parents at the inception of Middle English, or French children hearing Norse-speaking parents. Work in progress also indicates that implicational tests (of the sort exemplified in Elliott, Legum, and Thompson) offer a means of differentiating speakers within a language system from those outside it. Those outside the system present anything but the native pattern.

8. Of course the methods for sub-grouping languages (e.g., shared innovations) can be set aside in favor of the implicational scale as a way of relating lects.

9. Lehmann has pointed out to me (personal communication) that since most of the rules among which lects differ will be late rules, dialectologists could only deal with late rules. To get around this just observation, I have to stress that the phenomena usually utilized for dialectal studies—when not simply lexical items, as is usual in America—are very, very late rules of little systematic import for language relationships. Often they are but symptoms of deeper differences. For example, the lack of the $//t//$ → [d] rule in Hawaiian English appears to be the result of the lack in this lect of the sort of syllabification which would offer an environment for the operation of this rule. Similarly, the merger of *Mary, marry,* and *merry* in "r-ful" English may be just the result of a different syllabification from that found in lects which keep these items apart, as I have maintained elsewhere, since all lects merge the nuclei in question before word-final outputs of $//r//$. If these surmises are at all correct, dialectologists "discover" the wrong differentiators of dialects when they claim that these are the surface symptoms in question.

10. Less extensive analyses of Quechua and Rumanian lectal differences presented by Gary J. Parker 1969 and E. Vasiliu 1966 will be described elsewhere. They harmonize very neatly with the foregoing results.

REFERENCES

Bailey, Charles-James N. 1968. Optimality, positivism, and pandialectal grammars. *ERIC/PEGS* 30. Washington, D.C.: Center for Applied Linguistics.

——. 1970. A new intonation theory to account for pan-English and idiomparticular patterns. *Papers in Linguistics,* 2: 522-604.

Becker, Donald Allen. 1967. Generative phonology and dialect studies: an investigation of three Modern German dialects. Unpublished University of Texas at Austin dissertation.

Chafe, Wallace L. 1968. The ordering of phonological rules. *IJAL* 34: 115-36.

Chomsky, Noam. 1965. *Aspects of the Theory of Syntax.* Cambridge: M.I.T. Press.

——, and Morris Halle. 1968. *The Sound Pattern of English.* New York: Harper and Row.

DeCamp, David. 1968. Toward a generative analysis of a post-Creole continuum. Paper read at the Conference on Pidginization and Creolization of Languages, Jamaica, April 1968, unpublished. To appear in the published volume of those papers, Dell Hymes, ed.

Elliott, Dale, Stanley Legum, and Sandra Annear Thompson. 1969. Syntactic variation as linguistic data. *Papers from the Fifth Regional Meeting, Chicago Linguistic Society,* April 18-19, 1969, Robert I. Binnick, Alice Davison, Georgia M. Green, and Jerry L. Morgan, eds., pp. 52-59. Chicago: Department of Linguistics, University of Chicago.

Fasold, Ralph. 1970. Two models of socially significant linguistic variation. *Language* 46: 551-63.

Greenberg, S. Robert. 1969. An experimental study of certain intonation contrasts in American English. *Working Papers in Phonetics, 13.* Los Angeles: University of California, Los Angeles.

Kiparsky, Paul. 1968. Linguistic universals and linguistic change. *Universals in Linguistic Theory,* Emmon Bach and Robert T. Harms, eds., pp. 170-202. New York: Holt, Rinehart and Winston.

Labov, William. 1963. The social motivation of a sound change. *Word* 19: 273-309.

——. 1966. *The Social Stratification of English in New York City.* Washington, D.C.: Center for Applied Linguistics.

——. 1969. Contraction, deletion, and inherent variability of the English copula. *Language* 45: 715-62.

Parker, Gary J. 1969. Comparative Quechua phonology and grammar I: classification. *Working Papers in Linguistics,* 1, pp. 65-87. Honolulu: Department of Linguistics, University of Hawaii.

Saporta, Sol. 1965. Ordered rules, dialect differences, and historical processes. *Language* 41: 218-24.

Stampe, David. 1969. The acquisition of phonetic representation. *Papers from the Fifth Regional Meeting, Chicago Linguistic Society,* April 18-19, 1969, Robert I. Binnick, Alice Davison, Georgia M. Green, and Jerry L. Morgan, eds., pp. 443-54. Chicago: Department of Linguistics, University of Chicago.

Stockwell, Robert P. 1959. Structural dialectology: a proposal. *American Speech* 34: 258-68.

Vasiliu, E. 1966. Towards a generative phonology of Daco-Rumanian dialects. *Journal of Linguistics,* 2: 79-98.

Weinreich, Uriel, William Labov, and Marvin I. Herzog. 1968. Empirical foundations for a theory of language change. *Directions for Historical Linguistics: A Symposium,* W. P. Lehmann and Yakov Malkiel, eds., pp. 95-195. Austin: University of Texas Press.

3.

The Interaction of Speech
Perception and Grammatical
Structure in the Evolution
of Language

T. G. Bever,
Columbia University,

and D. T. Langendoen,
City University of New York

For use almost can change the form of nature.
                              [*Hamlet*, III, iv]

1. *Introduction and Summary: The Three Linguistic Capacities*

A person knows how to carry out three kinds of activities with
his language: He can produce sentences, he can understand sentences, and he can make judgments about potential sentences. Recent linguistic investigations have concentrated on describing the
facts brought out in speakers' predictions about the acceptability
and structural relations of potential sentences. Such predictions
have been assumed to reflect directly each speaker's knowledge of
his language ("competence"), while the capacities to speak and understand sentences have been viewed as revealing a person's linguistic knowledge only indirectly, because of the interposition of

This research was supported in part by the Advanced Research Projects
Agency, Grant No. DAHC15, and by the National Institutes of Health Grant
No. 1 PO1 GM 16735, to The Rockefeller University. This paper is an ex-
panded version of "A Dynamic Model of the Evolution of Language," *Linguistic Inquiry*, Fall 1971.

behavioral factors ("performance"). It is clear that the activities of talking and listening can obscure much of a person's linguistic knowledge, but judgments about potential sentences also are behavioral manifestations of linguistic knowledge, and as such are not different *in principle* from the more tangible uses of linguistic structures. Even though predictions about sentences may be the most direct evidence we have concerning linguistic structures, it cannot be claimed that such judgments are entirely free from behavioral effects.

Thus, linguists and psychologists can utilize three kinds of manifest speech behaviors as data relevant to the study of linguistic knowledge: speech production, speech perception, and the prediction of new sentences. In this paper, we shall discuss the evidence for the interaction of the systems of speech perception and sentence prediction in the history of the English language. We shall demonstrate that the history of a language, and therefore its synchronic state as well, are the products of a dynamic interaction between the rules required for the prediction of new sentences, and the behavioral mechanisms used to understand sentences.

2. *The Grammar of Relative Clauses in Modern English*

The major result from recent investigations of predictive linguistic capacity has been that every sentence of a language has distinct external and internal forms. Consider the English sentences in (1); they both have the same internal ("logical") relations of actor, action, object, although (1b) has an external form which presents the terms of these internal relations in a different order from (1a).

(1a) Harry ate a baklava.
(1b) A baklava was eaten by Harry.

The recent linguistic investigations have demonstrated that a grammar of a language (the device required for the prediction of new cases) is composed of a set of rules for generating possible internal structures, and a separate set of rules, called transformations, which map internal structures onto external ones. The organization of a grammar is given in (2).

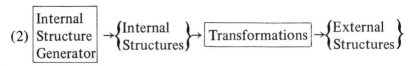

(2) $\boxed{\begin{array}{l}\text{Internal}\\\text{Structure}\\\text{Generator}\end{array}} \rightarrow \left\{\begin{array}{l}\text{Internal}\\\text{Structures}\end{array}\right\} \rightarrow \boxed{\text{Transformations}} \rightarrow \left\{\begin{array}{l}\text{External}\\\text{Structures}\end{array}\right\}$

In the case of (1), the mapping is one-many: The same internal structure is mapped onto several external ones. The mapping may also be many-one, as in the case of (3), in which the different internal structures are mapped onto the same external structure.

(3) Your mother was nice to visit.

In constructing grammars, linguists attempt to account for the predictions that people can make using the simplest instance of a grammar allowed by linguistic theory (Chomsky 1965, Postal 1970).

In this paper, we shall be concerned with the nature and history of the transformational rules governing the formation and reduction of relative clauses in English. These rules generate the various external forms exemplified in (4) from the same internal structure.

(4a) Harry ate a baklava; it was slowly disintegrating.
(4b) Harry ate a baklava that was slowly disintegrating.
(4c) *Harry ate a baklava slowly disintegrating.
(4d) Harry ate a slowly disintegrating baklava.

We assume that the internal structure corresponding to (4) is closest in appearance to that of (4a), and that the rules in (5) are among the transformations of English.[1]

(5a) Relative clause formation: Given a structure of the form:[2]

$$[_S [_S X_1 [_{Nom_i} X_2]_{Nom_i} X_3]_S ; [_S X_4 [_{Nom_i} X_5]_{Nom_i} X_6]_S]_S$$

convert it into the form:

$$[_S X_1 [_{Nom_i} X_2 [_S X_4 [_{Nom_i} X_5]_{Nom_i} X_6]_S]_{Nom_i} X_3]_S$$

That is, embed the second sentence as a constituent of the nominal in the first.

(5b) Relative pronoun formation: Copy the nominal in the relative clause containing the shared nominal at the beginning of the relative clause, and replace the shared nominal in this copy by the appropriate relative pronoun.[3]

(5c) Shared nominal deletion: Delete the original shared nominal (not the copy) in a relative clause.

(5d) Relative clause reduction: Delete any finite form of the verb *be* in a relative clause provided that it is the initial element of the clause (i.e., no relative pronoun has been added).

(5e) Modifier preposing: Move any reduced relative clause consisting of an adjective phrase (an adjective plus its modifiers if any) to a position preceding the noun it modifies.

The reader can easily verify that none of the transformations in (5) have applied in the derivation of (4a); that rules (5a, b, c) have applied in the derivation of (4b); (5a, c, d) in that of (4c); and (5a, c, d, e) in that of (4d).

Some of the rules in (5) have the property that when they can apply to a structure they must—these are called "obligatory" transformations—while the others need not apply to the structures to which they can apply—these are called "optional" transformations. Rule (5a) is optional, since there is no syntactic necessity for converting two conjoined sentences sharing a nominal into one sentence containing a relative clause. Rule (5b) is also generally optional, since a relative clause need not necessarily contain a relative pronoun.[4] However, the rule is obligatory in most contexts in which the shared noun is the subject of the relative clause and the finite verb of the relative clause is not *be*. Thus, for most speakers of English the sentences of (7) are not grammatically acceptable as counterparts of those of (6). (An asterisk indicates an ungrammatical sentence.)

(6a) The man that wants to see the boss is waiting downstairs.

(6b) The secretary discouraged the man that wanted to see the boss.

(6c) There is a man that wants to see the boss downstairs.

(6d) It was low wages and poor working conditions that caused the workers to strike.

(7a) *The man wants to see the boss is waiting downstairs.

(7b) *The secretary discouraged the man wanted to see the boss.

(7c) *There is a man wants to see the boss downstairs.

(7d) *It was low wages and poor working conditions caused the workers to strike.

Rule (5c), on the other hand, is obligatory, since sentences which retain shared nominals within relative clauses are ungrammatical (the shared nominal in the relative clause is italicized):

(8a) *Harry ate a baklava that *it* was slowly disintegrating.
(8b) *The man that I saw *him* was wearing a polka-dot shirt.

If the shared nominal occurs in a relative or noun-complement clause within the relative clause, the sentence is ungrammatical both if the shared nominal is deleted or if it is retained:

(9a) *The choir limped through the anthem (that) the organist couldn't make up his mind at what tempo *it* should be played.
(9b) **The choir limped through the anthem (that) the organist couldn't make up his mind at what tempo should be played.

Omission of the shared nominal in such sentences as (9b) leads to an even greater degree of ungrammaticality than its retention, as in (9a). This is due to the operation of the "complex noun-phrase constraint" discussed in Ross 1967, according to which a constituent cannot be deleted under identity within a clause wholly contained within a nominal expression if the identical element is outside that expression. If the shared nominal is retained, then the complex noun-phrase constraint is not violated; rather the violation is that of the obligatory shared-nominal deletion transformation. Obviously, the retention of the shared nominal in sentences like (9a) serves to remind the speaker and hearer of the grammatical source of the relative pronoun in a situation where the syntactic complexity is so great that it is both easy to forget and hard to tell what that source is.[5]

Rule (5d) is also generally obligatory, since sentences containing relative clauses beginning with finite forms of *be* are generally ungrammatical, just as sentences containing relative clauses beginning with other verbs, such as those in (7), are. However, to resolve this ungrammaticality, it is not necessary to add a relative pronoun (although this may be done); rather the relative clause may be reduced further by the deletion of *be*. Thus we have the sentences in (10) derived from those in (11).

(10a, i) The man that is waiting downstairs wants to see the boss.

(10a, ii) The man waiting downstairs wants to see the boss.

(10b, i) The secretary called the man that was waiting downstairs.

(10b, ii) The secretary called the man waiting downstairs.

(10c, i) There are few koala bears that are in captivity outside Australia.

(10c, ii) There are few koala bears in captivity outside Australia.

(10d, i) It is the mayor that is responsible for this mess.

(10d, ii) *It is the mayor responsible for this mess.[6]

(11a) *The man is waiting downstairs wants to see the boss.

(11b) *The secretary called the man was waiting downstairs.

(11c) *There are few koala bears are in captivity outside Australia.

(11d) *It is the mayor is responsible for this mess.

Finally, rule (5e) is obligatory when the modifier consists of an adjective or an adjective plus adverbial modifiers, and is inapplicable when the adjective is followed by a preposition phrase or clausal adjunct. Thus, while (4c) is ungrammatical, (12a, b) below are fully grammatical.[7]

(12a) Harry ate a baklava made with love.

(12b) Harry ate a baklava so rich that it gave him indigestion.

The rules in (5) are also ordered in a particular way. To a great extent, this ordering is a consequence of the form of the rules themselves. For example, rule (5a) must precede all the other rules of (5), since the others all make reference to the relative clauses created by rule (5a). By similar arguments, one can show that rule (5b) must precede (5c), and that (5c) and (5d) must precede (5e). On the other hand, there is nothing in the form of the rules themselves which tells us whether rule (5d) should precede or follow rule (5b). We have chosen initially to state the rules such that (5d) follows (5b) for purposes of exposition and following previous analyses. But what if we chose to order the application of (5d) before that of (5b)?

It turns out that we can effect a simplification of the grammar of English as a whole if we order (5d) before (5b); that is, if we have relative clause reduction precede relative pronoun formation. The reason is that we can then simplify the statement of the conditions under which rule (5b) is obligatory. It is obligatory when the relative clause begins with the shared nominal followed by *any* finite verb (before, it will be recalled, we were obliged to say any finite verb other than *be*). Moreover, relative clause reduction can now be stated as an optional, rather than as an obligatory, rule.

To summarize, the rules of relative clause formation and reduction apply in the following order: Relative clause formation (5a); Relative clause reduction (5d); Relative pronoun formation (5b); Shared nominal deletion (5c); and Modifier preposing (5e).

3. The Interaction between Universal Grammar and the History of Languages

The acquisition of grammar by children determines its historical development. In the view of Halle 1962 the child brings to bear on the sentences he hears around him his (presumably intuitive) knowledge of the universal form of linguistic grammars. He uses this knowledge to develop an internal grammatical representation of what he hears. The main constraint that he applies to the language as he learns it is that of *grammatical simplicity:* He attempts to find descriptive representations of the sentences he has experienced which are produced by a maximally simple grammar—one which uses linguistic universals in the most efficient way.

The view of language learning and language change proposed by Halle underlies most of the current attempts to describe historical changes in language in terms of changes in grammatical structures. Halle has proposed that people can develop a grammatical representation of their language in two different ways: Young children (presumably up to about age twelve, cf. Lenneberg 1967 for arguments that there is a critical period for language learning) develop a series of grammatical representations, taking as the basis for each grammar the sentences they have experienced. When new sentences do not conform to the predictions made by the grammar in a particular state of the child's development, he modifies the grammar appropriately to accommodate the new sentences as well. By the time the child is about twelve years old, he has experienced enough kinds of sentences for the predictive grammar he has developed to account for his linguistic experience to be the grammar of the complete adult language. Thereafter, his capacity to restructure his grammar is limited to the addition of rules to the end of the grammar, as opposed to adding rules within the grammar, or reordering existing rules.

The history of the conditions under which the relative pronoun formation rule (5b) was obligatory in English provides an illustration of the way in which grammatical restructuring is alleged to have occurred. There was a period of time in which sentences like (7b, c, d) were all grammatical; i.e., the subject relative pronoun did not have to be expressed when the clause modified an object nominal or a nominal following *be* in an existential or cleft sentence. Relative pronoun formation was therefore obligatory only under the conditions given in (13).

> (13) Add the appropriate relative pronoun obligatorily to a relative clause which begins with the shared nominal and a finite verb and which modifies a noun which precedes the verb in its own clause.

Somewhat later, however, sentences like (7b) became very infrequent, and presumably were viewed for a time as stylistic anachronisms. According to the theory of linguistic change we outlined above, there was a period when people learned the system described in (13) as children, but then added a rule to the end of their grammar, so that sentences like (7b) would be marked as ungrammatical. Such a rule is described in (14).

> (14) Add the appropriate relative pronoun obligatorily to a relative clause which begins with a finite verb and which modifies a noun which is an object of the verb in its own clause.

The complexity of a grammar which contains rule (5b) with the stipulation given in (13) and rule (14) is quite great, since rule (14) redoes obligatorily what rule (5b) does optionally. Thus, the children who heard adult speakers of the system described in (13)-(14) would restructure it to the simpler grammar containing the provision described in (15) as a condition under which rule (5b) is obligatory.

(15) Add the appropriate relative pronoun obligatorily to a relative clause which begins with the shared nominal and a finite verb, and which modifies a noun which either precedes the verb in its own clause or which is an object of the verb in its own clause.

The fact that language change can be described in this way has been used by Halle and others to justify the universal form of grammar in which there are ordered rules which transform internal structures into external structures. That is, the universal forms of grammar proposed for synchronic descriptions of languages provide the linguist with analyses relevant to the description of the history of languages. We agree that support for the claim that the history of a language is describable as a series of minimal changes in transformational rules is also empirical support for the form of specific synchronic descriptions; obviously a form of synchronic grammar which accounts only for the linguistic present and cannot be used to describe the recent linguistic past is unacceptable. The truth of the claim that the history of English can be described as a series of rule additions, simplifications, deletions, and reorderings justifies the use of ordered transformational rules to describe language in general.

However, no general principle of historical change itself emerges as a function of the rules. For example, many studies of language change explore possible principles needed as supplements for the principle of grammatical simplification to account for the historical development of languages. It is obvious that rule simplification itself is not a sufficient principle. Yet it is the only potentially explanatory device which the structure of a predictive grammar offers to the historical linguist in his quest for causes of historical developments. To find the causes of historical change we must therefore look beyond the structures offered by predictive linguistic grammars, to the structure of the interaction between the predictive and the behavioral system of language.

4. *The Independence of the Predictive and Perceptual Systems of Language*

Consider now the problem of understanding sentences. Recent psychological studies have shown that the form in which sentences are understood corresponds closely to their internal structure (Miller 1962, Mehler 1963). Thus, any model for speech perception includes a mechanism which isolates the internal structure corresponding to each external form (16).

(16)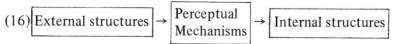

When transformational grammars were first proposed, it was thought that the grammatical mechanisms could be embedded within the operation of the perceptual mechanisms. A preliminary series of studies appeared to support this view; they showed that certain sentences which involve more transformations in the *grammatical* description of the relation between their internal and external structures are relatively hard to understand. For example, passive sentences like (17b) involve one more rule than corresponding active ones like (17a), and are indeed harder to understand. This was shown in many different kinds of studies; for example, McMahon 1963 demonstrated that generically true actives (17a) are verified more quickly than generically true passives (17b).

(17a) Five precedes thirteen.
        Thirteen follows five.
(17b) Thirteen is preceded by five.
        Five is followed by thirteen.

The basic principle at issue in these studies was that every grammatically defined rule corresponds to a psychological operation, and that therefore sentences with more rules mapping the internal-onto-the external structure should be relatively more complex psychologically.

However, this view of the relation between grammar and perception is incorrect. There are many examples of sentences which have relatively more transformations in their derivation and which are clearly *less* complex psychologically. Thus, in (18)-(20), the grammatical derivation of the second sentence of each pair (b) is more complex than the first (a), but is much easier to understand.

(18a) Harry ate the baklava that was green.
(18b) Harry ate the green baklava. (Relative clause reduction, Modifier preposing)

(19a) That Harry liked the green baklava amazed Bill.
(19b) It amazed Bill that Harry liked the green baklava. (Subject-clause extraposition)

(20a) The boy the girl the man liked hit cried.
(20b) The boy the girl liked by the man hit cried. (Passive)

In addition, recent reviews of the existing experimental literature (Fodor and Garrett 1967, Bever 1970a) have argued that the previous evidence which appeared to support the hypothesis that grammatical transformations are part of perceptual operations is inconclusive on methodological grounds.

This negative finding leaves open the question as to what the nature of the perceptual mechanism really is. Some of our most recent work has suggested to us that listeners make primary use of an ordered set of perceptual strategies which directly map external strings onto their internal structures. In this discussion we will consider evidence for one such perceptual rule used to establish the segmentation of external sequences into those sub-sequences which are related in the internal structure by such basic relations as actor, action, and object.

For a perceptual mechanism which maps external strings directly onto internal structures to operate efficiently, the actual string of words in a speech event must be segmented into those substrings which correspond to full sentences at the internal structure level. For example, if one hears the string represented phonetically in (21), one must decide that it contains two distinct sentences which correspond to clusters at the internal structure level, and not more or less.

(21) ðəbɔy l a y k s g ə r l z g ə r l z l ə v b ɔ y z (i.e., "the boy likes girls; girls love boys")

Failure to find the correct basic segmentation into strings which do correspond to internal structure sentences would seriously impair comprehension. For example, suppose that a listener were to assume that the second instance of *girls* in (21) was actually a spurious repetition; then he would be faced with the task of finding an internal structure for the following:

(22) The boy likes girls love boys.

The problem is that (22) has no corresponding internal structure representation.[8]

There is no known automatic procedure which insures the proper segmentation of external structures into those structures which correspond to sentences in internal structures. In cases like the above, however, pronunciation often provides many cues which indicate where the segmentation into internal sentences should occur. The operation of this segmentation strategy to separate sentences in a discourse like (22) can utilize many situational, semantic, and pronunciation cues. The segmentation problem is much more complex, however, for sentences embedded within other sentences.

   (23a) When he left the party became dull.

(23a) has two internal structure sentences, each one corresponding to one of the clauses in the external string: When he left and the party became dull. Let us represent this structural division into clauses in external structure with parentheses ( ), and the corresponding internal structure segmentation with brackets [ ]; thus (23a) has the structural organization assigned in (23b).

   (23b) ([When he left])   ([the party became dull])

If the wrong perceptual segmentation were attempted, then further perceptual analysis of the sentence would be impossible. For example, the listener could initially segment the first five words into a cluster (i.e., when he left the party), but then he would have two words left over (became dull), which cannot be analyzed as an internal structure cluster.

A recent series of experiments has given initial support to the claim that there exists a set of perceptual strategies which isolate lexical strings corresponding directly to internal structure clusters (Fodor and Bever 1965; Garrett, Bever, and Fodor 1966; Bever, Kirk, and Lackner 1969). These investigations have studied the perception of nonspeech interruptions in sentences with two clauses. The basic finding is that subjects report the location of a single click in a sentence as having occurred towards the point between the clauses from its objective location. For example, Fodor and Bever found that in sentence (24), a click objectively located in *yesterday* or in *the* was most often reported as having occurred between those two words.

(24) Because it rained yesterday the picnic will be cancelled.

Fodor and Bever argued that the systematic displacement of the click towards the point between the clauses shows that the clause has relatively high psychological coherence, since it "resists" interruption by the click.

Several experiments have shown that this systematic effect of the syntactic segmentation is not due to any actual pauses or cues in the pronunciation of the sentence. First, Garrett, Bever, and Fodor used materials in which the exactly identical acoustic string was assigned different clause structures depending on what preceded. Consider the string:

(25) . . . eagerness to win the horse is quite immature.

If (25) is preceded by *your*, then the clause break immediately follows *horse*. But, if that string is preceded by *in its*, then the clause break immediately follows *win*. We cross-recorded one initial string or the other and tested subjects on their ability to locate clicks in the different sentences. The results showed that the clause structure assigned each string "attracted" the subjective location of the clicks. In a second study, Abrams and Bever (1969) found similar results with sentences constructed by splicing words from a spoken list.

Various kinds of perceptual knowledge are involved in segmentation. An example of how generic semantic relations assist in perception is provided by a recent study by Schlesinger (1966), who found that center-embedded sentences in which the separate clauses are uniquely related semantically are easier to understand; (26b) is easier perceptually than (26a).

(26a) The boy the man the girl liked hated laughed.
(26b) The gift the girl the dog bit received glittered.

Semantic relations like those in (26b) can also restrict the possible segmentations of external strings into internal structure clusters. Compare, for example, (27a) with (23a); in (27a) the unlikeliness that the string when he undressed the party corresponds to a complete unit in the internal structure prevents a listener from segmenting that string together. On the other hand, unique semantic relations can force the opposite segmentation, as in (27b).

(27a) When he undressed the party became dull.
(27b) When he joined the party it became dull.

Bever et al. (1969) found that knowledge of the internal structure potentialities of specific lexical items can also affect immediate segmentation of external strings. For example, clicks located in verbs like *defy*, which take both a direct object and a complement, are located subjectively following the verb less often than clicks located in verbs like *desire,* which take just a complement.

(28a) <u>The general defied the troops</u> to fight.
(28b) <u>The general desired</u> the troops to fight.

Bever et al. interpret this result as a demonstration of the claim that listeners know that the sequence following a verb like *desire* can begin a new internal structure sentence (as indicated by the underlining in (28b)). By contrast, a verb like *defy* is known to permit only a direct object immediately following it (as indicated by the underlining in (28a)); accordingly, listeners have a greater immediate tendency to establish internal structure segmentation following verbs like *desire* than they do for verbs like *defy*.

In this paper we are concerned with the effects on perceptual segmentation of the external patterning of syntactic lexical categories. In particular, we argue that there are the following perceptual rules: (a) A string consisting of a nominal phrase followed by a finite verb whose inflection agrees with that nominal phrase is the beginning of an internal structure cluster (i.e., sentence). (b) The verb phrase (optionally including a nominal) is the end of such a cluster. These perceptual rules may be stated formally as in (29).

(29a) X_1 Nominal $V_f X_2 \rightarrow [_S X_1$ Nonominal $V_f X_2]$
(29b) $[_S X V_f (\text{Nominal}) \rightarrow [_S X V_f (\text{Nominal})]_S$

These strategies have interacted with the predictive grammar of English throughout its history in the development of the rules governing relative clause reduction.

At the moment we do not know what the appropriate formalism should be for such perceptual rules, so (29) should be taken only as suggestive. Clearly such strategies presuppose lexical-class identification, which in some cases may include syntactic subcategorization features. For example, (29a) must apply to the second sequence in (28b), but not (28a), reflecting the difference in the two main verbs. As written, the application of strategy (29a) must precede that of (29b). The reason is that people have no difficulty understanding sentences like (30). However, if the right bracket were assigned before the left bracket, then the incorrect initial bracketing in (31) would result, and the sentence would be incomprehensible.

(30) John believed Bill was a fool.

(31) $_S$[John believed Bill]$_S$ was a fool.

Thus, strategy (29a) applies first to an entire string, and then strategy (29b) applies. After application of (29a), example (30) would be analyzed as in (32).

(32) $_S$[John believed $_S$[Bill was a fool.

Strategy (29b) would then apply to produce (33).

(33) [$_S$John believed [$_S$Bill was a fool]$_S$

Notice that (29b) is prevented from assigning a right bracket after *Bill* in (33) because (33) does not meet the structural index of (29b).

The presence of the perceptual strategies having the effect of those in (29) is demonstrated by the existence of many sentences in English in which the strategies produce temporarily misleading analyses, thereby making them hard to understand. In each of the examples (34)–(36) below, (a) is hard to understand relative to (b) because there is a nominal-verb sequence presented in its structure which does not, in fact, correspond to any internal structure cluster, or which results in there being lexical material left over which cannot be assigned to such a cluster.

(34a) The umbrella the man sold despite his wife is in the room.
(34b) The umbrella the man sold despite his relatives is in the room.
(35a) The horse raced past the barn fell.[9]
(35b) The horse that was raced past the barn fell.
(36a) The paper was considered by John finished.

(36b) The paper was considered by John not finished.

While such examples demonstrate the activity of a principle like (29), there are also some experimental studies which give further direct evidence for it.

Blumenthal (1966) examined the kinds of error that subjects make when attempting to paraphrase center-embedded sentences like (26a). He found that the largest class of errors takes the three nouns as a compound subject, and the verbs as a compound predicate. For example, (26a) would be paraphrased as though it were (37).

(37) The boy, the man, and the girl liked, hated, and laughed.

That is, a simple "Nominal-Verb" schema is imposed on what is actually a complex sentence. In a related experiment, Bever et al. (1969) found that center-embedded sentences which have plausible, but misleading, noun-verb sequences in them are relatively hard to paraphrase (see (38)).

(38a) <u>The editor authors the newspaper</u> hired liked laughed.
(38b) The editor the authors the newspaper hired liked laughed.

Experiments like the ones just described serve to strengthen the claim that the strategies in (29) are present in adults (it is in fact unlikely that anyone would deny the existence of a strategy like (29a, b) even if the experimental evidence were not available). However, the presence of such perceptual strategies in young children cannot be taken for granted just because they appear in adult intuitions and behavior. Some of our recent experiments have explored the basic dependence in the child on a strategy like (29). For example, we have found that children less than two years old tend to recall (and act out) the first "nominal-verb" string that they hear, even if it is in a dependent clause (e.g., <u>dog jumped</u> in (39)). Older children, on the other hand, tend to recall the main clause "nominal . . . verb" and to drop the dependent clause (they recall <u>the dog fell</u> in (39)).

(39) The dog that jumped fell.

That is, older children assign priority on the basis of superordinate structure, while the younger children take the first nominal-verb string that they encounter as the most important. The main result of our investigations into the ways in which young children acquire perceptual strategies (see Bever 1970a for a review) is that the child from age two to five years is heavily dependent on perceptual strategies in speech perception, even to the point of overgeneralizing them to sentences where they should not be applied. For example, children of four years, *more* so than younger children, tend to take the first noun within a clause as the actor, even in passive (40b) or cleft (40c) sentences, in which that strategy leads to misperception.

(40a) The cow kisses the horse
(40b) The horse is kissed by the cow.
(40c) It's the horse that the cow kisses.

Thus, while adults have intuitive control over the application of such perceptual strategies in most cases, children are more often at their mercy.

5. *The Interaction of the Acquisition of Perceptual Strategies and of Grammar*

The relative dependence of the child on perceptual strategies of speech constrains the form of predictive grammars which can be learned. For example, a grammar which predicted every sentence to be ambiguous with respect to its internal structure could not be learned, nor could a grammar in which every predicted sentence violates universal perceptual principles. But existing grammars do predict sentences, *some* of which are ambiguous, and *some* of which do violate general perceptual principles. Thus, we cannot restrict the universal form of possible predictive grammars in any way except to say that sentences which it predicts must be *in general perceptually analyzable.*

This kind of restriction on the form of predictive grammar implies that certain universal features of such grammars are due to laws governing their actual use by young children and adults. This is distinct from the view that all the universal properties are internal to the predictive mechanism itself (such as the principle that transformational rules are ordered). The fact that the child is simultaneously acquiring a predictive grammar and systems for speech production and perception requires a conception of language learning, with corresponding principles of linguistic change, which is different from a view centered on the learning of predictive grammar constrained by formal simplicity. Since language learning includes the simultaneous acquisition of perceptual and predictive structures, the ultimate structure of the predictive system is partially a function of two kinds of simplicity: simplicity of the predictive system itself, and simplicity of the systems for speech perception and production.

In the next section, we illustrate how the predictive and perceptual systems can place conflicting constraints on a language, and produce historical changes which increase complexity in one language system in order to simplify another language system.

6. Informal Account of the History of Relative Clause Formation and Reduction in English

The historical changes we are concerned with are the rules of relative clause formation and reduction described (for contemporary English) in (5). It is convenient to distinguish six stages in the history of English relative clauses. Stage 1, Old English, dates from the time of the earliest manuscripts to about A.D. 1100. Stage 2, Early Middle English, runs from 1100 to 1400; Stage 3, Late Middle English, from 1400 to about 1550; Stage 4, Early Modern English, from 1550 to 1700; Stage 5, Late Modern English, from 1700 to the beginning of this century; and Stage 6, Contemporary English.

In Stage 1, the only element that could function as a relative pronoun was the demonstrative *se*, "that," which was declinable, and which had a masculine, a feminine, and a neuter form. In Stage 2, the demonstrative as relative, which now existed only in a single indeclinable form *þæt* (a continuation of the neuter form in Stage 1), was joined by various interrogative pronouns (the modern forms of which are *who, whom, which, whose*, etc.) a situation which has continued to the present day (the demonstrative is now, of course, spelled *that*). In addition, in Stage 1, a relative clause could be introduced simply by the indeclinable relative particle (n.b., *not* pronoun) *þe*, or by the demonstrative plus *þe*. The latter was also a possibility in Stage 2, but by Stage 3, the use of the relative particle had been discontinued.[10]

In Stage 1, the shared nominal could be retained in all syntactic positions in the relative clause except in clauses introduced by a word other than a particle or a pronoun; indeed in relative clauses introduced solely by the relative particle þe, the shared nominal could be deleted only if it was the subject of the relative clause. The situation was the same in Stage 2, except that since relative clauses could not be introduced just by the particle, the shared nominal was deletable everywhere. By Stage 3, however, the shared nominal had to be deleted if it occurred next to the relative pronoun, and was optionally deletable elsewhere. Still later, the shared nominal could only be retained in a subordinate clause within the relative clause, a situation which has continued until the present day.

We come now to a description of the historical development of the rule which introduces relative pronouns. As far as we can determine from the evidence cited by various grammarians, such as Abbott (A),* Curme (C), Jespersen (J), Mustanoja (M), Poutsma (P), Roberts (R), Sweet (S), Visser (V), and Wilson (W), at no stage in the history of English was a relative clause which modifies a nominal preceding the verb in its own clause allowed to begin with a finite verb.[11] As Curme himself argued, we may assume derivations of the sort given in (41) were never allowed.

(41) the girl [$_S$ she ate the baklava]$_S$ was fat. (SHARED NOMINAL DELETION)⇒
*the girl [$_S$ ate the baklava]$_S$ was fat.

On the other hand, it was possible up to the end of Stage 4 for a relative clause modifying a noun which followed the verb in its own clause to begin with a finite verb, so that derivations like (42) could be obtained.

(42) Harry ate the baklava [$_S$ it was disintegrating]$_S$ (SHARED NOMINAL DELETION) ⇒
Harry ate the baklava [$_S$ was disintegrating]$_S$

---

*The grammarian who was the source for the various citations given below is indicated by the first letter of his surname; the number is the page on which the citation may be found in the work listed in the bibliography.

Examples of this sort, in which the subject relative pronoun has apparently been omitted are, however, quite rare throughout the history of English.[12]

From Stage 4 to Stage 5 it became obligatory to introduce a relative pronoun into clauses modifying an object noun, a development which we analyzed above. In Stage 5, the subject relative could only be omitted in existential sentences like (7c) and (43a) below, and in cleft sentences like (7d) and (43b), including question-word interrogative cleft sentences, either direct, as in (43c), or indirect, as in (43d).[13]

(43a) There are lots of vulgar people live in Grosvenor Square.
[J 145; Wilde]
(43b) It was haste killed the yellow snake. [J 145; Kipling]
(43c) Who is this opens the door? [P 1001; Thackeray]
(43d) I wonder who it was defined man as a rational animal.
[J 146; Wilde]

Finally, in Stage 6, it seems that subject relative omission has become archaic or ungrammatical in existential and cleft sentences of the type (43a,b), and for some people also in interrogative cleft sentences of the type (43c,d).

Omission of the object relative pronoun, which necessarily leaves a nominal or some constituent other than the finite verb as the first element of the relative clause, has always been possible in English, although instances are very rare in Stages 1-3 (examples being even less frequent than those of subject relative pronoun omission in Stages 1-2, although in Stage 2, the formula represented in "by the faith I have to you" is fairly often instantiated). But, by Stage 4, the phenomenon had become quite common (see figures cited in note 12), and it is, of course, firmly established in idiomatic English today.[14]

Fig. 1 outlines the historical developments relating to the form of the relative pronoun, the retention of shared nominals, and the omission of the relative pronoun, and also information concerning the loss of most noun and verb inflections in English.

Before proceeding with a formal statement of the rules of concern to us, we may point out that nothing special about the history of the relative clause reduction rule need be mentioned, given our

Figure 1

Synopsis of Developments in Relative Clause Formation
in the History of English, Along with
Some Other Developments

Phenomenon	*Stage*					
	1 (OE) (to 1100)	2 (EME) (1100–1400)	3 (LME) (1400–1550)	4 (EMnE) (1550–1700)	5 (LMnE) (1700–1900)	6 (CE) (1900–)
Relative Clause introduced by:						
Particle þe	yes	no	no	no	no	no
Demons. pronoun + þe (*that* in 2)	yes	yes	no	no	no	no
Demons. pronoun (declinable)	yes	—	—	—	—	—
Demons. pronoun (indeclinable)	—	yes	yes	yes	yes	yes
Interrogative pronoun	no	coming	yes	yes	yes	yes
Shared nominal retainable:						
Obligatorily if not subject & no rel. pronoun	yes	going	no	no	no	no
Next to rel. pron.	yes	yes	going	no	no	no
Elsewhere	yes	yes	yes	no	no	no
Subject rel. pron. form. obligatory:						
On clause initial preverbal nouns	yes	yes	yes	yes	yes	yes
On obj. nouns	no	no	no	coming	yes	yes
On subjects of existential & cleft sentences	no	no	no	no	coming	yes
In interr. cleft sentences	no	no	no	no	no	coming
Nom./Acc. distinction	yes	going	no	no	no	no
Verb inflection	yes	yes	going	residual	residual	residual

decision to order that transformation before the rule of relative pronoun formation. The rule has remained optional in all environments throughout the entire history of English.[15]

7. Formal Account of the History of Relative Clause Formation and Reduction in English

In Stage 1 a relative clause could be introduced by the relative particle þe, by the inflected demonstrative pronoun se functioning as a relative pronoun, or by the two together in the order se þe. The shared nominal also was retainable except in clauses introduced by zero, and indeed had to be retained in clauses introduced by þe alone when it was not the subject of the relative clause.[16] (44) is a formal statement of the rules of relative clause formation and reduction in Stage 1. A verbal account of each rule follows each formal statement.

(44a) Relative clause formation:

$$[_S,[_S X_1 [_{Nom_i} X_2 ,\emptyset,]_{Nom_i} X_3]_S],;,[_S X_4 [_{Nom_i} X_5]_{Nom_i} X_6]_S],]_S$$

1	2	3	4	5	6	7 $\Rightarrow$
$\emptyset$	2 (þe+) 6	4	$\emptyset$		$\emptyset$	$\emptyset$

This is simply a formalization of rule (5a), together with a provision for the optional addition of the relative particle þe.

(44b) Relative clause reduction:

$$X_1 [_{Nom_i} X_2 [_S [_{Nom_i} X_3]_{Nom_i} ,\text{Tense} +be, X_4]_S]_{Nom_i} X_5$$

	1		2	3 $\Rightarrow$
	1		$\emptyset$	3

This is a formalization of rule (5d).

(44c) Relative pronoun formation:

$$X_1 [_{Nom_i} X_2 [_S, \emptyset, (þe)X_3 ,[_{Nom_i} X_4]_{Nom_i} X_5]_S]_{Nom_i} X_6$$

1	2	3	4 $\Rightarrow$
1	se_i	3	4

Conditions: (i) Not applicable when neither X_3 nor X_5 contains Tense.

(ii) Obligatory when X_6 begins with a Verb and 3 = $\emptyset$.

The demonstrative pronoun *se* is added at the beginning of a relative clause. It agrees in case and gender with the shared noun, something not explicitly provided for in this rule. The non-applicability condition is necessary to insure that the rule does not apply to reduced relative clauses. The obligatory condition insures that relative clauses on preverbal nouns do not themselves begin with a verb.

(44d) Shared nominal deletion:

$$X_1 [_{Nom_i} X_2 [_S, (se_i), (\text{þ}e), X_3 [_{Nom_i} X_4]_{Nom_i} X_5]_S]_{Nom_i} X_6$$

| 1 | 2 | 3 | 4 | 5 | 6 | $\Rightarrow$ |
| 1 | 2 | 3 | 4 | $\emptyset$ | 6 | |

Conditions: (i) Not applicable when $2 = \emptyset$; $3 \neq \emptyset$; $4 \neq \emptyset$.
(ii) Obligatory when $2 = \emptyset$; $3 = \emptyset$.

Shared nominals within relative clauses are deleted optionally except when the clause is introduced just by þe and the shared nominal is not the subject (if it is, $3 = \emptyset$). They are deleted obligatorily when there is no relative marker (either particle or pronoun).

(45) presents Old English examples of relative clauses containing shared nominals; (46) gives examples of clauses introduced by *se, þe*, and *se þe*; and (47), examples of clauses introduced by zero.

(45a) Nænig forþum wæs, þæt he æwiscmod eft siþade. [V 59] "No one previously was there, that afterwards departed ashamed"

(45b) þonne fisc þe . . . mine geferen mid anum slege he mæg besencean. [V 59] "than a fish that . . . can sink my companions with one blow"

(45c) Se god . . . þe þis his beacen wæs. [V 58] "the god whose beacon this was"

(45d) We, þe us· befæst is seo gyming Godes folces. [V 523] "we to whom is entrusted the care of God's people"

(46a) Geseoh þu, cyning, hwelc þeos lar sie, þe us nu bodad is. [Bede's *Ecclesiastical History*] "Consider, king, what doctrine this is, which now is preached to us"

(46b) He þæt beacen geseah <u>þæt</u> him geiewed wearþ. [S118]
"He saw the beacon that was shown to him."

(46c) Ond gif þu forþ his willan hearsum beon wilt, <u>þone</u> he
þurh me bodaþ ond læreþ, . . . [Bede's *Ecclesiastical History*]
"And if you henceforth are willing to be obedient to his desire
which he claims and teaches through me, . . ."

(46d) Ure ieldran, <u>þa þe</u> þas stowa ær hioldan, hie lufodon wisdom. [*Pastoral Care,* Preface] "Our forebears, who previously
possessed these places, they loved wisdom"

(47a) Hwa is <u>þæt þe</u> slog? [C 16] "Who is that [who] smote
thee?"[17]

(47b) Sum welig man wæs hæfde sumne gerefan. [C 25]
"There was a rich man [that] had a steward"

(47c) Alle mæhtiga þæm gelefes. [C 180] "All things are possible to him [who] believes"

(47d) Se fæder hire sealde ane þeowene Bala hatte. [J 133-34]
"Her father gave her a maid [who] was called Bala"

(47e) Her on þys geare gefor AElfred wæs æt Baþum gerefa.
[J 133] "In this year died Alfred [who] was reeve at Bath."

(47f) Se þæt wicg byrþ [V 537] "He [whom] that steed bears"

(47g) Wiste forworhte þam he ær wlite sealde [V 537] "He
knew to be guilty those [to whom] he previously had given
beauty"

(47h) Bed him þet he scolde him giuen ealle þa minstre þa
hæþen men hæfden ær tobrocon. [V 536] "He asked him to
give him entirely the monasteries [that] the pagans had earlier
destroyed"

The rules of relative clause formation and reduction for Stage 2
are the same as (44), except that relative pronoun formation is obligatory if the relative particle has been introduced, the demonstrative pronoun has become the indeclinable form þæt (modern
spelling, *that*), and the interrogative pronouns are beginning to
come into use as relative pronouns. Condition (i) on rule (44d) is,
of course, no longer necessary.

In Stage 3, the relative particle is no longer introduced by the rule
of relative clause formation. Shared nominal deletion is now obligatory when the shared nominal immediately follows the relative
pronoun. That rule had become (44d').

(44d′) Shared nominal deletion (Stage 3):

$$X_1 \, [_{Nom_i} X_2 \, [_S, \, (\text{Rel-pron}_i) \, \emptyset, \, X_3, [_{Nom_i} X_4 \,]_{Nom_i} X_5 \,]_S \,]_{Nom_i} X_6$$

1		2	3	4	5 ⇒
1		2	3	∅	4

Conditions: (i) Obligatory when 3 = ∅.
               (ii) Obligatory when 2 = ∅.

In (48), examples from Stage 2 of sentences in which the shared nominal immediately follows the relative pronoun are given; in (49), examples in which the shared nominal is separated from the relative pronoun. In (50) and (51) reduced relative clauses from both stages in which the subject relative and object relative pronouns, respectively, have been omitted are given.

(48a) ther no wight is that he ne dooth, or sei that is amys [V 59; Chaucer, *Canterbury Tales*]
(48b) he knew sir Blamour de Ganys that he was a noble knyght. [V 59; Malory, *Morte d'Arthur*]

(49a) Our Lord that jn hevene ne Erthe he hath non pere. [V 59; Merlin]
(49b) a jantyllwoman that semeth she hath grete nede of you. [V 59; Malory, *M. d'A.*]
(49c) it was þat ilk cok þat peter herd him crau. [V 59; *Cursor Mundi*]
(49d) seynt lucie . . . , þat þe holy gost made hire so hevy þat sche myght not be draw . . . to þe bordelhous. [V 522; c. 1400]
(49e) And this man began to do tristely in the synagoge, whom whanne Priscilla and Aquila herden, they token hym. [V 522; Wyclif]

(50a) He sente after a cherl was in the toun. [V 12; Chaucer, *C. T.*]
(50b) Ye ryde as coy and stille as dooth a mayde, Was newe spoused.[18] [W 41; Chaucer, *C. T.*]
(50c) Ther was noon auditour coude on him winne. [J 146; Chaucer, *C. T.*]
(50d) This es the loue bes neuer gan. [C 184; Cotton MS]

(50e) Whar es now Dame Dido was qwene of Cartage? [R 109; *Parlement of the Thre Ages*]

(50f) Where is the lady shold mete vs here? [J 147; Malory]

(50g) Lete fetche the best hors maye be founde. [J 143; Malory]

(50h) With a knyght full sone she mette hyght Syr lucan de bottelere. [V 12; Malory]

(51a) Sir be þe feith I haue to yow . . . [V 538; *Cursor Mundi*]

(51b) The tresor they hadden, he it hem reft. [V 538; *Brunne Chronicle*]

(51c) He had a sone men cald Ector. [V 538; *Brunne Chronicle*]

In Stage 4, the rule of shared nominal deletion had become effectively what it is today—a shared nominal was obligatorily deleted. Also in this period, the relative frequency of object relative pronoun to subject relative pronoun omission had become extremely great (see note 8), so that subject relative pronoun omission began to take on the appearance of something unusual.

In Stage 5, the necessity for subject relative pronoun formation in clauses modifying object and predicate nominals had become established. The rule of relative pronoun formation for this period had become (44c′).

(44c′) Relative pronoun formation (Stage 5):

$$X_1 [_{Nom_i} X_2 [_S, \emptyset, X_3 [_{Nom_i} X_4]_{Nom_i} X_5]_S]_{Nom_i} X_6$$

$$\begin{array}{ccc} 1 & 2 & 3 \Rightarrow \\ 1 & \text{Rel-pron}_i & 3 \end{array}$$

Condition: (i) Obligatory when X_6 begins with a Verb and $X_3 = \emptyset$.

(ii) Obligatory when X_1 = Nominal Verb (where the Nominal is not an expletive such as *there* or *it*) and $X_3 = \emptyset$.

In (52), we give examples from Stage 4, which include relative clauses beginning with a finite verb modifying an object, and in (53) examples from Stage 5, which represent archaisms (cf. Jespersen 1927:144). In (54) we give examples which include such relative clauses in existential and cleft sentences of the type given in (43a-d).

(52a) My father had a daughter lov'd a man. [J 143; Shakespeare, *Two Gentlemen* II, iv. 110]

(52b) I see a man here needs not live by shifts. [J 143; Shakespeare, *Comedy of Errors* III, ii, 186]

(52c) I've done a deed will make my story quoted. [J 143; Otway].

(52d) I bring him news will raise his drooping spirits. [J 143; Dryden]

(53a) I had several men died in my ship. [J 147; Swift]

(53b) I will advance a terrible right arm Shall scare that infant thunderer, rebel Jove. [J 144; Keats]

(53c) You beat that great Maryland man was twice your size. [P 1001; Thackeray]

(53d) I knew an Irish lady was married at fourteen. [P 1002; Meredith] [19]

(54a) Some men there are loue not a gaping pigge. [J 134; Shakespeare, *Merchant of Venice* IV, i, 47]

(54b) There's one did laugh in's sleepe. [J 146; Shakespeare, *Macbeth* II, ii, 24]

(54c) 'Tis the God Hercules, whom Antony loued, Now leaves him. [J 145; Shakespeare, *Antony and Cleopatra* IV, iii, 16]

(54d) 'Tis thy design brought all this ruin on us. [J 144; Dryden]

(54e) See who it is lives in the most magnificent buildings. [J 145; Fielding]

(54f) 'Tis I have sent them.[20] [J 145; Hardy]

(54g) Grandpa, what is it makes your eyes so bright and blue like the sky? [V 13; G. Cannan (1913)]

Finally, in Stage 6, we observe that sentences like (43a,b), in which the subject relative pronoun has been omitted from relative clauses modifying the subject of existential and nonquestion word cleft sentences, are felt to be ungrammatical. Nevertheless, there are some speakers of Contemporary English, the authors included, who find the question word cleft sentences of the sort (43c,d), with subject relative pronouns omitted, grammatical. For such persons, the rule of relative pronoun formation has become (44c'').

(44c″) Relative pronoun formation (Stage 6):

$$X_1 [_{Nom_i} X_2 [_S ,\emptyset, X_3 [_{Nom_i} X_4]_{Nom_i} X_5]_S]_{Nom_i} X_6$$

$$\begin{array}{cccc} 1 & 2 & 3 & \Rightarrow \\ 1 & \left\{\begin{array}{c} that \\ Interr \end{array}\right\}_i & 3 \end{array}$$

Condition: Obligatory when $X_3 = \emptyset$, except when $X_2 = \emptyset$ and X_1 = Interrogative *it* Tense + *be*.

For those speakers of Contemporary English who, unlike us, find (43c,d) also ungrammatical, the condition on rule (44c″) lacks the *except*-clause.

The following is a summary of the rules for each stage (structural indices are renumbered to facilitate stage-by-stage comparison).

Stage 1.

a. Rel. clause formation:

$$[_S ,[_S X_1 [_{Nom_i} X_2 ,\emptyset,]_{Nom_i} X_3]_S ,;, [_S X_4 [_{Nom_i} X_5]_{Nom_i} X_6]_S ,]_S$$

$$\begin{array}{ccccccc} 1 & 2 & 3 & 4 & 5 & 6 & 7 \Rightarrow \\ \emptyset & 2 & (þe +)6 & 4 & \emptyset & \emptyset & \emptyset \end{array}$$

b. Relative clause reduction:

$$X_1 [_{Nom_i} X_2 [_S [_{Nom_i} X_3]_{Nom_i} , \text{Tense} + be, X_4]_S]_{Nom_i} X_5$$

$$\begin{array}{cccc} & 1 & 2 & 3 & \Rightarrow \\ & 1 & \emptyset & 3 \end{array}$$

c. Relative pronoun formation:

$$X_1 [_{Nom_i} X_2 [_S ,\emptyset,(þe) X_3 , [_{Nom_i} X_4]_{Nom_i} X_5]_S]_{Nom_i} X_6$$

$$\begin{array}{ccccc} 1 & 2 & 3 & 4 & \Rightarrow \\ 1 & se_i & 3 & 4 \end{array}$$

Conditions: (i) Not applicable when neither X_3 nor X_5 contains an unembedded instance of Tense.

(ii) Obligatory when X_6 begins with a Verb and $3 = \emptyset$.

d. Shared nominal deletion:

$$X_1 [_{\text{Nom}_i} X_2 [_S, (se_i), (þe), X_3, [_{\text{Nom}_i} X_4]_{\text{Nom}_i}, X_5]_S]_{\text{Nom}_i} X_6$$

1	2	3	4	5	6	$\Rightarrow$
1	2	3	4	$\emptyset$	6	

Conditions: (i) Not applicable when $2 = \emptyset$; $3 \neq \emptyset$; $4 \neq \emptyset$.
　　　　　　(ii) Obligatory when $2 = \emptyset$; $3 = \emptyset$.

Stage 2.

　a. Same as Stage 1.
　b. Same as Stage 1.
　c. Add condition:
　　(iii) Obligatory when þe is present.
　　Change se_i to $\begin{Bmatrix} that_i \\ \text{Interr}_i \end{Bmatrix}$
　d. Omit Condition 1.
　　Change se_i to $\begin{Bmatrix} that_i \\ \text{Interr}_i \end{Bmatrix}$

Stage 3.
　a. Omit (þe) from structure change.
　b. Same as Stage 1.
　c. Omit (þe) from structure index. Omit Condition (iii).

d. $X_1 [_{\text{Nom}_i} X_2 (\begin{Bmatrix} that \\ \text{Interr} \end{Bmatrix}_i), X_3, [_{\text{Nom}_i} X_4]_{\text{Nom}_i}, X_5]_S]_{\text{Nom}_i} X_6$

1	2	4	5	6	$\Rightarrow$
1	2	4	$\emptyset$	6	

Conditions: (i) Obligatory when $4 = \emptyset$.
　　　　　　(ii) Obligatory when $2 = \emptyset$.

Stage 4.

　a. Same as Stage 3.
　b. Same as Stage 1.
　c. Same as Stage 3.
　d. Replace Conditions (i) and (ii) by:
　　(i) Obligatory

Stage 5.

　a. Same as Stage 3.

b. Same as Stage 1.

c. $X_1 [_{Nom_i} X_2 [_S ,\emptyset, X_3 [_{Nom_i} X_4]_{Nom_i} X_5]_S]_{Nom_i} X_6$

$$1 \qquad 2 \qquad 3 \Rightarrow$$

$$1 \qquad \left\{ \begin{matrix} that \\ Interr \end{matrix} \right\}_i \quad 3$$

Conditions: (i) Obligatory when X_6 begins with a Verb and $X_3 = \emptyset$.

(ii) Obligatory when X_1 = Nominal Verb, but when Nominal is not an expletive such as *then* or *it*, and $X_3 = \emptyset$.

d. Same as Stage 4.

Stage 6.

a. Same as Stage 3.

b. Same as Stage 1.

c. $X_1 [_{Nom_i} X_2 [_S, \emptyset, X_3 [_{Nom_i} X_4]_{Nom_i} X_5]_S]_{Nom_i} X_6$

$$1 \qquad 2 \qquad 3 \Rightarrow$$

$$1 \qquad \left\{ \begin{matrix} that \\ Interr \end{matrix} \right\}_i$$

Conditions: (i) Not applicable when neither X_3 nor X_5 contains an unembedded instance of Tense.

(ii) Obligatory when $X_3 = \emptyset$, except when $X_2 = \emptyset$ and X_1 = Interr *it* Tense + *be*. *

8. *The Interaction of These Developments with Speech Perception*

The development of the relative-clause formation system over the last millenium can be described straightforwardly in terms of slight changes in the description of rules and their domain of application. As we argued above, this fact in itself is an empirical demonstration of the appropriateness of the form of grammar used to describe each stage of the language. Clearly, a form of grammar which required that each stage be represented as radically distinct from every other stage would be less satisfactory. Thus, our investigation to this point constitutes an empirical demonstration in favor of the

---

*For some speakers, omit the *except*-clause.

use of a transformational grammar to describe diachronic aspects of language and (by direct inference) to describe synchronic aspects as well.

However, our formal outline of the historical developments is less satisfactory as the basis for an *explanation* of what has happened. Indeed, there is no general sense in which the changes we outline demonstrate any overall tendency for grammars to evolve in a particular formal way. The major historical shifts are outlined in (55). The formal reflex of these changes in the statements of the rules does not offer any insight as to why these changes occurred and whether they are related developments.

(55a) Disappearance of inflections, first in nouns then in verbs.
(55b) Appearance of restrictions on the absence of relative
      clause markers on clauses modifying postverbal nouns.

There is no general trend towards formal rule simplification or elaboration to be found in these developments, and examination of the formal rules alone leaves us without any understanding of the processes which might be involved. For example, the shift from Stage 4 to Stage 6 represents a generalization of the restriction on the absence of the relative pronoun in relative clauses. This generalization is represented formally as a simplification of the rule which inserts relative pronouns. However, the shift from Stage 3 to Stage 5 represents a reduction in the generality of the restrictions on relative pronoun insertion since the relative pronoun is still optional before a verb in the relative clause if the head noun is preceded by an expletive construction. This loss of generalization is represented formally as an addition to the rule which inserts relative pronouns. (We should emphasize that the oscillation of the formal complexity underlying the description of the relative pronoun system in English is not a consequence of our decision to treat the presence of relative pronouns as due to the operation of a single rule of relative pronoun formation as opposed to an early rule of formation and then optional deletion proposed in previous accounts (Smith 1964). If one adopted the previous solution then one would find that the formal complexity of relative pronoun restrictions decreased from Stage 3 to Stage 4 but increased from Stage 4 to Stage 6.)

Of course, we do not want to prejudge the possibility that some formal aspect of the rules might be found which represents a generally observed historical shift, nor do we wish to claim that our formalization of the developments is not potentially subject to reformulation in the light of data that we have not considered. Such a reformulation might offer a formal characteristic which would allow a satisfactory generalization about the historical developments. However, whatever formal account is found in terms of transformational rules it will fail to represent that the two historical changes in (55) are related. Yet it is the presence of such a relation which partially explains the historical changes themselves.

In Section 5 we argued that the child's system for the use of language is reflected formally in constraints on the grammatical rules that he can learn. We concentrated on the nature and acquisition of the child's system of speech perception and suggested that at certain points the learning of the perceptual system and of the system for the prediction of new sentences would come into conflict with each other. The first area for such conflict of concern to us is the perceptual and predictive use of a rich system of inflectional endings. The current research on speech perception argues that the primary goal of speech perception is to extract the internal relations from an external sequence—the more explicit and unique the markers in the external sequence of the internal relations, the easier it is to perceive the sentence. For example, a language in which the first noun is *always* the internal subject would be perceptually simple. Or a language in which the subject is invariably marked by one sort of case marking while the object is marked by another, regardless of their order, would also be perceptually simple: The listener would not need to attend to the order of the words; only the inflectional markers would be at issue. While there may be no language which is entirely dependent on the use of case markings or entirely dependent on surface order, Old English was a relatively extreme case-marking language with a variety of inflectional paradigms.

From the standpoint of language learning it is clear that a rich inflectional system is a mixed blessing. On the one hand, if the inflectional system is extremely general and without exception then the child need learn only one inflectional system for nouns and for verbs, and then can apply it ubiquitously. However, in the evolution of most inflectional systems (Jespersen 1940: 59), it appears that even if inflections are small in number at one stage, they tend to multiply and become differentiated into many different systems of inflection, which vary according to the syntactic, semantic, or phonological property of each lexical item. Once learned, such a varied inflectional system may increase the perceptual simplicity of the language as a whole, since the inflectional endings themselves carry partial lexical information (see below for a discussion of this). However, the learning problem is considerably complicated. Many authors have noted that even in an inflectionally simple language like modern English children go through a period of great difficulty with exceptional forms for which they overgeneralize the inflectional regularities (e.g., they say "wented" instead of "went," or "childrens" instead of "children"). A language in which there is greater variety of inflections than Modern English must be more difficult to learn, at least in that respect.

This was the state of affairs in Old and Early Middle English; the variety of distinct paradigms of noun declensions was high. Depending on the delicacy of the criteria one wishes to apply, one can speak of anywhere from four to ten basic paradigms without including any of the more marginal classes. Thus the child was faced with a formidable learning task. When the opportunity for some restructuring of his language arose it is not surprising that noun inflections were leveled. Of course, we have not explained what the basis of the opporunity to change the language was, only why it was utilized in this particular way.

Subsidiary evidence for this interpretation of the loss of inflectional endings in English is found in the fact that noun inflections disappeared before verb inflections. Indeed, a system of verb inflection is residual in Modern English. Our argument is that the basic pressure to change the noun system came from the fact that there were so many different paradigms. But the verb system was far more regular: There were two main classes, each with its own system of inflectional endings.[21] Thus, the learning problem for the verb system was far less complex than for the noun systems, and the verb inflections dropped out of the language at a later time.

Of course, many languages persist in maintaining complex irregular declension systems. Consequently, we cannot claim that the emergence of an intricate set of declension systems was the direct cause of the loss of all inflections. One might be tempted to argue that the *real* "cause" of the loss of inflections was the Germanic tendency for word-initial stress. This "caused" a reduction of stress on other syllables, which "caused" the ultimate loss of phonetic differentiation of the inflectional endings, which "caused" their ultimate deletion. Such an "explanation" would merely beg the question as to why the inflectional endings were dropped entirely: There are many examples of neutralized vowels which remain in English and have not disappeared. Thus vowel reduction *may* be a prerequisite for the loss of inflectional distinctions, but to take it as a direct cause would be as naive as to take the complexity of the declension system as the single direct cause. It is unlikely that linguistic evolution has single causes of this sort.

Consider now the implications of the loss of inflections for the marking of subordinate and superordinate clause relations in general and the relation of a relative clause to its head noun in particular. First, it was apparently the case in Old English as well as Modern English that the first Nominal Verbal sequence in a sentence was almost always part of the main clause unless specifically marked otherwise. Thus, if the first verb introduced a relative clause there had to be *some marker* present in the surface structure. Of course, in Stage 1 the number of different possible relative clause markers makes difficult the formal statement of the restriction that at least one of them must be present, since they are introduced by at least partially independent rules.[22] However, it is predictable that such a constraint exists if the perceptual principles in (29) are to be useful. For example, if there were no marker on an initial relative clause which has subject order, then it would be confused with the main clause of the sentence, as in (7a).

Cases in which the verb-initial relative clause modified a non-subject noun would have created less ambiguity in Stages 1 and 2, since in many instances the noninitial nominal was inflected either in the noun or the article or as an inflected pronoun. Thus, the absence of a relative clause marker in such cases did not lead to perceptual difficulty because the nominals were often marked by their inflected case endings as nonsubject. Of course, proper names and plural inflections in most noun declensions were phonologically the same for the nominative and accusative cases, so that the language would not have been entirely without the possibility of generating cases which would be perceptually difficult. But as cases like (34-36a) show, one cannot require of a language that it never generate a sentence which violates a perceptual generalization, only that the actually uttered sentences be *in general* perceptually recoverable.[23]

When the declensions were entirely leveled at Stage 3 (except for personal pronouns, as in Contemporary English) the frequency of the kinds of ambiguity increased, especially since the number of alternative ways of marking a relative clause had diminished by the end of Stage 3 to the interrogative relative pronoun and the indeclinable demonstrative "that," as in Contemporary English. We interpret the appearance of an obligatory relative clause marker on noninitial nouns that are subject of the relative clause as a response to the increase in perceptual ambiguity occasioned by the loss of declensions.

Thus, in our view the two historical trends in (55a) and (55b) are directly related since the first is a precondition for the second. As the number of false *NV = Subject verb* segmentations determined by perceptual strategy (29) became too great the independent marking of the relative clause became obligatory. There are several subsidiary facts which strengthen our interpretation that the restrictions on the presence of relative markers are due to perceptual confusions, some of which we can observe at work in the modern development of the language. Consider the sentences in (56). According to the data we have collected, sentences like (a) are grammatically unacceptable for most speakers, and sentences like (b) are unacceptable for a subset of those speakers.[24]

(56a) ?? $\left\{ \begin{matrix} \text{It's} \\ \text{There's} \end{matrix} \right\}$ a boy wants to see me.

(56b) ? Who is $\left\{ \begin{matrix} \text{there} \\ \text{it} \end{matrix} \right\}$ wants to see me?

Consider the operation of perceptual strategies (29) on the last part of a sentence like (56a). It would yield the segmentation in (57).

(57) There is [$_S$ a boy wants to see me] $_S$

It is important to note that this segmentation is appropriate to the meaning of the sentence, unlike the inappropriate segmentations which the strategy would yield on cases like (6) (see above): (56a) is synonomous with (58).

(58) A boy wants to see me.

That is, in cases like this operation of strategy (29) interferes little with the recovery of the internal grammatical relations. What is lost by such a preliminary segmentation of (57) is the information that the sentence is an existential statement about *a boy*. This information, however, is uniquely recoverable from the expletive use of the initial word *there*.[25] If the locative use of *there* is intended then the absence of the relative clause marker involves a much less acceptable sequence, because the operation of strategy (29) leads to a nonsynonomous sentence (60).

(59) ? (Over) there is the boy wants to see you.
(60) The boy wants to see you.

Further evidence that it is the temporarily incorrect segmentation which makes these sentences (56) unacceptable is shown by the fact that any feature of the sentence which either reduces the salience of *there* as an expletive or heightens the salience of the "Noun-verb" association increases the unacceptability of the sentence. For example, in (61a) the constraint between *dog* and *bark* makes the operation of strategy (29) more powerful and makes the sentence less acceptable than (61b). In (62a) the intervening phrases reduce the force of the sentence as an existential statement and make it relatively less acceptable.

(61a) It was a dog barked at the cat.
(61b) It was a dog fell on the cat.

(62a) There is according to the secretary on the phone a boy wants to see you.
(62b) There is a boy wants to see you according to the secretary on the phone.

Furthermore, if an adverb intervenes between the noun and the relative clause verb the sentence also is more acceptable, as in (63a) compared with (63b). According to our interpretation this also is due to the fact that the intervening adverb reduces the force of *the boy* as subject of the verb *wants*.

(63a) There's a boy outside wants to see you.
(63b) Outside there's a boy wants to see you.

Consider now questions like (56b), which are still fully acceptable in many modern dialects. We interpret this as due to the fact that the *it* in such sentences functions as an "expletive" (analogous to *there*) rather than as a referential pronoun. This is not true for the unacceptable questions with pronouns or nouns and no relative clause markers in (64).[26]

(64a) *Who is he saw the fire?
(64b) *Who is the one saw the fire?
(64c) *Who is the person saw the fire?
(64d) *Who is the boy saw the fire?

In (56b) the *it* is unambiguously an expletive, since it cannot be coreferential with the personal pronoun *who*. However, if the interrogative pronoun used is *what*, the resulting questions, such as (65), are less acceptable than (56b), presumably because of the uncertainty as to whether *it* is a personal pronoun or an expletive.

(65) What was it fell on you?

Thus cases like (56b) are acceptable only because they do not lead to a false segmentation.

Given that cases like (56a) and (56b) do not involve perceptual difficulty, we might ask why they appear to be in the course of becoming ungrammatical. Presumably this active development could be taken as an example of the pressure for simplification of a rule of predictive grammar—that is, if cases like (56a) and (56b) always required a relative pronoun, then the relative pronoun insertion rule would be as stated in Stage 6, but without *any* qualifications. Thus, this generalization can be taken as an instance in which the pressure to simplify the predictive rules is forcing a grammatical restructuring.

One other historical change remains for discussion—the evolution of the system of relative clause markers themselves, in particular the disappearance of the shared nominal and the appearance of the relative pronoun. The shared nominal could be deleted in a set of environments which are superficially heterogenous:

(66a) if the shared nominal was the subject of the relative clause verb

(66b) if the shared nominal is the object and the relative clause was introduced by (i) an inflected form of the demonstrative *se* or (ii) an inflected interrogative pronoun

(66c) obligatorily for both subject and object shared nominal if there is no relative clause marker (either þe or *se* or interrogative pronoun)

There is no representation offered by the rules themselves which reveals what generalization underlies these facts—the statements that account for the different deletion environments are simply presented as a list in (66). Yet it is clear that what is at issue in case (66b,i) and (66b,ii) is that there be *some* marker in the surface structure as to what the shared noun is and what its function in the relative clause is. Since the system of verb inflections was fully developed during Stages 1 and 2, a great deal of information about the shared noun could be gathered simply by examination of the particular inflectional ending on the verb in the relative clause. Furthermore, the relation in the relative clause of the (deleted) shared nominal is presumably perceptually recoverable because of the fact that only subjects of inflected verbs are ever deleted—as in the hortative or imperative constructions. However, no information about the object is revealed in the verb inflection. Accordingly, object pronouns could be deleted only if there was some other signal as to the fact that the shared nominal is the object—namely the presence of the relative pronoun or demonstrative inflected to be in the accusative case.

The fact that shared nominals *must* be deleted if there is no other relative clause marker may be interpreted as due to the confusion that would arise between compound and subordinate constructions. For example, if (67a) and (68a) were to appear as (67b) and (68b), the meaning would not be affected but the sequences would be interpreted as a compound of two independent sentences:

(67a) He hit the boy likes Mary

(67b) He hit the boy he likes Mary

(68a) He hit the boy Mary likes
(68b) He hit the boy Mary likes him

Thus, the obligatory deletion of the shared nominal when there was
no other relative clause marker had the effect of creating a sequence
which could *only* be interpreted as a subordinate (relative) clause
rather than being mistaken as an independent sentence.

The details of the formation of the relative pronoun itself pose
quite a difficult formal problem in their own right. What occurred
is represented in (69).

	Stage 1	Stage 2
(69) undeclined rel. marker	þe	demonstrative (that)
declined rel. marker	demonstrative (se)	interrogative (who, what, etc.)

It is clear that in Stages 1 and 2 (indeed even in Modern English)
there was both a declined and undeclined function word available
to introduce relative clauses. However, at Stage 2 the demonstrative
marker *se* that had been declined at Stage 1 now appeared in the
form *þæt* as the (undeclined) relative clause marker, while the inflected interrogative pronoun was now used as the inflected relative
clause marker. Furthermore, just as *se* could optionally precede þe
in Stage 1, the interrogative pronoun introducing a relative clause
could appear optionally before *þæt* in Stage 2. Thus the only change
between Stage 1 and Stage 2 in the relative clause markers themselves was that þe became *þæt* while the inflected demonstrative
as relative clause initial was replaced by interrogative pronouns.

The facts are straightforward, as is their functional interpretation.
However, their formal description in terms of changes in rewrite
rules does not reveal the fact that the syntactic pattern of the language remained the same in this respect while the individual words
used in that pattern changed. While the formulation in (69) above
represents these facts of each stage, it does not appear to do so in
a way that naturally represents the changes, nor does it offer any
explanation as to the cause of the developments. In this respect
we can only offer the conjecture that with the general leveling of

inflections on the demonstrative pronoun (often used as the article) and nouns, that the *se* converged on þe in the form þæt, leaving no inflected form except the interrogative pronouns to be used as inflected relative clause markers. But this does not explain *why* there was a continued pressure for an inflected relative clause marker.[27]

9. *Some Synchronic Effects of the Perceptual Parsing Principle*

So far we have outlined the way in which the perceptual operations used to isolate the main clause of sentences have constrained the historical development of the rules governing the insertion of relative pronouns and particles in English. The main result of the currently operative constraints on English grammar is that young listeners are not misled into parsing a noun together with a subordinate verb form as an independent clause. There are other aspects of modern English structure which appear to reveal the same constraints. For example, R. Kirk and others have observed that the grammar of English is such that a sentence-initial subordinate clause is always marked in the surface structure so as to be distinguishable from the main clause.

The most obvious mark of subordination is a clause-initial subordinating conjunction, as in (70).

(70a) <u>While</u> I was listening to E. Power Biggs, I had a vision of the Virgin Mary.
(70b) <u>Since</u> he comes from Brooklyn, John knows how to stiff a cabbie.

Sentence-initial subject complements, on the other hand, are marked by clause-initial complementizers, as in (71).

(71a) <u>The fact that</u> the rattlesnake had been milked did not make me like him.
(71b) <u>For</u> the man to introduce the speaker was nice.
(71c) The boy<u>'s</u> winning the race so handily delighted the coach.

At first glance, such facts could appear to be a coincidental manifestation of unrelated rules which place morphemes like *while*, *that*, *'s*, etc., at the beginning of sentence-initial subordinate clauses. However, the patterning of these morphemes makes it clear that their appearance is governed by the general constraint that an initial subordinate clause not be confusable with a main clause. Notice that in sentences like (71a), either one of the two initial complementizers may be deleted, but not both, as illustrated in (72).

(72a) <u>The fact</u> the rattlesnake had been milked did not make me like him.
(72b) <u>That</u> the rattlesnake had been milked did not make me like him.
(72c) *The rattlesnake had been milked did not make me like him.

Moreover, there are situations in which the clause-initial subordinating conjunction may be deleted, but if so, the subject and the verb of the subordinate clause are also deleted and the verb of the subordinate clause becomes nonfinite. This is illustrated in (73); the examples are synonymous with those in (70).

(73a) Listening to E. Power Biggs, I had a vision of the Virgin Mary.
(73b) Coming from Brooklyn, John knows how to stiff a cabbie.

In our interpretation, sentences like those in (73) are acceptable versions of those in (70) just because the verb forms in their subordinate clauses are nonfinite. Note that this situation is exactly parallel to that created by the rule of relative-clause reduction; (74b) is an acceptable version of (74a) just because the verb of the relative clause is nonfinite, whereas (74c) is unacceptable, because the verb is finite and hence would mistakenly be taken to be the main verb of the sentence.[28]

(74a) The man who maintains a fleet of six cars deserves to be taxed at the highest rate.
(74b) The man maintaining a fleet of six cars deserves to be taxed at the highest rate.
(74c) *The man maintains a fleet of six cars deserves to be taxed at the highest rate.

In section 5 above, however we pointed out that certain sentences which are complex perceptually because they contain subordinate clauses which may be mistaken for main clauses are nevertheless grammatical, for example (35a), which is repeated here for convenience.

(35a) The horse raced past the barn fell.

Such sentences would appear to weaken our claim that there are constraints operating on all derivations which block the generation of sentences which are perceptually confusing because of the lack of markers to indicate the subordinate status of subordinate clauses. How is it that the grammar allows sentences such as (35a) to be generated as fully grammatical? The answer has to do with the difficulty one would encounter in ruling out as ungrammatical perceptually confusing sentences such as (35a), while admitting large classes of sentences which are structurally parallel but which are not confusing.[29] For example, (75a), which is completely parallel to (35a), is not at all confusing.

(75a) The horse ridden past the barn fell.

In order for a grammar to block the derivation of (35a) while admitting (75a) and similar sentences, relative-clause reduction would have to include a restriction so as to disallow it only when the past participial form of the verb in the relative clause is homophonous with its past of present finite form (thus blocking clause reduction when the main verb of the relative clause is the passive of a verb like *race, walk, sell, run,* etc.). However, as (75b) reveals, this restriction is too strong: Although *sold* is homophonously the past participle and past tense form of *sell*, the sentence is not confusing, since if *sold* were acting as the main verb of the sentence, it would require a direct object.

(75b) The horse sold at the barn fell.

Consequently, the constraint on relative-clause reduction would have to be stated so as to allow reduction of clauses containing a homophonous verb form when the syntax of the verb would rule out the particular initial string as a possible main clause. But even this constraint is too strong, since it would block both (75c) and (75d), when only the latter is confusing:

(75c) The pillows tossed in the bed stayed there all night.

(75d) The men tossed in the bed stayed there all night.

Thus the constraints blocking clause reduction which would be appropriate to the perceptual facts are of the following sort:

(76) Relative-clause reduction may not apply within a passive relative clause if:
- (a) the past participle of the verb is homophonous with a finite form of the verb appropriately inflected to have the preceding noun as subject, and
- (b) the constituents which follow the verb form are permitted by the strict subcategorization of the active form of the verb, and
- (c) the sentence formed by the string including the object phrase(s) following the verb is a semantically plausible independent sentence.

In other words, anything that would allow the listener to interpret the first subordinate clause as a main clause would have to be blocked, but not otherwise. The formulation given in (76) is furthermore probably incomplete as it stands, but it does give a good idea of the complexity that would be involved in stating the appropriate restriction on relative-clause reduction, and it is this complexity which has maintained sentences like (35a) as grammatical in English. Having to learn restrictions like those in (76) is more problematic than the occasional perceptual embarrassment caused by sentences like (35a).

Another problem is raised by sentences like (71b,c), in which the markers *for* and *'s* may not be deleted even though such deletions would leave distinctive markers: In such sentences the initial clause is redundantly marked as subordinate by the elements *to* and *ing* as well as the *for* and *'s*. Nevertheless (77a,b) are disallowed as variants of (71b,c):

(77a) *The man to introduce the speaker was nice.

(77b) *The boy winning the race so handily delighted the coach.

The reason is that although the verb phrase is marked as subordinate (by the *to* or *ing*), the subject of the subordinate clause would mistakenly be taken as a reduced relative clause modifying that subject. In other words, (77a,b) are taken to be variants of:

(78a) The man who was to introduce the speaker was nice.

(78b) The boy, who was winning the race so handily, delighted the coach.

It is because of this confusion that the grammar does not contain special deletion rules that would exploit the apparent redundancy in the subordinate clause marking of sentences like (71b,c). Moreover, the absence of these deletion rules is formally parallel to the absence of a rule which would delete one or the other of the clause-initial complementizers *the fact* or *that,* and so does not occasion any additional complexity in the grammar of English— indeed it would involve added complexity in the grammar to have rules to delete them. We conclude that the addition of rules that would create ambiguities, increase the complexity of the grammar, and resolve no behavioral or structural complexities (other than to reduce apparent redundancy) would be linguistically quixotic and an unlikely historical development.[30]

In the foregoing discussion we have shown some consequences for present-day English of the perceptual parsing principle (29b) with regard to sentence-initial subordinate clauses and clauses which modify the subject noun phrase. The principle also has some grammatical consequences for subordinate clauses in English which follow the verb.

Consider verbs such as *mention* and *say* (which we shall call class "M") which occur with indirect objects obligatorily introduced by the preposition *to* and with *that*-clause object complements, as in (79).

(79) I $\begin{Bmatrix} \text{(a) mentioned} \\ \text{(b) said} \end{Bmatrix}$ to Marsha (that) Frieda was crazy about Harvey.

(The parentheses around *that* in (79) indicate that this complementizer is optional.) Suppose one were to question the indirect object. Two possibilities arise. First, the preposition may be fronted along with the question-word, resulting in sentences like (80).

(80) To whom did you $\begin{Bmatrix} \text{(a) mention} \\ \text{(b) say} \end{Bmatrix}$ (that) Frieda was crazy about Harvey?

Second, the preposition may be left behind, or stranded, but in this case, the expletive *it*, acting as a dummy direct object, must be inserted directly following the main verb, as in (81).

(81a) Who(m) did you $\left\{\begin{matrix}\text{(i)} & \text{mention}\\ \text{(ii)} & \text{say}\end{matrix}\right\}$ it to (that) Frieda was crazy about Harvey?

(81b) *Who(m) did you $\left\{\begin{matrix}\text{(i)} & \text{mention}\\ \text{(ii)} & \text{say}\end{matrix}\right\}$ to (that) Frieda was crazy about Harvey?

From a purely syntactic point of view, the obligatory insertion of the dummy direct object *it* following verbs of the class M when and only when the indirect-object preposition *to* has been stranded[31] is certainly a curious and inexplicable state of affairs.

There is, however, a straightforward explanation on the basis of the perceptual parsing principle. Whenever a preposition is stranded, there is a danger that if a noun phrase immediately follows it in the surface string, that noun phrase will mistakenly be taken to be the object of the preposition. In (81) that situation obtains: A stranded preposition is directly followed by a noun phrase which is nevertheless not its object. What is needed is a marker in the surface structure which signals that the entire clause which follows the stranded preposition is the complement of the main verb. English grammar can provide such a marker, namely, the expletive pronoun *it*, which independently of the sentences under consideration, functions as a signal that a complement clause follows. It also signals what grammatical relation that clause bears to the main verb: If the *it* is the surface subject, then the clause is subject; if the *it* is the surface object, then the clause is object, as the examples in (82) indicate.

(82a) It is likely that the Latvians will reach the moon before the Lithuanians do.
(82b) I have it on good authority that the budget cuts will not be restored.

Accordingly, in cases like (81), the grammar of English requires that the expletive *it* be inserted before the preposition exploiting its general capacity to act as a signal that that which follows the stranded preposition is necessarily the object complement of the verb and not the object of the preposition.[32]

10. *A Speculative Smorgasbord*

A. SUMMARY

We have argued that the constraints which a child and adult have on the utilization of language in speech behavior limit the kinds of sentences that are understood and therefore restrict the kinds of grammatical structures which are learned. The history of the grammatical restrictions on relative clause markers in English has been our example of the effects on linguistic evolution of this interaction between the systems for understanding sentences and learning sentence structure. As the nominal inflections disappeared between the 11th and 15th century, certain constructions with relative clauses became perceptually complex. This complexity was counteracted by changes in the restrictions on the presence of relative clause markers, which removed most of the perceptually difficult cases from the language.

Such developments exemplify the historical competition between what makes a language easy to understand and what makes it easy to learn. Between the 11th and 15th centuries the overall tendency with respect to the subcomponent of grammar we have been considering was to simplify the learning of grammatical structures by leveling the different systems of inflection—as we pointed out above, a rich inflectional system may make sentences easier to comprehend but it also makes the language harder to learn. Thus, the disappearance of all inflections had the effect of simplifying the learnability of one part of the language. Similarly the gradual disappearance of the shared nominal in relative clauses also had the effect of making the language easier to master, although harder to understand. The disappearance of shared nominals increased the generality of the shared-nominal-deletion rule (44d), but made certain sentences more confusing. (It is clear that in those cases in which the shared nominal appears in modern English, e.g., (9a), it is retained in order to remind the speaker or the listener of the grammatical source of the relative pronoun.)

In the 15th century the first change in the restrictions represented an increase in the grammatical complexity (and a decrease in the corresponding "syntactic regularity") of the restrictions on the

presence of the relative pronoun. Finally, the modern generalization of the restrictions represents a grammatical resimplification.

These developments in the past millenium are not susceptible to
any generalization about the evolution of formal grammars as such.
No tendency appears always to simplify rules or to maximize a
formal property of the rules, such as the extent to which the output of one rule is part of the input to a subsequent rule (cf. Kiparsky 1968 for a discussion of this principle as a formalized motivating force underlying certain linguistic developments). Thus, while a
plausible account can be found in the consideration of the interaction of the ease of learning and of understanding the language,
the structure inherent in the formal account of what is learned and
perceived does not itself reveal any plausible formal account of the
historical changes.

However, in all these examples of the interaction of perceptibility
and learnability we have only considered one small subcomponent
of the grammatical structure and the perceptual mechanisms. How
the whole language maintains a balance between learnability and
perceptibility cannot be formulated at the moment since there is
no common theoretical language available in which to compare
the two kinds of complexity. Unfortunately, languages cannot as
yet be rated for their overall "usability." Consequently, we cannot
predict *a priori* which languages are highly "unusable" and likely
to undergo some sort of evolution that will simplify learnability or
perceptibility. (Note that this problem arises even within the consideration of synchronic "structural" facts, such as the comparison
of the relative complexity of a change in a phonological rule with
the use of several lexically-marked exceptions to that rule.) The
inevitable incompleteness of every grammar is particularly damaging
to the formulation of a univocal explanation of historical developments.

B. THE MUTATIONAL BASIS OF LINGUISTIC EVOLUTION AND
THE COMPETENCE/PERFORMANCE DISTINCTION

Recent linguistic theorists have drawn a rigid distinction between
linguistic structure ("competence") and speech behavior ("performance"). The corresponding theories of linguistic evolution have
concentrated on the changes that take place within linguistic struc-

ture. The main proposal has been that suggested by Halle (1962), that children *restructure* their grammar to provide simpler accounts of the language than they hear in the grammar of their parents. This presupposes that new forms appear in languages spontaneously (at least from the standpoint of the grammar), which then motivate a grammatical restructuring. This picture of linguistic change is outlined in (83). (See also the discussion in section 3, pp. 38–40 above.)

(83) Stage   Sentence Types   Grammatical Structures
     (a)   a. . . . . .z   A. . . . . .Z
     (b)   b. . . . . .z+ⓒ B. . . . . .Z+#
     (c)   a. . . . . .z+ⓒ A' . . . . .Z'

In this model there is a period when adults may have one grammar (e.g., 83b) while children have advanced to a restructured grammar (e.g., 83c). Such a model follows directly from three claims:

(84a) Children can replace learned grammatical structures, while adults can only add rules to already learned structure.
(84b) Grammars learned by children are maximally simple representations of the linguistic forms the children hear.
(84c) New linguistic forms appear spontaneously.

The first claim (84a) is related to the psychological hypothesis that there is a "critical period" for "creative" language learning, which cuts off about age 12. After that point new language learning is viewed as a relatively artificial process, in which it is easier to learn new forms as a function of old structures than to restructure the already learned grammar *de novo*. This hypothesis has both clinical and anecdotal evidence in its favor (cf. Lenneberg 1967). However, it is a moot point whether or not children from 2–12 are themselves willing to restructure their own grammars totally when presented with new linguistic forms. Recent investigations of the development of grammatical structure (at least as revealed by speech production; cf. Brown, Bellugi, Bloom) have demonstrated that the child's linguistic ability itself develops at each point by minimal changes in highly articulated grammatical rules. Thus the fact that the adult appears not to be able to change his grammar in a major way may also be true of the child at every point in his language development: It may simply be the case that during the ten years that the child is acquiring language he has the lability to perform many more slight grammatical restructurings than an adult. That is, principle (85) governs the restructuring that a child will carry out at each point.

(85) The child's grammar at one stage is a minimal change from the grammar at the preceding stage.

(85) raises an old theoretical problem: What constitutes a "minimal" change in grammatical structure? Detailed examination of the ontogenetic restructurings in the course of language acquisition may provide some empirical data which will clarify this theoretical question.

Proposal (84b) that children always learn the maximally "simple" grammar would provide a natural basis for constraining the extent of restructuring that a child applies to his own grammar when he hears linguistic forms that are novel to him. The problem left open by (84b) is this: How does a child decide which of the sentences he hears are relevant data for a grammatical restructuring and which are not? Clearly if a child is presented with a foreign language at age four he does not learn it as a function of his already-mastered linguistic structures. He recognizes intuitively that the difference between the foreign language and what he knows already is *so* great that it must be considered as entirely distinct (even if the same people in his environment speak both the first and second language). Presumably at each point in his speech development, there are certain possible additions to his first language that he will also be unable to learn as part of his language because their grammatical description represents too great a departure from the grammar he has already mastered. Thus, the possible novel forms that a child will try to take account of within his grammar are limited in part by the following sort of principle (86):

(86) Neologisms that are recognized by children as motivating a restructuring, (a) must be comprehensible, and (b) imply grammatical structures that are "close" to the already-learned structure.

Of course, like (85), this principle leaves open the definition of structural "closeness."

The third proposal, (84c), that neologisms occur, is not intended as an explanation of their occurrence or of their form. No doubt new forms may be introduced into a language by cross-cultural contacts, as well as by creative individuals within the culture. Whatever the source of a particular neologism the problem remains to characterize the general constraints on what kind of neologisms are likely to occur. Part of the argument in the present paper is that non-structural behavioral constraints modify linguistic evolution by their presence in the language-learning child. Another way in which these behavioral systems influence language change is by limiting the neologisms that adult speakers themselves will produce and accept as "semi-sentences." Clearly semi-sentences (potential neologisms) which are incomprehensible or which violate some general behavioral laws will tend not to be uttered or picked up as part of a new argot (87).

(87) Possible neologisms are limited by the systems of speech behavior ("performance").

Of course the main burden of this paper has been to point out that language learning and linguistic evolution are the learning and evolution not merely of grammatical structure but also of the perceptual and productive systems for speech behavior. The novel structures that the child recognizes as relevant motivation for restructuring his grammar must be sentences he can (at least partially) understand, desire to say, and learn from. Thus, we can see that there are at least two sorts of requirements that the child applies to a novel sentence before attempting to modify his grammar to predict it: (1) It must be comprehensible. (2) Its grammatical description must not be radically different from the grammar the child has already mastered. In this way we can view the child as "filtering" constructions that are new to him, and learning those that meet the conditions in (86). Sometimes constructions are novel to a child merely because he has not heard them, and at other times because they are new to the language as a whole. Certain otherwise possible neologisms will never be incorporated into a language because they will be filtered out at all points in the child's development.

In this respect linguistic evolution can be interpreted as an interaction of systematically constrained neologisms with the ontogenetically shifting filter in the child: Those neologisms that are appropriate to the particular stage in the child "survive"; they are picked up by the child and incorporated into the predictive grammar of his language. In this sense the effect of linguistic neologisms is analogous to the role of biological mutations in species evolution: Their form is somewhat constrained by existing synchronic structures, and if they create a structure which is too much at variance with existing structures they "die out" and do not become part of the structural evolution. In brief, the linguistic future is highly constrained by the structural and behavioral systems implicit in the linguistic present.[33] One consequence of this is that certain universals of language which appear to be aspects of synchronic "linguistic structure" have sources in the ways in which language is learned and used. There is other evidence that this theoretical entailment of our empirical investigation of the history of English is correct. (See Bever 1970b for empirical investigations of the ways in which linguistic structures can be interpreted as linguistic reflections of cognitive structures.)

Once we have taken into consideration learning and perceptual factors as part of the explanation for linguistic evolution we are faced with the question of how to interpret language history in terms of changes in formal linguistic structure. One recent proposal (Kiparsky 1970) is to include such factors as "functional roles" (and presumably perceptual mechanisms) as part of the linguistic structure ("competence"), since such factors obviously play a part in linguistic evolution and consequently determine certain universal properties of language. Such a claim must be carried out in its entirety. That is, one cannot accept one part of the perceptual system as being within linguistic competence and exclude other parts from competence because they do not appear to interact with formal structure. To do this would allow for completely circular explanations of historical changes—every time we observe a particular perceptual or functional constraint motivating a linguistic change we could merely postulate it as part of linguistic "competence" and take that as our explanation. Surely this will not do. If we are to take certain nonstructural factors ("performance") into account at all in explaining linguistic evolution we cannot pick and choose what is relevant *post hoc*. Rather, the entire range of behavioral aspects of language must be considered simultaneously as constraining the possible changes a language structure can exhibit. But to include all systematic behavioral properties of language within "competence" would be to claim that there is no such aspect of language as "performance"—that is, that linguistic structure does not have a reality distinct from its use except as a subcomponent of its use. It is doubtful that such an all-inclusive notion of "competence" is fruitful. We will understand more about linguistic structures by carefully drawing distinctions between linguistic systems, rather than by blurring them together.

C. SOME TRADITIONAL ISSUES

Our investigations also bear on several issues which have been of traditional interest for all students of linguistic change: (1) the notion of "functional load" as an explanation for linguistic developments; (2) the claim that languages tend to change from depending on inflections to express internal relations to depending on superficial word order; and (3) the relative importance of factors external and internal to a culture in triggering linguistic change.

(1) Various scholars have appealed to the notion of "functional load" as an explanation for the appearance of particular changes in the evolution of a language (cf. Martinet 1962). Basically, the proposals depend on a notion of optimum distribution of information-bearing features in a language: If a particular sound or distinctive feature becomes too important in distinguishing words or sentences, the disproportion of the "functional load" on that sound or feature can be taken as forcing a restructuring of the language so that other units or sentences can take over some of the information load. The interest of such arguments depends entirely on the postulated nature of the language in which functional load is optimally distributed. Clearly, maximum equality of distribution across sound types or syntactic constructions is not an intuitive linguistic *desideratum*, since many languages reveal large disproportions between the most and least frequent structures. Our arguments in this paper suggest that optimum *frequency* of a construction or *informational* load must be measured vis-à-vis the particular mechanisms for language perception and production. With this proviso, we agree with those who argue that the motivation for linguistic change can be found partially in the ways in which the structure of

language is used. However, our position is that it would be circular to define changes in language structure in terms of its function (cf. Jespersen 1941, Martinet) or function in terms of structure (cf. Kiparsky 1970). Rather, the two systems of linguistic organization must be defined and studied independently in order to understand how they interact within the speaking child and adult. Our advantage today over earlier scholars concerned with this interaction is that we have available independently motivated theories of linguistic structure and speech performance.

(2) The change from relative dependence on inflections to relative dependence on surface order to indicate the internal structure relations between phrases has been a traditional topic for linguistic historians. Our argument is that the secondary cause of such a development can be the relative difficulty of learning a language in which there is a large number of phonologically different nominal declensional systems (as opposed to one with a highly regular declensional system). This pushes the question back as to why simple declensional systems have a tendency to become elaborated at all. We have suggested that this may be due to the increased perceptual ease of a language in which there are many different cues as to the particular lexical items which are being heard. But of course other factors such as the introduction of new vocabulary items or sets of irregular forms from foreign languages may be even more important.

The evolutionary pattern of inflectional systems described by Jespersen is that inflectional systems characteristically evolve from simple to complex and then are leveled. This pattern may be interpreted as resulting from the conflict between the perceptual and the predictive systems of language. We assume that there is continual evolutionary pressure for a language to maximize the recoverability of deep structure relations in individual sentences. These languages tend to develop both surface order constraints (using function words) *and* inflectional markings. Consider a (hypothetical) language in an initially stable stage, having both inflections and ordering restrictions. If this language has one regular declension class it is easy to learn—but the homogeneity of a single-class inflectional system contributes information only about the logical relations within a sentence and this information is also generally recoverable (by hypothesis) from surface order (and special morphemes). However, the perceptual simplicity of each individual sentence would be increased if the inflectional endings contributed differential information about each phrase and attributive relations between words separated from each other (e.g., as between adjectives and their head nouns). (Note that this would be relatively difficult to attain through proliferation of ordering restrictions—there is an upper limit to the number of possible lexical-class orders within an average size clause, but there is no theoretical limit to the possible number of inflectional classes in the lexicon). Accordingly, the second phase of the hypothetical language is one in which the ordering restrictions are somewhat tightened and there is a large number of inflectional classes. This in turn strains the learning process, which provides the conditions for leveling all the inflections, with order restrictions remaining.

This description of a pattern of linguistic evolution in terms of competition between language learning and perception leaves open too many questions to count as an explanation. Rather, its value lies in articulating the explanation of the evolution into specific questions concerning the interaction of the learning and of the perception of language—questions which may be answered through further research.

(3) It is obviously premature to pinpoint specific external causes of linguistic change, although we can try to describe the *kinds* of nonlinguistic event that can trigger linguistic developments. One extra-linguistic factor that is often referred to is being conquered by or conquering a group of speakers of a different language. In addition, our claim that linguistic evolution is in part a function of the balance between learnability and perceptibility raises the possibility that certain internal cultural developments can themselves motivate a linguistic shift by changing what the language is used for. Suppose that there were a cultural change in the relative importance of the learnability of a language and its perceptibility? This would in itself place a new set of constraints on the evolution of the language since it would upset the previous balance in the culture between the language's learnability and perceptibility. For example, an increase in the relative importance of "educated forms" of sentences (e.g., sentences with many embeddings) might place a greater relative emphasis on perceptibility constraints, and motivate those linguistic shifts which increase the perceptibility of individual

sentences, even though such shifts would increase the complexity of the predictive grammar which must be learned.[34]

D. CONCLUSION

Such questions await further empirical and theoretical investigation. The main focus of this paper is to emphasize the fact that linguistic evolution is a joint function of the various systems for the use of language. Attempts to explain linguistic development as a formal function of just one of these systems are doomed to incompleteness whether the system considered is that of speech perception, production, or the grammatical prediction of new sentences. We cannot explain a linguistic restructuring as a function only of an out-of-balance perceptual load, or of a learning difficulty, or of the formal complexity of the predictive grammar. All the systems of speech behavior interact in the child and naturally constrain each other as the language evolves.

NOTES

1. For arguments that relative clauses are formed from internal structure conjoined sentences, see Thompson 1971.

2. The subscript i indicates reference; accordingly, the formula requires that the two nominal expressions mentioned make the same reference. We call these the "shared nominals." The symbols X_1, X_2, etc., are variables.

3. If the nominal containing the shared nominal is in fact just the shared nominal, then the relative pronoun is either the word *that,* or one of the interrogative pronouns *who, whom,* or *which* (the choice of the *who/whom* vs. *which* having to do with whether or not the shared nominal is assumed to designate a sentient being, and the choice of *who* vs. *whom* having to do with the syntactic functioning of the shared nominal in the relative clause).

If the shared nominal is wholly contained within a larger nominal expression, then the relative pronoun *whose* is chosen, and sentences like (i) are obtained.

(i) A man whose reputation I admire is looking for a job.

4. Here, we depart from the position of recent investigators of relative clause formation in English, according to whom relative pronoun formation is obligatory, there being also an optional rule of relative pronoun deletion. We contend that the grammar of English is simplified, and that a more unified account of the history of English is possible, if it is assumed instead that relative pronoun formation is made optional.

5. Ross's complex noun-phrase constraint and similar "derivational constraints" in grammar (Lakoff 1969) all seem to be reflections of perceptual strategies of one sort or another. To show this, however, would require extended discussion, which would go far beyond the scope of this paper. See also note 22 and Bever 1970a, b.

6. The ungrammaticality of example (10d, ii) is accounted for independently as follows. First, note that the relative clause does not modify the preceding noun, but rather that the internal structure of this sentence is also that of the sentence:

(i) The one that is responsible for this mess is the mayor.

Example (10d, i) is obtained from (i) by rules which first delete the elements *the one,* and second extrapose the relative clause to the end of the sentence, leaving behind the expletive *it.* But the rule which deletes *the one* requires the presence of a relative pronoun immediately following those elements; hence neither (10d, ii) nor (11d) will be generated. On the other hand, if the relative pronoun is not added, the relative clause will automatically be reduced, and (ii) will be obtained.

(ii) The one responsible for this mess is the mayor.

7. Modifier preposing does not, however, apply if the modified noun is an indefinite pronoun such as *someone,* etc. It also applies only optionally to a very small set of particular noun-adjective combinations such as *life eternal,* and to certain other combinations in lyrics and poetry (e.g., *fiddlers three* in "Old King Cole").

8. At least, it has none in contemporary English. We shall return to consider examples like (22) in the history of English below in Section 6.

9. In order to explain the difficulty one has in understanding examples like (35a), we need recourse to another perceptual strategy besides that of (29), one which states in effect that the beginning of a sentence is the beginning of a sentence:

(i) $\# X \rightarrow \# [_S X$

The perceptual difficulty of (35a) is that strategies (i) and (29a) together assign only one left sentence boundary to that sentence, leaving the listener in a quandary as to what to do with the leftover verb *fell.*

10. In Stages 2 and 3 there were also relative clauses introduced by a string consisting of an interrogative followed by the demonstrative (*who that, which that,* etc.); quite possibly this use of *that* in second position was a continuation of *be* in second position. It is worth noting that this construction fell into disuse about the same time that subject-verb inversion began to be restricted to interrogative and a few other main clause types. The reason is that prior to this time the *that* was useful in signaling that the preceding pronoun was a relative and that the following clause was subordinate. Later, word order could be used to tell whether the pronoun was interrogative or relative, and the following clause main or subordinate.

11. Two sentences from the works of Shakespeare may be cited as counter-examples to this claim:

(i) Yet I'll move him to walk this way: I never do him wrong But he does buy my injuries to be friends, Pays dear for my offences. [A 166; Shakespeare, *Cymbeline* I, i, 105] " . . . but he [who] does buy . . ."

(ii) Those men blush not in actions blacker than the night will shun no course to keep them from the light. [C 16; Shakespeare, *Pericles* I, i, 135] "Those men [who] blush not . . ."

But, as Curme argued, we may assume that the omission of the subject relative pronoun in these cases was done deliberately and consciously by Shakespeare, and that they do not reflect the rules of English syntax which he normally followed. Besides these, we have encountered very few other examples of this sort in all of English literature; one occurs in the writings of the Irish playwright John Synge:

(iii) A lad would kill his father, I'm thinking, would face a foxy devil with a pitchpike. [V 14; Synge, *Playboy of the Western World*, (1907)] "A lad [who] would kill . . ."

Another (called to our attention by Fred Householder) is from a recent detective novel:

(iv) Anybody knows Harry'd say the same (i.e., Anybody *who* knows Harry'd . . .) [E. Livington, *Policeman's Lot,* 1968]

12. In Stages 1 and 2, omission of the subject relative pronoun in nonreduced relative clauses was largely limited to constructions involving the verbs *hatan* or *clepan* "be named," and even here because of the possibility of having the object before the verb, the result was not always that the verb came first in the relative clause. For Middle English, Mustanoja (1960: 205) refers to a dissertation by G. Winkler, in which it is observed that "the relative subject-pronoun is more frequently left unexpressed in Chaucer than the object-pronoun but the ratio is reversed in Caxton." On the next page, he cites figures from a dissertation by J. Steinki on the ratio of nonexpressed to expressed object relative pronouns in the works of various late Middle and early Modern English writers. The figures he gives are Pecock 1: 950; Capgrave 53: 1250; Cely Papers 4: 172; Caxton 8: 2800; Fortescue 1: 245; Latimer 19: 3100; Bacon 15: 490; Sidney 331: 2180. From these figures, we may conclude that both subject and object relative pronoun omission were quite rare for Chaucer, Caxton, and the other writers of the late ME period. Mustanoja claims further, however, that there was a rise in the frequency of subject relative omission early in the Early Modern English period (our Stage 4).

13. Some examples which exhibit subject relative omission in relative clauses modifying direct objects can be found in the writings of certain nineteenth-century novelists and poets, such as Keats, Mrs. Browning, Thackeray, and Meredith, but they are deliberate archaisms. The construction has also been

preserved dialectally, if we are to believe the testimony of Wright (1905: 280): "The relatives are, however, often omitted in the dialects, not only in the obj[ective] case in the lit[erary] language, but also in the nom[inative], as *I know a man will do for you.*" In support of this, Visser (1963: 14) supplies a number of examples from Synge, and examples can also be found in modern detective stories, as Householder has pointed out to us.

14. According to Visser (1963: 538), in about 98% of the cases of object relative omission found in Early Modern English texts, the relative clause begins with a pronoun, rather than with a full nominal expression. That is, sentences like (i) occur about fifty times as often as sentences like (ii):

(i) John saw the man she admires.
(ii) John saw the man the woman admires.

Visser assumes this is so for metrical reasons; the omission of the object relative (*whom* or *that*) before a pronoun insures that two weakly stressed elements do not occur together. This explanation cannot be true, however, since nominal expressions also generally begin with a weakly stressed element (*a* or *the*). The explanation probably has to do with a perceptual strategy which leads one to expect that when two independent nominal expressions of the same type (i.e., both full noun phrases or both pronouns) occur next to one another, they are part of a larger coordinate structure. The omission of an object relative before a full nominal expression modifying a full nominal expression leads to a violation of that strategy; e.g., when one hears (iii)

(iii) John saw the man the woman _____

one expects that it will be completed by another nominal, e.g., "and the child," rather than by a verb, e.g., "admires."

15. If we were to remain with our earlier decision to have the rule follow relative pronoun formation, we would find that the rule would have to be stated differently for each of the last two stages. We shall not discuss developments concerning the rule of modifier preposing.

16. An explanation for these facts about shared nominal retention is given in the next section.

17. Notice that in the examples in (47a) and (47e) the relative clause without an introducer modifies a subject nominal that has been inverted with its verb.

18. See note 17.

19. Examples (52b) and (53d) are not to be interpreted as containing complements, according to the secondary sources.

20. Jespersen (1927: 145) points out that a number of authors who use the accusative of the predicate nominal pronoun in simple sentences like:

(i) 'Tis me.

use the nominative (as in (53f)) when the pronoun is followed by a relative clause with the subject relative pronoun omitted. This observation provides additional independent evidence for the interaction of strategy (29) on grammar.

21. The traditional analysis of the verbal inflections would appear to show that there were many different idiosyncratic kinds of verb inflections among both strong and weak verbs. These complexities have been shown to be more apparent than real. The interested reader should consult Bever (1963) and Keyser (1966) to see the demonstration that there was actually an extremely small number of underlying classes in the strong and weak verb systems, respectively.

22. This sort of restriction on the surface structure expression in internal relations could be interpreted, following Perlmutter 1968, Lakoff 1969, Ross 1967, and Langendoen 1969, as an example of an "output constraint," which restricts the kind of derivation which is possible from an internal relative clause to an external form, and which explicitly marks that clause as relative. We see nothing wrong with such a formulation except that it merely restates the facts at issue. Our quest is to explain such features of sentences rather then enumerate them. For example, Bever (1970a) has suggested that it is characteristic of such "output constraints" that they reflect general perceptual processes which are true of the perception of stimuli other than language.

23. It is interesting to note that in all the cases of unmarked relative clauses in OE that we have found in the texts in which the object noun is the object of a finite verb and confusable with a nominative, the relative clause verb is either a form of *be* or a modal. That is, the allowed ambiguity may have been restricted even further than we claim by actual grammatical rule or simply by conventions of usage. This interpretation of the constraint would be further supported if it is true that sentences which began in initial nouns in the objective case could have a relative clause following with verb initial but without any relative clause marker, e.g., (i):

(i) Him likes me nobody likes.

Cases like this would not have run afoul of the segmentation strategies in (29) since the fact that the first noun is not in the nominative case shows that it cannot be the subject of any following verb. So far we have not found any data that would decide this question.

24. All the intuitions in this section of our discussion are relatively evanescent. We suggest that the reader compare the two versions of each sentence, with and without the relative clause marker, in order to convince himself that our statements are correct, at least about the *relative* acceptability of the sentences. For example, in our dialects the difference in acceptability between (56a) and (a$'$) is greater than the difference between (56b) and (b$'$). Indeed, while it is clear that (a$'$) is more acceptable than (56a), it is not at all clear to us that (b$'$) is more acceptable than (56b).

(a$'$) $\left\{ \begin{array}{l} \text{It's} \\ \text{There's} \end{array} \right\}$ a boy $\left\{ \begin{array}{l} \text{who} \\ \text{that} \end{array} \right\}$ wants to see me.

(b$'$) Who is $\left\{ \begin{array}{l} \text{it} \\ \text{there} \end{array} \right\} \left\{ \begin{array}{l} \text{who} \\ \text{that} \end{array} \right\}$ wants to see me?

25. Notice that the cases with expletive *there* and *it* ought to have caused trouble in OE as well, since the initial noun is in the nominative case and therefore should have been segmented as the subject of the following verb. However, as we are arguing for Modern English, this segmentation would not have involved a semantically inappropriate segmentation of the first clause.

26. We have no data on this kind of construction in OE.

27. J. Thorne has pointed out to us some evidence that suggests that "who/which" is an inflected relative clause-marker, even in Modern English, which would account for the continued presence of some inflections. In relative clauses prepositions can precede "who/which" but not "that," as shown below.

(a) The room in which we stayed was small.
(b) *The room in that we stayed was small.
(c) The man with whom we spoke was small.
(d) *The man with that we spoke was small.

Thorne suggests that if we view a noun phrase with an initial preposition as "case marked" then (b) and (d) are inadmissible because "that" is undeclinable; prepositions may *precede* "who/which" if they are viewed as being the modern form of an inflected clause introducer.

28. Similarly, we get in Current English the paradigm:

(i) Anyone who owns a fleet of six cars deserves to be taxed at the highest rate.
(ii) Anyone owning a fleet of six cars deserves to be taxed at the highest rate.
(iii) *Anyone owns a fleet of six cars deserves to be taxed at the highest rate.

Note that (iii) is ungrammatical, even though, as it turns out, the initial sub-sentence anyone owns a fleet of six cars is not a possible English main clause. What this example reveals is that the constraint in question is a grammatical one and not merely a perceptual one, since if it were merely perceptual, (iii) would be both grammatical and acceptable. We have not investigated the question whether, in earlier stages of English, sentences like (iii) were acceptable. If they were, we would still be faced with the question whether they were ungrammatical, but acceptable because of their usability, or fully grammatical.

29. The critical question here, to which we cannot give a completely satisfactory answer, is "How large is large?" As we have already seen, whenever a perceptual difficulty is grammatically codified into a grammatical restriction, certain sentences which are structurally parallel to the difficult sentences but which are themselves not so perceptually difficult are also rendered ungrammatical (see, for example, the discussion above in connection with the examples in note 28). However, it is apparent that the class of ruled-out sentences which are not difficult is small compared with the class of ruled-out difficult ones. In the situation under discussion (reduced relative passive clauses) the opposite situation obtains: The class of perceptually difficult sentences is small compared with those structurally parallel ones which are not

difficult. The task remains, of course, to give a more precise meaning to these remarks about relative sizes of classes of sentences, but their import should be clear.

30. Note that the potential ambiguity of (77a, b) could be resolved by blocking their derivation from (78a, b), rather than from (71b, c). However, such a mechanism would involve the same sorts of complexities as those discussed in the text in connection with the problem of blocking the derivation of (35a) by relative-clause reduction.

Also observe that the fact that the markers *for* and *'s* may be (and in the case of *for* generally are) deleted when the subordinate clause is an object complement, as in examples (i) and (ii),

(i) I expect the man to introduce the speaker.
(ii) The coach approved of the boy winning the race.

is in conformity with our expectations, since if there is temporary ambiguity as to whether the verb phrase is to be taken as part of the complement of the main verb or as a modifier of the object noun phrase, it would be resolved by what follows, as in (iii) and (iv):

(iii) I expect the man to introduce the speaker to come late.
(iv) The coach approved of the boy, winning the race, taking a shower.

Or, the ambiguity involved has to do with lexical ambiguity of the main verb itself, as in (v):

(v) I know the man to be the hero in tomorrow night's play.

31. That this is the correct generalization can be seen from other types of sentences, for example, cleft sentences, in which the preposition is also stranded:

(i) It was Marsha (that) I $\left\{\begin{matrix}\text{(a) mentioned}\\\text{(b) said}\end{matrix}\right\}$ it to (that) Frieda was crazy about Harvey.

(ii) *It was Marsha (that) I $\left\{\begin{matrix}\text{(a) mentioned}\\\text{(b) said}\end{matrix}\right\}$ to (that) Frieda was crazy about Harvey.

32. It is interesting to note that the grammar of English does not simply constrain *that*-deletion to accomplish the objective of separating a stranded preposition from a following noun phrase which is not its object. Apparently the presence of *that* as in:

(i) *Who(m) did you mention to that Frieda was crazy about Harvey?

is insufficient in itself to prevent confusion (perhaps because of its homophony with the demonstrative pronoun). Note, in this connection, the grammaticality of both variants of (ii), i.e., with or without the *that:*

(ii) Who(m) did you learn from (that) Frieda was crazy about Harvey?

We have no explanation for the failure of the expletive object *it* to appear in cases like (ii).

33. Such a view allows us to interpret the occurrence of particular developments in one language and their non-occurrence in a closely related language. For example, German is highly inflected, such that singular nouns are uniquely marked as being in the objective case if they are not the internal structure subject of their verb. Yet relative pronouns may not be dropped in German sentences analogous to those in (7) above. This would seem to be at variance with our explanation that deleting relative pronouns in those positions in Old English is allowable because of the presence of noun inflections at the time. That is, while Old English had a rule for deletion of relative pronouns in certain positions German has no such rule. Thus to delete a relative pronoun in German even in positions which would not create perceptual confusions would be to change an exceptionless rule into a variable one. (Note that the argument has the same form if one takes the view that relative pronouns are transformationally introduced in German since there is no rule that deletes them.) That is, if an adult or child makes a slip of the tongue in German and produces a relative clause without a relative pronoun it tends not to be picked up as a productive neologism since it is too much at variance with the existing linguistic structure. It would be tempting to argue for a principle like (a) as a specific subpart of (86), but the evidence is far too scanty to do any more than suggest it as a hypothesis for further investigation.

(a) Changing an ungoverned (universal) rule into a governed rule (optional or restricted to certain environments), is not a minimal grammatical change.

Also, at present we cannot explain why relative pronouns could be omitted in the older Germanic languages generally, e.g., Old High German, Old Saxon, etc., but not in Modern German.

34. The reader may have noticed that we do not discuss the putative effects of the interaction of structure learning and perception with the system of speech production. This is not because we think that such effects do not exist, but because the system of speech production has been largely unstudied.

REFERENCES

Abbott, E. A. 1870. *A Shakesperian Grammar.* New York: Macmillan.

Abrams, K., and T. G. Bever. 1969. Syntactic structure modifies attention during speech perception and recognition. *Quarterly Journal of Experimental Psychology,* 21: 280-90.

Bellugi, U. 1967. The acquisition of interrogative and negative constructions. Harvard University Ph.D. dissertation.

Bever, T. G. 1963. The E/O ablaut in Old English. *Quarterly Progress Report,* M.I.T. 69: 203-207.

——. 1970a. The cognitive basis for linguistic structures. *Cognition and the Development of Language,* J. Hayes, ed., pp. 279-362. New York: Wiley.

——. 1970b. The influence of speech performance on linguistic competence. *Advances in Psycholinguistics,* G. D'Arcais and W. Levelt, eds., pp. 21-50. Amsterdam: North-Holland.

Bever, T. G., J. Lackner, and R. Kirk. 1969. The underlying structure sentence is the primary unit of speech perception. *Perception and Psychophysics* 5: 225-34.

Bloom, L. 1970. *Language Development.* Cambridge: M.I.T. Press.

Blumenthal, A. 1966. Observations with self-embedded sentences. *Psychonomic Science* 6, 10: 453-54.

Brown, R. 1965. *Social Psychology.* New York: Free Press.

Chomsky, Noam. 1965. *Aspects of the Theory of Syntax.* Cambridge: M.I.T. Press.

Curme, G. O. 1912. A history of the English relative constructions. *Journal of English and Germanic Philology* 11: 10-29, 180-204.

Fodor, J., and T. G. Bever. 1965. The psychological reality of linguistic segments. *Journal of Verbal Learning and Verbal Behavior* 4: 414-20.

Fodor, J., and M. Garrett. 1967. Some syntactic determinants of sentential complexity. *Perception and Psychophysics* 2: 289-96.

Garrett, M., T. G. Bever, and J. Fodor. 1966. The active use of grammar in speech perception. *Perception and Psychophysics* 1: 30-32.

Halle, M. 1962. Phonology in generative grammar. *Word* 18: 54-72. Reprinted in *The Structure of Language,* J. Fodor and J. Katz, eds., pp. 334-52. Englewood Cliffs, N.J.: Prentice-Hall, 1964.

Jespersen, O. 1927, 1940. *A Modern English Grammar on Historical Principles,* vols. III, VII. Heidelberg: Carl Winters Universitätsbuchhandlung.

——. 1941. *Efficiency in Linguistic Change.* Copenhagen: Ejnar Munksgaard.

Keyser, S. J. 1966. Unpublished manuscript.

Kiparsky, P. 1968. Linguistic universals and linguistic change. *Universals in Linguistic Theory,* E. Bach and R. Harms, eds., pp. 170-202. New York: Holt, Rinehart and Winston.

——. 1970. Explanation in phonology. To appear in S. Peters, ed., *Goals of Linguistic Theory.*

Lakoff, G. 1969. On derivational constraints. *Papers from the Fifth Regional Meeting of the Chicago Linguistics Society,* R. I. Binnick, et al., eds., pp. 117-42. Chicago: Department of Linguistics, University of Chicago.

Langendoen, D. T. 1969. The "Can't seem to" construction. *Linguistic Inquiry* 1: 25-36.

Lenneberg, E. 1967. *Biological Foundations of Language.* New York: Wiley.

Martinet, A. 1962. *A Functional View of Language.* London: Oxford University Press.

McMahon, L. 1963. Grammatical analysis as part of understanding a sentence. Harvard University Ph.D. dissertation.

Mehler, J. 1963. Some effects of grammatical transformations in the recall of English sentences. *Journal of Verbal Learning and Verbal Behavior* 2: 346-51.

Miller, G. A. 1962. Some psychological studies of grammar. *American Psychologist* 17: 748-62.

Mustanoja, T. F. 1960. *A Middle English Syntax,* Part I. Helsinki: Société Néophilologique.

Perlmutter, D. 1968. Deep and surface constraints in syntax. M.I.T. Ph.D. dissertation.

Postal, P. 1970. On the surface verb "Remind." *Linguistic Inquiry* 1: 37-120.

Poutsma, H. 1916. *A Grammar of Late Modern English.* Groningen: P. Noordhoff.

Roberts, W. J. F. 1937. Ellipsis of the subject-pronoun in Middle English. *London Mediaeval Studies* 1: 107-15.

Ross, J. R. 1967. Constraints on variables in syntax. M.I.T. Ph.D. dissertation.

Schlesinger, I. 1966. The influence of sentence structure in the reading process. U.S. Office of Naval Research Technical Report 24.

Smith, C. S. 1964. Determiners and relative clauses in a generative grammar of English. *Language* 40: 37-52. Reprinted in *Modern Studies in English,* D. Reibel and S. Schane, eds., pp. 247-63. Englewood Cliffs, N.J.: Prentice-Hall, 1969.

Sweet, H. 1924. *A Short Historical English Grammar.* Oxford: Clarendon Press.

Thompson, S. A. 1971. The deep structure of relative clauses. *Studies in Linguistic Semantics,* C. J. Fillmore and D. T. Langendoen, eds. New York: Holt, Rinehart and Winston.

Visser, F. T. 1963. *An Historical Syntax of the English Language,* vol. I. Leiden: E. J. Brill.

Wilson, L. R. 1906. *Chaucer's Relative Constructions.* Chapel Hill: University of North Carolina Press.

Wright, J. 1905. *The English Dialect Grammar.* Oxford: Clarendon Press.

4.

Rule Precursors and Phonological Change by Meta-Rule

James Foley,
University of British Columbia

I claim that historical change occurs not by the addition of rules to a grammar, but rather by changes in rules already existing in the parent language; and that historical changes are not unrelated to each other, but rather occur in groups definable by meta-rules. These ideas are illustrated by the Spanish phenomena of lenition, syncope, and facilitation.

Lenition is the voicing of intervocalic stops, e.g., Latin *aqua*, Spanish *agua*; Latin *vita*, Spanish *vida*; Latin *capere*, Spanish *caber*. Within Spanish itself compare *amado*, past participle of *amar* from **amato,* with *muerto,* past participle of *morir.* The continuant *s* also becomes voiced intervocalically, as in Latin, though this development is obscured by subsequent conversion of *z* to *r*: *querer*, but *quisto*; *rural*, but *rústico*; *sugerir*, but *sugestión*; etc. Note Latin *amare* from **amase*, cf. *esse*; *amaverunt* from **amavesunt*, cf. *amavistis*; *cineris* from **cinisis*, cf. *cinis.*

I claim that the Latin rule which voices intervocalic continuants (it is clear from the development of IE voiced aspirates in Latin that *s* is the only example) is the precursor of the Spanish rule which voices all intervocalic consonants.

I can establish a set of distinctive features which are not based on articulatory or acoustical data but on processes which occur in natural languages. Thus, for example, there are languages in which *g* becomes a fricative, but *d* and *b* do not (North German *saɣen,* but *baden, beben*), and there are languages in which *g* and *d* drop, but *b* does not (Spanish *leer, caer, haber* corresponding to Latin *legere, cadere, habere*). Assuming that the order of spirantization and elision represents relative strength, I can establish the scale

g d b

$\longrightarrow$

1 2 3

relative strength

It is important to emphasize that this scale does not refer to the phonetic properties of the segments but to abstract phonological relationships. Since our goal is the study of the human psyche, of which language is one manifestation (along with behavior and mythopoesis), we surely want to construct our linguistic system in a manner which will allow correspondences to be established with other psychic systems. A phonological theory which includes a set of distinctive features based on phonetic data, because of its parochialism, its inapplicability to other fields, will not allow us to reach this goal.

Observation of natural languages suggests many such scales (see my Morphophonological Investigations II), of which one is

stops   continuants   nasals   liquids   glides

$\longrightarrow$

∅   1   2   3   4

relative resonance

Exposition of the arguments for these scalar positions is beyond the scope of this paper, but intuitively, glides, the counterparts of vowels, are the most resonant consonants. Nasals and liquids are more resonant than oral stops and continuants. The existence of rules such as ln → ll, but not ln → nn (e.g., Lithuanian *kalnas*, Latin *collis*), in view of the relatively stronger position of *n* (cf. Latin *dictus* > Italian *detto*, not *dekko*), suggests that liquids are relatively stronger than nasals. The possibility of *s* becoming syllabic (e.g., Turkish *spirto > ṣpirto > ispirto, Spanish *scala > ṣcala >

escala, parallel to Latin *agr > agr̥ > ager) suggests that continuants
are more resonant than oral stops. For evidence from English concerning the relative position of segments on this scale see the paper
by Arnold Zwicky in this volume.

With reference to this scale, the Latin rule which voices intervocalic continuants is

$$[-\text{syllabic, resonance value} \geq 1] \rightarrow [+\text{voice}] \; / \; V\_\_V$$

whereas the Spanish rule is

$$[-\text{syllabic resonance value} \geq \emptyset] \rightarrow [+\text{voice}] \; / \; V\_\_V$$

Latin and Spanish possess the same rule,

$$[-\text{syllabic, resonance value} \geq n] \rightarrow [+\text{voice}] \; / \; V\_\_V$$

but for Latin $n = 1$, for Spanish $n = \emptyset$.

The source of the lenition innovation in Spanish is the advent of
the meta-rule (rule which applies to rules)

$$n \rightarrow \emptyset / \text{ resonance value} \geq n$$

Syncope results from the elision of a short unstressed vowel, e.g.,
Spanish *feble,* Latin *flebilis*; Spanish *deuda*, Latin *debita*, where
lenition applies first (debida), then syncope (debda), and finally
vocalization of the *b*.

In Latin, as a general rule, elision occurs after a liquid, as in the
verb conjugations *duco, ducis, ducit, ducimus, ducitis, ducunt,* but
fero, fers from **feris*; *fert* from **ferit*; *ferimus, fertis* from **feritis,
ferunt*; as well as nouns *ager* from **agros* (cf. Greek *agros*), *puer*
from **pueros* (cf. *amicus* from **amicos*). Without concerning ourselves with the nature of the vowel, other than that it be short and
unstressed, the rule is

$$V \rightarrow \emptyset / [-\text{syllabic, resonance value} \geq 3] \; \_\_C$$

whereas in Spanish the conditions are relaxed to allow elision when
the vowel is preceded by any consonant (*debita > deuda, dubitare >
dudar*), and the rule is

$$V \rightarrow \emptyset / [-\text{syllabic, resonance value} \geq \emptyset] \; \_\_C$$

The origin of Spanish syncope is the Latin elision of short unstressed vowels after a liquid. Latin and Spanish have the same rule

$$V \rightarrow \emptyset \ / \ [-\text{syllabic, resonance value} \geq n] \_\_C$$

but with different values for the variable n (for Latin n = 3, for Spanish n = $\emptyset$). Once again, the Spanish innovation is due to the application of the meta-rule

$$n \rightarrow \emptyset \ / \ \text{resonance value} \geq n$$

Facilitation is manifested here as the development of a liquid to a glide when followed by a consonant; e.g., Spanish *otro* (French *autre*), Latin *alter*. Examination of the conjugation of *velle* reveals the Latin source of this rule:

volō	volumus
vīs	vultis
vult	volunt

The thematic vowel drops when preceded by a liquid unless it is followed by a nasal, and *o* becomes *u* when followed by tautosyllabic *l*. The radical vowel *e* becomes *o* under the influence of the preceding *w*, except in the infinitive and second singular. The underlying forms are

welō	welimus
welis	welitis
welit	welunt

After syncope, *l* becomes *y* when followed by a continuant (second singular *wels* > *weys*), but not when followed by a stop (third singular *welt* remains). Then *ey* yields long *ī* (note *dīcō* from *deicō*, cf. Greek *deiknūmi*).

The Latin rule is

$$l \rightarrow \text{glide} \ / \ \_\_ [-\text{syllabic, resonance value} \geq n], \text{where n = 1}$$

(The nature of the glide does not concern us here. *ln* becomes *ll* before glide formation can apply.)

In Spanish, since **altro* > *awtro* > *otro*, the rule is

$$l \rightarrow \text{glide} \ / \ \_\_ [-\text{syllabic, resonance value} \geq n], \text{where n = } \emptyset$$

The transition from the Latin rule to the Spanish rule is achieved by the operation of the meta-rule.

$$n \rightarrow \emptyset \ / \ \text{resonance value} \geq n$$

The Spanish innovations discussed above are not arbitrary accretions to the grammar of Latin, but rather have their source in Latin
rules, and although apparently disparate and unrelated, in fact form
a natural group defined by a single meta-rule in a system of nonphonetic distinctive features.

5.

The Internal Evolution of Linguistic Rules

William Labov
University of Pennsylvania

1. *The Transition Problem for Generative Rules*

It is generally understood that one of the most important contributions of generative grammar is a precise notion of "rule of language." In earlier periods, few linguists appreciated the complexity and depth of the ordered rules involved in syntax or morphophonemics. Even the exceptional linguists who did operate at this level of complexity, like Stanley Newman, did not have available a theory to delimit and specify the kinds of rules which operate in linguistic structure. But as the concept of the linguistic rule became sharper, the problem as to how one rule changes into another became more difficult to handle. This is the generative aspect of the *transition problem*—"the attempt to discover the intervening stage by which Structure A evolved into Structure B" (Weinreich, Labov, and Herzog 1968: 184).

The problem was no less baffling to those who worked in terms of discrete, invariant categories rather than invariant rules. To cite the well-known passage of Hockett:

A phonemic restructuring . . . must in a sense be absolutely sudden. No matter how gradual was the approach of EME /æ:/ and /ɔ:/ towards each other, we cannot imagine the actual coalescence of the two other than a sudden event: on such-and-such a day . . . the two fell together as /a:/ and the whole system of stressed nuclei . . . was restructured. Yet there is no reason to think that we would ever be able to detect this kind of event by direct observation. [1958: 456-57]

The transition from quantitative to qualitative change is not made easier when we turn from categories to rules. The notion of a categorical rule also implies that at a certain point in history a rule was dropped, was added, or was reordered. We also speak of the simplification of rules by deletion of features in the environment, but these are also categorical, discrete changes which must be conceived as occurring at a discrete time.

Halle's solution to this problem is to relate discrete breaks in language learning to gaps between generations. A father necessarily forms his basic rule system several decades before his son. It therefore follows that a son may formulate a radically different set of rules, reorganizing all the late accretions and modifications in his father's speech into a more systematic, simpler version of the grammar (Halle 1962). But the discreteness of generations is a property of the family, not of the speech community. Preadolescent children do not speak like their parents, but like their age-mates in the neighborhood. The effect is most easily observed when the parents were raised in a different dialect area; it may be seen in high prestige and low prestige speech communities, in England, France, or America. That is not to deny that some parental influences can be observed, and it is hard to believe that the mechanism proposed by Halle does not actually operate to some extent. But in general, we find that preadolescent children restructure the grammar learned from their parents to match that of their peers, and peer groups form a continuous, relatively unbroken series. We are left with the problem of accounting for discrete differences in rule systems between successive cadres of speakers who form a continuous linguistic tradition.

For many linguists, the period of change is conceived of as one of disruption. Thus Moulton cites as obviously true the remark of Hans Kurath that all linguistic change inevitably involves disruption. ("A language cannot pass from one system to another without temporary disorganization"—Moulton 1967: 1405.) The difficulty here is that change is not rare or occasional. Every speech community that has been examined with any degree of attention shows extensive variation in rules; and many of these variables show evidence of change in progress. Each time that a linguist begins to observe a speech community with any degree of care, we receive a report of "exceptional" variation, dialect mixture, and unusual heterogeneity. Such variation would theoretically seem to be disadvantageous to the speakers, since the Saussurian model of language calls for homogeneous rules shared by all members of the speech community. How then do people use their language as it changes? Can we point to any real examples of linguistic impairment as a result of the disruption of rules in the process of change? Traditionally, members of the community speak of the decay and corruption of their language from a former state of excellence, but linguists have rightly looked at such complaints with scepticism.

In this paper, I will argue that the solution to the problem lies in extending the notion of rule of language to include orderly differentiation over a range of linguistic environments. In a more general presentation, we have argued that a rational conception of language change must provide for such orderly differentiation within the speech community. The competence of a native speaker must include the command of such heterogeneous ways of speaking: it is a homogeneous system which would be dysfunctional (Weinreich, Labov, and Herzog 1968). The rule-governed aspect of language includes the differentiation of speakers according to age, sex, social class, and other aspects of ascribed and achieved status. But this discussion will be confined to the central area of the internal constraints on linguistic rules—primarily the phonetic and syntactic conditions which govern phonological rules. This is the area where the categorical view of discrete, invariant structure is most clearly established, and where the difficulties in accounting for change are most severe.

In section 2 of this paper I will consider the possible models of linguistic change in terms of various combinations of regularity and discreteness. The third section will take up the types of linguistic rules which can formally account for such models, using as an example the consonant cluster simplification rule of nonstandard Negro English, which evolves internally with age. The fourth section will take up the centralization of /aw/ on Martha's Vineyard, using spectrographic measurements to study the evolution of the rule through three generations, and the final section will consider the raising of short *a* in New York City as it moves from low to high

KEY

to Spectrographic Vowel Charts

o i,	bit	⬤ ihr,	beer		o u,	put	⬤ uhr,	boor
O iy,	be	⬤ ih,	idea		O uw,	do	⊖uw,	dew*

▽ e,	bet	▼ehr,	bare		▽ ʌ,	but	▼ohr, four
▽ey,	bay	▼eh,	yeah		▽ow,	know	▼ɔhr, for*
							▽oh, law

☐œ,	bat	☐œhN,	man*		◇a,	got	◈ahr, guard
☐̰œ,	had***	☐œh$,	bad*				◈ah, god*
		☐œhF,	bath*				◈äh, father

⬂ay,	buy	⬀ aw,	now		⬁oy,	boy	⊏yuw, you

ᶜO front**   Oˣ back**

As indicated above, the following values hold for all symbols:

```
o O circles . . . . . . . . . . . . . high vowels
▽ ▽ triangles . . . . . . . . . . . . . mid vowels
◇ ☐ squares, diamonds . . . . . . . . low vowels
⬂ ⬀ wedges . . . . . . . . . . . . . upgliding true diphthongs

☐ o small symbols . . . . . . . . . . short or lax
O ▽ large symbols . . . . . . . . . long or tense
   ▼☐ open . . . . . . . . . . . upgliding
   ◆■ shaded . . . . . . . . . . before /r/
   ◆■ hatched . . . . . . . . . . ingliding
```

Word classes are identified not by their underlying forms, but
by their position in a broad phonetic representation, which is the
common input to sound changes for all of the dialects concerned.

---

*   distinguished only in some dialects
** distinguished only where front and back are in close proximity
*** class of "weak words", which may have [ə] as the only vowel

position, again using spectrographic data taken from our larger study of sound changes in progress. Although most of the data will be drawn from cases of sound change, with more or less complex grammatical conditioning, the general application of the findings is not confined to phonology. Our knowledge of syntactic change is much less advanced, but the few indications we have suggest that the mechanism of change will involve rules of the same kind as those discussed here.

2. Models of sound change

Linguistic systems are complex enough to provide many possible ways and routes and manners of change. The situation can become more than a little confusing when one begins to discuss regular or irregular change, since there are so many ways in which a changing system can depart from uniformity. Fig. 1 shows five simple models of phonological change, with terminology which may help to abbreviate the discussion which follows. We consider a simple speech community with only three speakers, S1, S2, S3, and a homogeneous word class with three items, represented by ○, △, and □. The top diagram is the state of the language before the change. The rule which governs the change may produce gradual or discrete movement of a segment in these words through a given dimension of phonological space. The issue of gradual or discrete movement will not be considered here, but the change will be taken as a whole. The height of each column represents the proportion of occurrences of members of the word class in natural speech for which the rule applies, ranging from 0.0 to 1.0. In the categorical models on the left, only these two values are considered—either the rule applies or it does not. On the right are variable models, in which we take into account intermediate values of the frequency variable.

Model A is "regular sound change" in the neogrammarian sense: All three speakers move together and the word class is intact. The variable Model A' is similar, except that we can see the rule applying with intermediate frequency to all speakers and members of the word class. Model A is the kind of construct we may find useful for viewing completed changes, or remote cases where the data is insufficient. But no such cases have ever been observed in progress.

Fig. I. Five models of
phonological change.

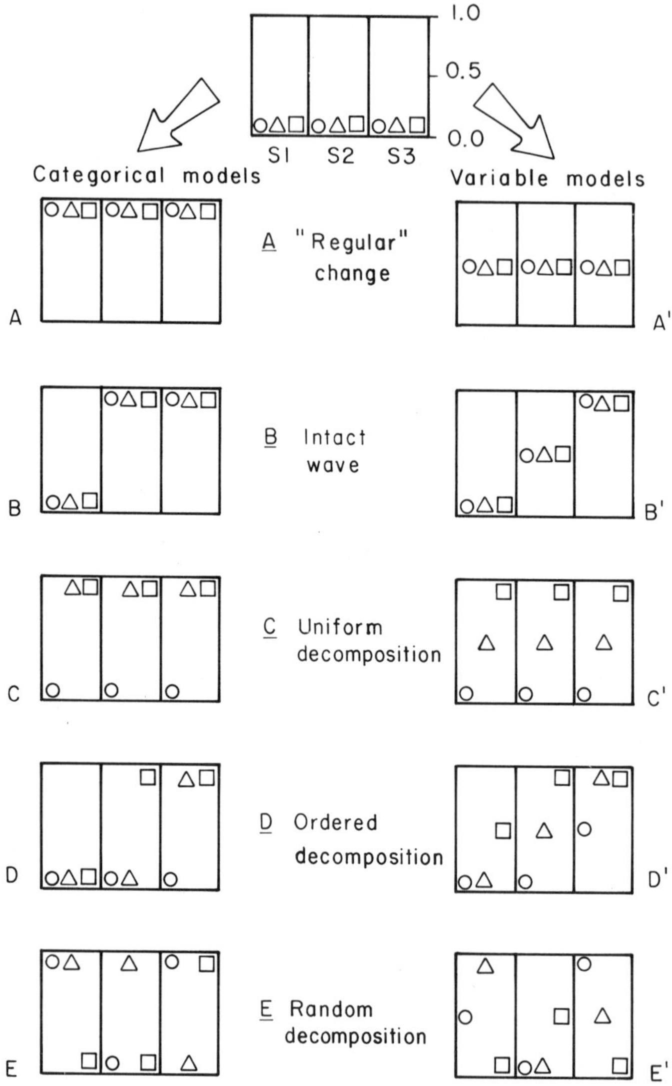

Model B shows the word class still behaving as a unit, but the change moving gradually through the three speakers who form this population is an "intact wave." The fact that the three speakers are different does not necessarily contradict the regularity of sound change; it can be asserted that they speak different "dialects." The fact that the original class of words moves together is the important thing. This is what is meant by Bloomfield's observation that "Phonemes change." The class may be large or small, a phonetically conditioned subclass or a whole phoneme (or even a whole feature), but model B preserves the notion that it is the class (or the rule) which changes, not the individual words.

The converse of model B is also logically possible—that the change will move through the entire population at the same rate, but through the word class one at a time. Thus we have model C, or "uniform decomposition." This model would in fact create a new word class. If everyone in the community decomposed the original set of words in the same way, it would not be possible to restore the original class if the change did not, for any reason, affect the entire class. This is obviously true in the categorical version of the model. In the variable model C', the second word is sometimes pronounced in the older manner, sometimes in the newer manner. This fluctuation would let the current generation of speakers suspect that ○ and □ were once members of the same class—unless the change merges □ with another class. In that case, there would be no way of separating the completely changed □ from the other class, which had never undergone the change.

We can find cases of such uniform decomposition in which a word class was disrupted in the same way for all members of a speech community. The tensing rule for short *a* in Philadelphia offers a striking example. Monosyllables ending in anterior voiceless fricatives are affected by this rule, raising [æ] to [ɛ:ə] in *pass, bath,* and *laugh* but not *cash.* The corresponding rule in New York City affects all voiced stops as well, but in Philadelphia, only three such words, all ending in -*d*, are involved. These are *bad, mad,* and *glad,* contrasting [ɛ:ə] with lax [æ] in *pad, grab, Brad,* etc. We might try to rationalize this decomposition by saying that "common adjectives" are affected, but this attempt fails because *sad* is always pronounced with [æ] in this dialect (Ferguson 1968).

This Philadelphia situation is uncommon. If all word classes were decomposed in such a uniform and inexplicable manner, we would be faced with an insoluble problem: How are word classes maintained? It is well established that the neogrammarian hypothesis is an effective working assumption for comparative reconstruction. It follows that word classes are in general reconstituted, no matter how much they may be fragmented in the course of change. Model D, "ordered decomposition," is therefore a more likely possibility than C. In this model, word classes are decomposed in a given order, in an ordered wave passing through the population. Words form an implicational series: If $\triangle$ is changed, then $\square$ is bound to be so. In the variable model, if the change begins to affect $\triangle$, we can be sure that $\square$ is affected at least to that extent and probably more so. S2, a native speaker of a community in which model D′ is operating, is never in any doubt about the composition of the original word class. From his own speech, there might be no way of knowing whether $\bigcirc$ and $\square$ were members of the same class. But knowing how S1 and S3 speak, he may be able to use this native knowledge to conclude that $\bigcirc$, $\triangle$, and $\square$ are all members of a class which can have either the older or the newer form. It is this possibility—that a knowledge of variation is a part of his competence—that we will explore further in sections 3, 4, and 5 of this paper.

Model D (and D′) assumes that the decomposition of the word class proceeds from some principle that we can grasp as linguists or as native speakers. No matter how small the class is, it is still possible for phonetic conditioning to be at work—for in the long run, every word is its own phonetic class, and can affect the change by some phonetic factors. Our discussion will revolve about such ordered phonetic decomposition—model D′—in which grammatical conditioning is only an incidental factor.

On the other hand, we must now be ready and willing to accept grammatical conditioning as part of the rationale of the decomposition. There is now a large body of empirical evidence which contradicts the neogrammarian notion that only phonetic factors influence sound change, and no reasonable person can proceed on the older assumption. The several cases cited by Postal (1968) from Mohawk are certainly valid examples of grammatical conditioning where the argument of analogy cannot apply. Even more persuasive are developments where the course of a sound change is directly modified by the need to preserve an important grammatical distinction, as in the case discovered by P. Eckert (1969). In one area of south central France, unstressed *a* was raised to *o*, and in a sizable core area, this rule applied in all grammatical environments. But to the north of this region, in exactly those areas where the loss of final -*s* eliminated the distinction between the feminine singular and plural, the sound change a→o took place only in the singular and not in the plural.[1] And as a third instance of grammatical conditioning, we can look again at the raising of short *a* in Philadelphia. The rule affected all words ending in front nasals except the three irregular verbs *ran, swam,* and *began.*[2]

The last model to be considered is E: "random decomposition." It is not always the case that word classes are decomposed in a regular order: There are some cases in which words fluctuate from speaker to speaker in a completely unpredictable way. There are elements in every sound change which would seem to answer this description. For example, there is a residue of unpredictable open *o* words in English formed by the irregular lengthening of *cloth, lost, foster,* and *Goth,* which rhyme for very few speakers of American English. The irregular shortenings of long *o* and *e* gave us such oppositions as *flood, good,* and *brood,* and *bread, dead,* and *mead.* In the case of the raising of short *a* in New York City to be discussed in section 5, the two-member word class of *jazz* and *razz* shows this unpredictable distribution, though the other word classes seem to behave in a more regular way. The randomness of model E does not refer to the fact that the pronunciation of a particular word may be unpredictable in a given sentence—that is true for all the variable models A' through E'. The reference here is to the unpredictable position of a particular word, where S1 may always apply the change to it, and S2 never, or vice-versa, literally without rhyme or reason. Model E is of course the enemy to rational explanation, which must be feared by all linguists. It implies that sound change is the product of such a vast number of historical accidents that we will never be able to account for the data we find.

In every sound change that we have observed closely we find ordered decomposition; yet within the smallest word classes, there is usually unordered decomposition of the model E or E' type. No matter how many new subclasses and new conditioning factors we discover, there will most likely be a residue of exceptions and non-conforming items. Examples can be found in any thorough histori-cal investigation: I cite one case as an example. In the reconstruction of Proto-Lolo-Burmese, Matisoff (personal communication) finds that Lahu ε corresponds to Old Burmese *a*, reconstructed as Proto-Lolo-Burmese (PLB) **a*.

	Lahu	*Old Burmese*	*PLB*
"bee"	pê	pyâ	*pyâ
"mountain field"	pê	hya	*ya
"eye"	pê	myak	*myak

However, there are "exceptions":

	Lahu	*Old Burmese*	*PLB*
"cold"	kâ	krâ	*krâ
"between"	ká	krâ	*krâ

The exceptions themselves can be seen here to form a regular sub-class. It is PLB *Kya* which becomes Lahu *Kε*, while *Kra* becomes Lahu *Ka*. Here regular rules are re-established, but there still re-mains a residual case:

	Lahu	*Old Burmese*	*PLB*
"many"	mâ	mya	*mya

No regular rule can be adduced to explain this last case. Within our present knowledge we cannot hope to reduce this residue of Model E behavior to the more regular types of sound change.

We can take three policies in regard to this evidence of unordered decomposition: We can be overwhelmed by the irreducibility of the Model E cases and conclude that there can be no explanatory theory of sound change; we can exclude all such cases from our data by labeling them as "dialect mixture"; or we can consider such limited cases as given, and look at the large body of ordered cases as problematical. Instead of asking why all sound change is not per-fectly regular, we can look at the matter the other way around: Given the fact that word classes are normally decomposed in the process of change, how do we account for the fact that they are al-most always reconstituted? What is the competence of native speakers which leads to this result?

In order to answer this question, it will be helpful to examine a typology of linguistic rules which can produce the models we have just considered.

3. *Types of linguistic rules*

Phonological rules that fit the categorical view outlined above are of the form:

(1) X → Y / A __ B

Given the environment A__B, the rule always applies. This is an *invariant* rule, which will be called here "Type I." The most important property of such invariant rules are that violations or exceptions do not naturally occur. If we construct a violation, it is not heard as coherent language, but as a meaningless sequence of sounds; more often, it is not heard at all. For example, there is an automatic Type I rule of English which determines the voicing of final inflections. To pronounce *cats* as [kætz] would not only be difficult, but odd in the extreme. The appropriate reaction is confusion ("Wha'?"), failure to hear ("I didn't get you"), or assignment of the speaker to another rule system ("What kind of an accent is that?"). The problem of interpretation is more pointed when we consider Type I rules of syntax. All dialects of English share an invariant rule of Negative Attraction, which asserts that a negative must be incorporated into a subject indefinite. If we construct a violation such as *Anybody doesn't sit there, do they?* many listeners find it almost impossible to hear, repeat, or interpret. They simply cannot figure out what we are up to.[3]

Not all rules have this invariant character. There are also semi-categorical, "Type II" rules, which are sometimes violated—such violations are rare but interpretable. For example, we know that the unstressed, indefinite quantifier is normally *some* in a positive sentence. Expressions such as "Ice cream? I hope there's any!" are heard as violations. But they are interpretable; some speakers will even accept them as English, and from other evidence we see that the use of *any* in positive sentences is just over the horizon.[4] We also observe a phonological rule that *-st-* clusters are not simplified directly before a vowel within a morpheme. Yet pronunciations such as [ɪnsɪns] for *instance* are heard from native speakers.

We can interpret them: We know that the speaker is extending the rule of consonant cluster simplification one step beyond normal. Metaphors are such Type II extensions—rare and reportable but interpretable breakings of the rules of English. "The soul had bandaged moments," according to Emily Dickinson, and we follow perceptively the violation of the rule that only [+ concrete] nouns are bandaged.

In recent work in the speech community we have found it necessary to utilize a third type of rule: "Type III," or variable rules, which extend the generative notion of "rule of grammar" to account for a larger range of data. In previous treatments of "free variation" we are confined to labeling certain rules as optional in their application, but forbidden to consider under what circumstances they apply more or less often. Type III rules are more than statements that a rule may or may not apply; they are lawful co-occurrence relations. In place of the strict co-occurrence statements which determine Type I and II rules, the Type III rule states that for every speaker of the language (and for reasonably small numbers of utterances), the rule will apply more often in one environment than in another—though "optional" in both.

Type III rules may be indicated formally by the use of angled brackets around the right-hand expression of the rule:

(2) $X \rightarrow <Y> / A\_\_B$

We associate with each rule a quantity ϕ, which expresses the proportion of cases in which the rule applies out of all those cases in which it might apply; e.g., all occurrences of AXB. To each rule of the form (2) we give an automatic interpretation that $\phi = 1 - k_0$, where k_0 is some factor which interferes with the rule going to completion. It follows that for Type I rule, $\phi = 1$, or $k_0 = 0$. The k_0 factor may be governed by such social constraints as age, sex, class, or ethnic group; the determination of such factors forms part of the embedding problem (Weinreich, Labov, and Herzog 1968: 101), but that will not be considered further here.

A characteristic Type III phonological rule of English is that which governs the deletion of final stops -t, d when a vowel does not follow.[5] In its most general form, this rule reads:

(3) $[-\text{cont}] \rightarrow <\emptyset> / [+\text{cons}] \_\_\#\#{\sim}V.$

Thus we may delete the final consonant in *just, find,* or *told.* Rules such as (3) will account for the intact wave of Model B'. But most of the cases that we have studied show *variable constraints:* The word class is decomposed into a number of phonological and/or grammatical subcategories which affect k_0 in a regular manner. For some members of the general word class AXB, the rule applies more often than with others. In the case of *t, d* deletion, we observe that for many dialects, there is no absolute prohibition against the rule applying before a following vowel; the rule does apply to such cases as *just a minute, most of the time,* and *find out,* but much less often than to *just now, most guys,* or *find me.* We can indicate such a regularity by writing angled brackets around the variable feature, and adopting a convention that the *presence* of this feature favors the rule.

(4) $[-\text{cont}] \rightarrow <\emptyset> / [+\text{cons}] \_\_ \#\# <\sim V>$

As the rule is now written it cannot apply to such past tense forms as *miss#ed* or *roll#ed,* since the inflectional boundary # is not indicated. But in many dialects of English, including nonstandard Negro English, such forms are affected by the rule. Again, we will want to indicate a variable constraint, for we find that for every speaker and every group, the rule applies less often to such past tense forms.

(5) $[-\text{cont}] \rightarrow <\emptyset> / [+\text{cons}] <\emptyset> \_\_ \#\# <\sim V>$

By this notation, we indicate that the rule applies more often to words like *mist* than to forms such as *miss#ed.* The angled bracket in the environment may be thought of as a cross reference to the original angled bracket around the right-hand member, reading "in reference to this variability, the rule applies more often when this element is present." The convention we have adopted leads us to expand both brackets first, with the most favored case that of *mist spray,* and least favored that of *missed us.* When one factor is favorable and the other unfavorable, as in *mist on it* or *missed me,* we have an intermediate ordering intermediate values of ϕ.

↑	-KK##K-	mist spray
ϕ	-KK##V; -K#K##K-	mist over it; missed me
	-K#K##V-	missed us

This is the simplest version of the rule, one which applies with great generality to all dialects of English. Indeed, such a rule may have universal implications; the constraints involved apply to a wide range of phonological variables in English and other languages, past and present. The constraint of a following vowel applies in English to the vocalization of /l/ and /r/, in Spanish and French to the aspiration and loss of /s/. The grammatical status of /s/, for example, has been shown to be an important constraint in Puerto Rican Spanish (Fishman et al., 1968). Without attempting to document this point with a long list of examples, one can turn the argument around and ask if there are any known cases of these constraints being reversed: a final consonant being dropped more often when a vowel follows or when it is a separate morpheme. Without such counter-examples one can say generally that whenever a phonological process removes a consonant variable at the end of a word, this process will be favored (a) if the consonant is part of a cluster, (b) if it is part of the word stem—not a separate morpheme, and (c) if it is not followed by a vowel at the beginning of the next word. Thus

(3a) [+cons] → <∅> / <+cons> <∅> __##<~V>

may lay claim to being a very general constraint on language and language change, and as such might not need to be written into the grammar of any particular language. But it is not practical or desirable to raise such rules into the realm of an as yet unrealized universal grammar. To begin with, the output constraints suggested by (3a) will apply to rules of epenthesis and vowel deletion as well,[6] so that one cannot condense such statements into a single rule which is at all coherent. Secondly, we are interested in more than the possibility of a change occurring and its direction—that is, the "constraints" problem (Weinreich, Labov, and Herzog 1968). We will want to attack the "transition problem"—to discover the route by which one state of the language passes into another; we will be concerned with the "embedding problem"—to locate the change within the linguistic and social matrix which governs its development; and finally, we hope to make some progress on the "actuation problem"—to say something about why this particular change took place at this particular time. Thus if we want to understand the wholesale loss of inflections in the history of English or German, we will want to analyze more than general tendencies. A general constraint such as (3a) will not allow us to trace the history of the change through successive stages, to show the relation between the grammatical and phonological factors at any particular time, to show the relation of this rule to compensating changes in the rule as it goes to completion, or to show the relative progress of the rule in various subgroups of the population. If our formal analysis of language is to give us insight into the process of linguistic change, we will need to design the general rules in the grammar so that they can serve as a framework on which to build specific detail.

In the case of consonant cluster simplification, we note that there is a great advantage in adding information on the relative ordering of the two variable constraints in (5). The convention of expanding angled brackets first will not help us in ordering two angled brackets located in different segments, yet such ordering can be strikingly different for different subgroups. For some groups of speakers, the phonological constraint is stronger and we can write

$$\text{(5a) } [-\text{cont}] \rightarrow <\emptyset> / [+\text{cons}] <\beta\,(\emptyset)> \underline{\quad} \#\#<\alpha(\sim V)>$$

while for others, the grammatical factor predominates, and we can write

$$\text{(5b) } [-\text{cont}] \rightarrow <\emptyset> / [+\text{cons}] <\alpha\,(\emptyset)> \underline{\quad} \#\#<\beta\,(\sim V)>$$

If the two types of ordering shown as (a) and (b) above were scattered irregularly through the speech community, the additional detail would be of little interest. But this is not the case: Those who speak the nonstandard Negro vernacular characteristically show the pattern of (a), while white speakers from a wide variety of dialects show (b). Furthermore, we find that as Negro speakers grow older, the order of the variable constraints is reversed. The effect of the grammatical constraint becomes stronger, which may reflect greater influence from standard English pattern. In any case, we witness in Table 1 a clear case of the internal evolution of a linguistic rule in the age-grading of this particular speech community.

Age-grading is one kind of linguistic change which often reflects the historical processes of change in progress, or at least the same kind of rule differences which occur in the course of linguistic evolution. The difference between younger and older speakers of this dialect is plainly a difference in the structure of their language, with definite behavioral consequences (see Labov et al. 1968: 3.2).

Table 1

Frequency of -t, d Deletion Rule for Five Groups of Speakers from South Central Harlem

Group	Age range	Monomorphemic clusters		Past tense clusters	
		__#(K)	__#V	__#(K)	__#V
Thunderbirds	9-13	.94	.59	.74	.24
Aces	10-13	.98	.64	.83	.43
Cobras	11-17	.97	.76	.73	.15
Jets	12-17	.94	.49	.44	.09
Oscar Bros.	15-18	.97	.69	.44	.09

—From Labov et al. 1968, Table 3-6, p. 128, single style only.

It cannot be expressed by adding rules, subtracting them, or re-ordering them as a whole. We could separate the past tense case from the monomorphemic case, write them as separate rules, and then set up a new convention that whichever of these two optional rules applies first would be used more frequently. But such a procedure would achieve nothing in the way of simplicity, and would be entirely against the spirit of generative grammar, which impels us to combine the separate rules into a single schema in the light of their obvious similarities (and thus "capture the generalization" that final -t, d obeys the same constraints in both monomorphemic and past tense clusters). This example of internal development in the age-grading of a dialect will be matched by parallel cases in the study of change in progress in the following section. But first we must consider the formal relations of variable and categorical constraints.

The decision to order the variable constraints for particular dialects must be reflected in the formal interpretation of the notation used. For a variable rule without any variable constraints in the environment, we have noted that $\phi = 1 - k_0$. The variable constraints are written so that the presence of the feature indicated favors the rule; that is, they diminish the limiting factor k_0

$$\phi = 1 - (k_0 - \alpha k_1 - \beta k_2 \ldots - \nu k_n)$$

where the Greek letters have their usual + and – values, and the constants $k_1 \ldots k_n$ are ordered so that $k_1 > k_2 > \ldots > k_n$. The strongest type of order would be the geometric ordering described in Labov 1969: 741, but there is not yet enough evidence to see what degree of order is usually imposed on these constraints, and whether the underlying model may not in fact be multiplicative rather than additive as shown here. If geometric ordering holds, or if the correct model shows that k_0 is to be multiplied by $1/k_1$, etc., change in the values of the variable constraints will never convert a variable rule to a categorical one.[7] The linguistic change will approach completion asymptotically, yet never reach it. But at some point in the course of linguistic evolution, there does occur a qualitative change in the rule, or in the effect of a variable constraint, so that the rule applies categorically. The formalization adopted here raises many questions concerning the way in which the variable constraints interact to approach the limiting values. Whether sum or product models are required may be revealed by further analysis of data now available.

For almost every synchronic rule that we have studied, there is such a case: a categorical constraint on a variable rule. For example, the rule of consonant cluster simplification in NNE always applies if the following word begins with a sibilant.[8] We can indicate this fact by writing.

$$(6)\ [-\text{cont}] \rightarrow <\emptyset> / [+\text{cons}] <\beta\,(\emptyset)> \underline{\quad} \#\# \begin{array}{l} <^*\text{strid}> \\ <\alpha(\sim V)> \end{array}$$

where the *signifies that if the feature [+strident] begins the next word (necessarily $\sim V$), then the rule always applies, regardless of whether $\emptyset$ or $\#$ precedes. To complete the formal interpretation of this symbolism we can say that for (6),

$$\phi = 1 - \left(\frac{-1^*1}{-2}\right)(k_0 - \alpha k_1 - \ldots \nu k_n)$$

The additional factor has the effect of canceling all constraint on the rule if $^* = +$, and no effect at all if $^* = -$. Subrules of this sort are essential if we are to account for one of the most difficult aspects of linguistic development, the gradual evolution of invariant, Type I rules out of the variable, Type III situation. Subrules which show the * feature are sometimes completely categorical,[9] but more often we might call them semi-categorical: They apply in 98-99 percent of the cases, so that violations are rare and reportable. If a

vernacular speaker of NNE pronounces the *t* in *I just saw him,* that
is indeed a rare event, which carries considerable information. Rules
which go to completion in this way—synchronically or diachronically—may be called Type II rules. They are the immediate end result
of the process of linguistic change which we are about to consider.
The transition from Type III to Type II, and eventually to Type I,
is a formal mode of depicting the transition from quantitative to
qualitative change.

4. *The Centralization of /aw/ on Martha's Vineyard*

One of the earliest and most famous studies of change in progress
was that of Gauchat (1905), who investigated the Swiss French
town of Charmey in 1899-1903. He observed six variables across
three generations, as summed up in Table 2. In the case of the
palatalization of *l*, the oldest generation I has [l′], and the youngest
has [j]. If this were the classical model of regular change, we would
expect some intermediate phonetic value from generation II. But
the middle generation does not show some intermediate degree of
palatalization; instead, Gauchat observed fluctuation between [l′]
and [j]. This result forced the neogrammarians to argue that Gauchat had not observed true sound change, but rather a complicated series of dialect borrowings, where generation II lost its original form and borrowed sometimes from I and sometimes from III
(see Goidanich 1926 and Bloomfield 1933: 361). Such intellectual
gymnastics were necessary because sound change by definition was
regular and admitted of no such alternations—that is, only Model
A could apply. The same argument holds for the other variables
in Table 2. Note that each change passes through a variable stage;
the timing is dictated by structural factors that will be obvious to
anyone who examines the relation between the monopthongization
of a^0 and the diphthongization of $ɔ$. It is a typical case of chain
shifting in phonological space as described by Martinet 1955: a^0
must lose its glide before $ɔ$ can shift to the same phonetic form a^0.

The situation at Charmey suggests that there is an intermediate
period of disruption and chaotic behavior which accompanies
change. Yet before coming to this conclusion, one may want to examine Table 3, which is a parallel development taken from my own
observations on Martha's Vineyard. The centralization of /ay/ and

Table 2

Six Phonological Variables in Three Generations
of Speakers of Swiss French: Charmey, 1899

	I 90-60 yrs.	II 60-30 yrs.	III under 30
(l′)	l′	l′ -j	j
(aw)	$a^0 \sim (a^{\cdot})$	$a^{\cdot}$	$a^{\cdot}$
(ey)	$\epsilon \sim (\epsilon^i)$	$\epsilon \sim \epsilon^i$	ϵ^i
(ɔ)	ɔ	$ɔ \sim a^0$	a^0
(θ)	θ → h, 2 items	θ → h, 3 items	θ → h, 4 items
(θr)	θr	$θ \sim (hr)$	θr ~ hr

—Adapted from L. Gauchat, *L'unité phonétique dans le patois d'une commune*
(Halle, 1905).

Table 3

Centralization of (ay) and (aw) in Three Generations
of English Speakers on Martha's Vineyard, Mass.

Generation	(ay) index	(aw) index
Ia (over 75 yrs.)	0.25	0.22
Ib (61-75 yrs.)	0.35	0.37
IIa (46-60 yrs.)	0.62	0.44
IIb (31-45 yrs.)	0.81	0.88
III (14-30 yrs.)	0.37	0.46

/aw/ passed through a comparable period of fluctuation; /aw/ was somewhat behind /ay/ but came on stronger in some groups, for reasons discussed elsewhere (Labov 1965). These indices of centralization are based on impressionistic transcription with a simple numerical system of low vowels as (aw-1,2) = [aut] and fully centralized nuclei as (aw-3) = [əut]. The case of /aw/ is the clearest example of a sound change in progress, since /aw/ was not centralized at all in the 1930s, according to the Linguistic Atlas records. We can set aside all questions of dialect mixture, and obtain a finer

Figure 2.   Development of a centralized allophone of
/aw/ before voiceless consonants in three
generations: Chilmark, Martha's Vineyard

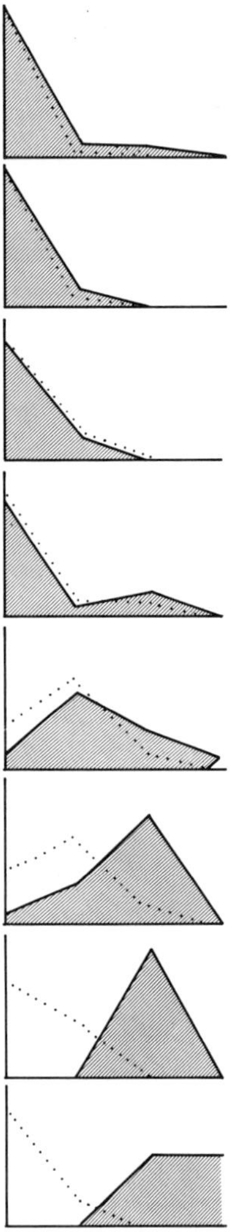

		(aw−) 0	1	2	3	(aw) index
(a) Four LANE informants, av. 65 yrs.	__C°	15	I	I		.10
	else	22	I			
(b) Mrs. H.H., Sr. 92 yrs.	__C°	15	2			.10
	else	14	I			
(c) Mrs. S. H. 87 yrs.	__C°	8	2			.20
	else	12	3			
(d) Mr. E. M. 83 yrs.	__C°	19	2	4		.41
	else	20	3	3		
(e) Mr. H.H., Jr. 60 yrs.	__C°	I	6	4	I	1.12
	else	4	8	2		
(f) Mr. D.P., Sr. 57 yrs.	__C°	I	3	10		1.07
	else	9	15	3		
(g) Mr. P. N. 52 yrs.	__C°			17	2	1.14
	else	10	6			
(h) Mr. D.P., Jr. 31 yrs.	__C°			9	9	1.67
	else	7	2			

view of this change by selecting individuals from the rural Yankee fishing community of Chilmark.[10] We could not find a better opportunity to observe a classic sound change at work.

Fig. 2 shows the development across three generations. The top diagram is an average for the four informants of the Linguistic Atlas of New England in the 1930s; the second is my oldest informant, who was of the same age grade. Both show no particular centralization of /aw/. In each diagram, the solid line represents the distribution of variants before voiceless consonants, and the dotted line all other environments. Next to them are the actual numbers of impressionistic transcriptions. Moving down the diagram to younger and younger informants, we can observe the development of more and more centralized forms of /aw/. For D. P., the median is at (aw-2), [ɐ], with strong indication of differentiation between voiceless and voiced environments. For P. N. and D. P., Jr. (the son of D. P.), centralization has proceeded further before voiceless consonants, but receded in other environments. These last two speakers show a perfectly regular system similar to that found in many sections of the South and Canada, with no overlap between voiceless and voiced environments.

Let us examine this classic case of a neogrammarian sound change in the light of the questions raised at the outset: What is the mechanism by which a change goes to completion? How does language change without disruption? We can recognize that H. H., Sr., at the beginning of the change, has a regular system, which does not require any special rule for centralization of /aw/. It is also apparent that P. N. and D. P., Jr., have an obligatory centralization rule:

$$(7) \ [+\text{voc}] \rightarrow [-\text{low}] \ / \ \underline{\quad} \ \begin{bmatrix} -\text{cons} \\ +\text{back} \end{bmatrix} \begin{bmatrix} +\text{cons} \\ +\text{tens} \end{bmatrix}$$

But what shall we say about H. H. and D. P. in the middle generation? Rule (7) does not apply, since some /aw/ are not centralized before tense consonants, and some are centralized before lax consonants. We could simplify the environment, and write an optional rule (8):

$$(8) \ [+\text{voc}] \rightarrow [-\text{low}] \ / \ \underline{\quad} \ \begin{bmatrix} -\text{cons} \\ -\text{voc} \\ +\text{back} \end{bmatrix}$$

On the face of it, rule (8) looks like a generalization of (7), a simpler form, such as we might obtain at a later stage of the change; yet because it is optional, it clearly says much less about the state of the language. The vowel /aw/ can be [a^0] or [$ə^0$] according to (8), and it makes no difference which; the two forms are in free variation. To say that this is a case of free variation is actually a very strong claim. It is equivalent to saying that the situation shown in Fig. 2(f) is a chance variation, no more likely than a situation in which we reverse the __C^0 and *elsewhere* environments. There would seem to be much less structure or determination in D. P.'s system than in the speech of others: His /aw/ is less narrowly constrained by rule. But if we examine the distribution of forms carefully, it appears that there is not *less* structure in the speech of D. P.; on the contrary, there is more. The variable rule which controls his use of /aw/ has a number of variable constraints which show the influence of the following and (to a lesser extent) the preceding consonant.[11] In general, we can say that most of the phonetic features of the consonantal system enter into this conditioning rule in one way or another. Our impressionistic phonetic transcriptions of /aw/ in the middle generation as a whole indicate that centralization was favored if the /aw/ was followed by

> a segment rather than no segment
> an obstruent rather than a sonorant
> a voiceless obstruent rather than a voiced one
> a stop rather than a fricative obstruent
> an oral rather than a nasal sonorant

The variable constraints on /aw/ are given roughly in the order of their relative importance. From the preceding discussion of consonant cluster simplification, it should not be surprising that the ordering of these constraints varies from one speaker to another, although the direction of the influence for each is invariant.

It is not possible to specify these environments for /aw/ as completely as for /ay/, because /aw/ is only one-third as frequent and is restricted in its distribution. We cannot determine, for example, whether apicals favor centralization in the case of /aw/, since this vowel does not occur before labials and velars.[12] Within these limitations, it would appear that the rule for the middle generation is much less vague than (8), and shows the more specific shape of (9):[13]

$$(9)\ [\text{+voc}] \rightarrow <\text{-low}> / \underline{\quad} \begin{bmatrix} -\text{cons} \\ +\text{back} \end{bmatrix} \begin{bmatrix} \alpha\ \text{obstr} \\ \beta\ \text{tens} \\ \gamma\ \text{cont} \\ \delta\ \text{seg} \end{bmatrix}$$

When several variable constraints are found within one segment, as in (9), we can simplify the notation by adopting the convention that the items within angle brackets are ordered in their effect from top to bottom, and thus eliminate the Greek letters.[14]

$$(9')\ [\text{+voc}] \rightarrow <\text{-low}> / \underline{\quad} \begin{bmatrix} -\text{cons} \\ +\text{back} \end{bmatrix} \begin{array}{l} <\text{+obstr}> \\ <\text{+tens}> \\ <\text{-cont}> \\ <\text{+seg}> \end{array}$$

or equivalently we may write:

$$(9'')\ [\text{+voc}] \rightarrow <\text{-low}> / \underline{\quad} \begin{bmatrix} -\text{cons} \\ +\text{back} \end{bmatrix} <\text{+obstr}> \text{+tens}> \text{-cont}> \text{+seg}>$$

where the right-hand member of the angled brackets does double duty as an inequality sign.

It should be apparent that the features which favor centralization are the inverse of those which control length in English vowels (House 1961). It might therefore be possible to simplify (9) by allowing centralization to be predicted from a single feature, length. This would involve moving the rule downward to the point where phonetic effects apply on a linear scale in a continuous phonetic dimension. Since rule (9) develops into a discrete phonological rule at a higher level of abstraction, a drastic case of rule reordering between generations II and III would be necessary. Furthermore, it appears that the preceding consonants, which do not affect length, also influence centralization to some extent—in the inverse direction from that seen in the following segment. Thus the most favored words would not be *doubt,* or *tout,* but *out* and *house,* and the least favored are not *hour* or *growl,* but *down* and *tower.* These minor effects will not be considered further, since they do not add to the basic argument.

Our main concern is with two transitions between three states: (1) from the absence of a centralization rule in Generation I to the presence of a variable rule in Generation II; (2) from the variable rule of Generation II to the semi-categorical rule of Generation III. It would be possible to describe the second transition in terms of

Figure 2a. Two different orderings of variable
constraints on the −t,d deletion rule

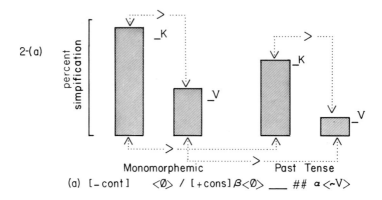

2-(a)

(a) [−cont]   <∅> / [+cons] β<∅> ___ ## α <~V>

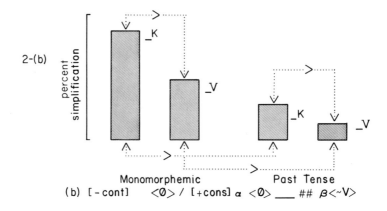

2-(b)

(b) [−cont]   <∅> / [+cons] α <∅> ___ ## β<~V>

simplification. It is obvious that (9) is more complex than (7). At the same time, it can hardly be said that (9) shows less *structure* in any conventional sense. Most of the distinctive feature system of the sound pattern is built into this rule. To pass from (9) to (7), it is necessary for the variable constraint of <+tense> to rise in the hierarchy of (9′) until we can enter <*tense> into the rule. At the same time the other constraints appear to decrease, receding to the phonetic horizon. Though the net result is simplification

$$(10) \ [\text{+voc}] \rightarrow <\text{-low}>/\underline{\quad} \begin{bmatrix} -\text{cons} \\ +\text{back} \end{bmatrix} \begin{bmatrix} +\text{cons} \\ <\text{*tense}> \\ . \\ . \\ . \\ . \end{bmatrix}$$

the process which leads to this result appears to have a different character: It is the magnification of the effect of one feature on the rule, and diminution of the others. The forces operating behind this movement are not well understood, but their strong impression on the phonetic system can easily be observed.

The first transition can have nothing to do with simplicity. To begin with, there are always minor phonetic influences on any vowel by the surrounding consonants. In the development of (9), these phonetic influences are magnified so that formerly insignificant, sublinguistic effects can now add up to the difference between a mid vowel and a low vowel, as in [əut] vs. [da^{0}n]. It would seem that the course of the sound change exaggerates the inherent conditioning effects of consonant on vowel, much as the difference between the swiftness of runners is exaggerated in the course of a race. To begin with, they are all bunched up at the starting line; as the race proceeds, they are strung out along the course, but finally they all gather together at the end into two groups: the winner and the losers.

The application of generative grammar to historical linguistics produces a dangerous tendency towards simplistic solutions. Thus it has been argued (King 1969) that rule simplification explains many linguistic changes, and even provides an explanation for the long-term drift which has puzzled linguists for so long (p. 202). In the outline given here, it can be seen that the pressures towards simplification may very well exist, but as weak forces in this development. The paper of Bach and Harms in this volume shows that there are many developments in completed sound changes which cannot be accounted for by any simplification argument. But the strongest argument against the use of *simplicity* as an explanation for sound change has been stated by Wang (personal communication): Let us suppose that we grant that the gradual development of a change is a form of generalization, eliminating features one by one until we reach the stage of the most favored or probable kind of rule, such as (7). This is equivalent to asserting that the rule which enters the system at the beginning of the change is the *least probable* one. Clearly our explanations of sound change must look for other phonetic, grammatical, and social factors if we are to understand what is happening, whether we are dealing with the transition, embedding, or actuation problem.

INSTRUMENTAL STUDIES OF CHANGE IN PROGRESS

The original investigation of Martha's Vineyard (Labov 1963) used spectrographic evidence to calibrate the impressionistic transcriptions and reduce the number of degrees of height to the most reliable series. We are currently engaged in extensive instrumental studies of sound change in progress, reviewing the data acquired in earlier studies of New York City and other areas, and adding further explorations in various dialects of England, France, and the United States.[15] We have returned to the original data from Martha's Vineyard, and re-analyzed it with an eye to the mechanisms discussed above. Fig. 3 shows the relative phonetic position of all the /aw/ vowels used by D. P. on a two-formant plot. The vertical axis shows the first formant position, increasing from top to bottom, and the horizontal axis the second-formant position, increasing from right to left. The array of /aw/ vowels which is formed shows the same orientation as our impressionistic transcriptions of the nucleus, but with considerably more precision and detail.[16]

Vowels before voiceless consonants are shown with open circles, and those before voiced consonants or final with shaded circles. The phonetic environments are given before and after the circle, except for the two most common items, *out* and *down*. An open circle with

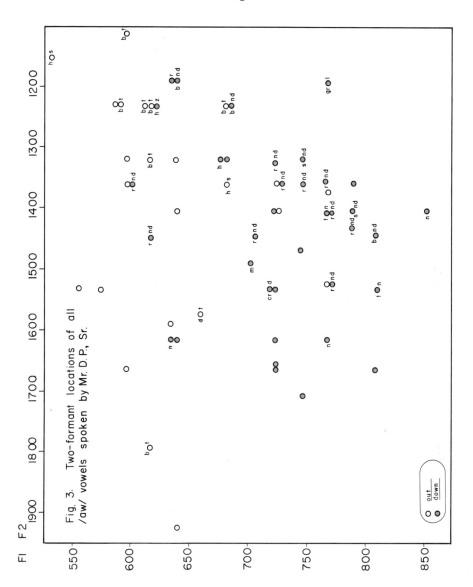

Fig. 3.   Two-formant locations of all /aw/ vowels spoken by Mr. D. P., Sr.

no environment marked indicates *out,* and a shaded circle with no marking represents *down.* Fig. 3 shows that D. P. has a clear tendency to centralize more before voiceless consonants. There is an average difference in first formant position of 70 c.p.s. But the separation is not absolute; we are dealing with a variable constraint. Furthermore, there are other variable constraints present. Table 4 shows the distribution of first formant positions for six phonetic environments on which we have more than two items measured. The average position of the first formant is shown at the bottom of

Table 4

Distribution and Average Location of First Formants of /aw/ Vowels for D. P.

range in c.p.s.	_t	_s	_d, z	_nd	_n	_#
650	16	1	1	3	1	1
700–650	2	1		1	1	1
750–700	2		1	5	7	1
750	2			6	5	2
Average c.p.s.	628	606	681	724	746	724

each column. From this fragmentary but reasonably accurate data,[17] we can construct the outline of a rule such as (11) for D. P.

$$(11)\ [+\text{voc}] \rightarrow <-\text{low}>/ \underline{\quad} \begin{bmatrix} -\text{cons} \\ +\text{back} \end{bmatrix} \begin{matrix} <+\text{obstr}> \\ <+\text{tens}> \\ <-\text{nas}> \end{matrix}$$

As far as middle generation speakers are concerned, D. P. seems to be well advanced in centralization, and much of the phonetic detail may be disappearing from the rule. We can obtain a clearer picture of the variable constraints on the centralization of /aw/ by taking a short step backward to a slightly older friend of D. P.'s, N. B., of Lambert's Cove, 63 years old. The distribution of his /aw/ vowels by first and second formant with the phonetic environments added appears in Fig. 4. The overall distribution of the /aw/ variants by environments is shown in Table 5, with the average formant positions again indicated at the bottom of each column. The pattern

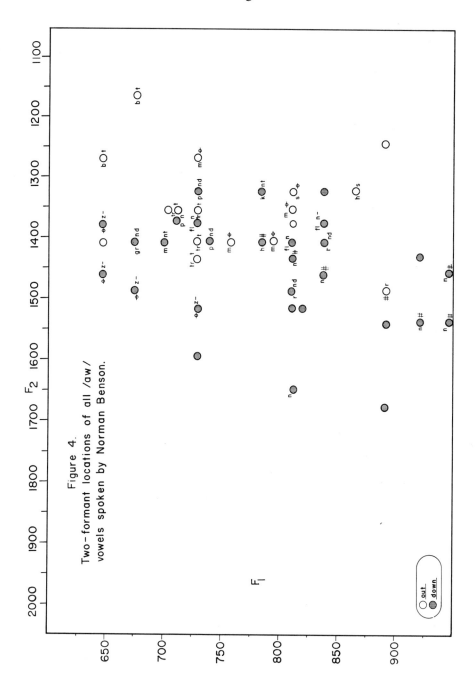

Figure 4.
Two-formant locations of all /aw/
vowels spoken by Norman Benson.

Table 5

Distribution and Average Location of
First Formants of /aw/ Vowels for N. B.

range in c.p.s.	_t	_nt	_θ	_nd	_n	_#
650	2					
700–650	3	1		2		
750–700	3	1	2	2		
800–750	1	1	3	3	3	3
850–800	1			4	1	1
850					3	3
Average c.p.s.	730	758	785	785	839	866

is very much like that of D. P., transferred to higher first formant positions, but with some additional detail. The five examples of /aw/ before /θ/ show that voiceless fricatives are intermediate between voiceless stops and voiced continuants. In Fig. 4 they are grouped in the middle range. The quantized distribution of Table 5 may leave some doubt as to whether absolute final position, __#, is different from the effect of a final nasal. But in Fig. 4, we see that the three lowest symbols are for *now,* and we are justified in entering as the lowest level constraint <+seg>.

It appears that a final nasal has more effect in preventing centralization than a pre-consonantal nasal. For -*nt* and -*nd* the distribution seems to be governed by the stop more than the nasal. There are several ways in which this effect can be symbolized, but the simplest, and the truest to the phonetic situation, is to suggest that the environment is transparent to nasals because nasality in pre-consonantal position is transferred to the vowel. Thus we have a rule such as (12)

$$(12) \ [+voc] \rightarrow <-low>/\_\_ \begin{bmatrix} \_\_ \\ <-nas> \end{bmatrix} \begin{bmatrix} -cons \\ +back \end{bmatrix} \begin{matrix} <+obstr> \\ <+tens> \\ <-cont> \\ <-nas> \\ <+seg> \end{matrix}$$

A study of Fig. 4 shows that the distribution of the various environments is rather tightly grouped, but with enough exceptions to indicate that we are plainly dealing with a variable rule. N. B. is a good example of the expansion of the phonetic spectrum.

Since we have displayed the /aw/ vowels for the middle generation in some detail, the question arises whether these phonetic variations represent a significant change, or whether they enlarge only slightly on phonetic tendencies which we would find in the oldest generation. Fig. 4a takes the longest possible backwards step to our oldest informant, H. H., Sr., 92 years old. Here we have none of the fluctuation or ordered decomposition characteristic of N. B. and D. P. Half the vowels are located at a first formant position of 675 c.p.s., and the other half are collected in a narrow range between 600 and 730. If we take the average first formant position for the most favoring environment, _t, we get 675 c.p.s. The average for the least favoring environments for centralization, _n and _#, are both 675 c.p.s. We conclude that there is no basis whatsoever for the centralization rule in the speech of H. H., Sr., as our impressionistic phonetics had indicated, and that the variable rule operating for N. B. and D. P. is altogether new to Chilmark in the middle generation.

If we now move to the other end of the scale, to the pattern of D. P., Jr. (Fig. 5), it is immediately apparent that the picture has been simplified in the other direction. There is no overlap between the voiced and voiceless environments, shown again as open and shaded circles. The two allophones meet along a line at 600 c.p.s., showing no more contact than many adjacent phonemes (Peterson and Barney 1952). We can then say with some confidence that the categorical rule (7) applies to D. P., Jr., in Generation III.

$$(7) \ [+voc] \rightarrow [-low] / \underline{\quad\quad} \begin{bmatrix} -cons \\ +back \end{bmatrix} \begin{bmatrix} +cons \\ +tens \end{bmatrix}$$

That is not to say that minor phonetic tendencies do not exist in the height of each allophone; the data here is not sufficient to make any strong statement about this. But such tendencies are minor in comparison with the effect of [+tense].

Our view of the centralization of /aw/ on Martha's Vineyard is thus complete, beginning with a uniform uncentralized norm for

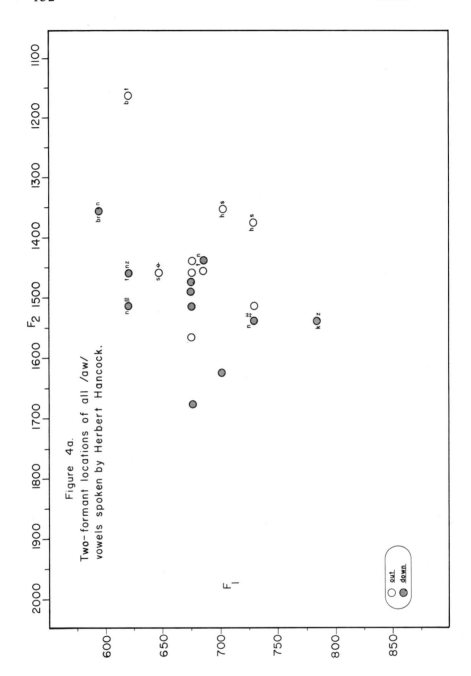

Figure 4a.
Two-formant locations of all /aw/
vowels spoken by Herbert Hancock.

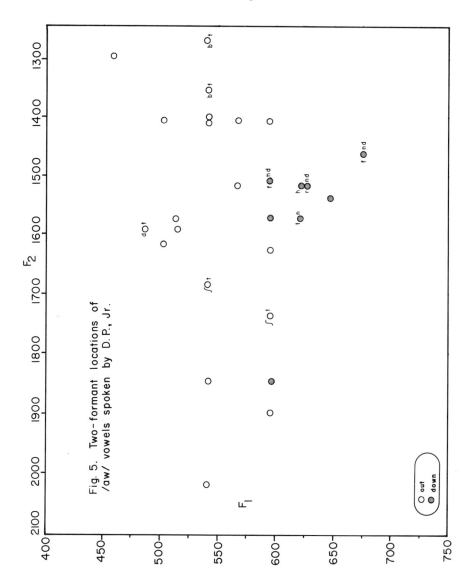

Fig. 5. Two-formant locations of /aw/ vowels spoken by D. P., Jr.

the oldest speakers passing through a period of ordered decomposition of the word classes, and ending with an invariant rule based on a single feature of tenseness. Our instrumental studies have allowed us to delineate the state of the rule system through this transitional period. The existence of variable rules for the centralization of /aw/ in the middle generation has been clearly demonstrated, and we have seen how a rule proceeds to completion through the reordering of variable constraints on such rules.

5. *The Raising of Short a in New York City*

One of the most complex conditioned sound changes which has been described to date is the tensing and raising of short *a* in the middle Atlantic states from New York to Baltimore. In section 2 several examples of ordered and unordered decomposition were drawn from this rich and varied assemblage of rules. We are fortunate to have a series of descriptions and analyses by linguists native to the dialect areas (Trager 1942 for northern New Jersey, Ferguson 1968 for Philadelphia, Cohen 1970 for New York). The basic outline of the New York City rule is that in closed syllables short *a* is raised before voiced stops, voiceless fricatives, and front nasals *m* and *n*. The rule does not apply to auxiliaries and other function words which can have schwa as the only vowel in unstressed position (weak words). Nor does it apply in open syllables as in *fabric* or *dragon* except when an inflectional boundary follows, as in *draggin'*. We thus have a series of long, ingliding vowels ("tense") vowels opposed to a series of short ("lax") monophthongs.

There are two aspects to the evolution of the rule. The selection of the lexical subclasses shows broad geographic variation from New York to Philadelphia and Baltimore, relatively stable but with subtle idiolectal variation within each sub-area. The raising of the affected word classes to higher and higher vowels appears to be in more rapid flux. This process will be the focus of the discussion to follow. In this discussion of the evolution of the rule, I will be concerned with three major subclasses to which the rule applies: when short *a* occurs before

voiced stops [$]	voiceless fricatives [F]	front nasals [N]
bad	laugh	man
cab	bath	ham
bag	pass	land
badge	ask	.
.	last	.
.	cash	.
	.	
	.	

The historical evidence, as summarized in Labov 1966, shows that the sound change began well before 1900, when some words had already reached mid position. By the 1930s, it seems that this phase had been completed. These short *a* words continued to rise past mid position, until in the 1960s, many younger speakers showed a merger of *bad, bared,* and *beard* in high position (Labov 1966: 557 ff.).

The original study of the social stratification of English in New York City (Labov 1966) provides us with a representative sample of informants whose social and linguistic characteristics are well established. From this sample we can select speakers in an age range from 73 to 12 years old, showing a distribution in "apparent time" that reflects the actual course of the sound changes in New York City. The historical evidence gives us a fixed time from which we can interpret this evidence in general. But for detailed arguments on the internal evolution of the rule, it will be necessary to evaluate each piece of evidence, and to state the relations of this evolution in apparent time to changes in real time with some degree of precision.

As the vowel system of New York City evolves, some older speakers show stylistic shifting to reflect the norms of younger speakers. One such shift is towards the higher vowels and mergers characteristic of the evolving vernacular of younger speakers; thus a middle-aged Italian working-class woman shifts to the merger of *bad, beard,* and *bared* as [bɪːᵊd], whereas her own basic pattern distinguishes *beard* [bɪːᵊd] from *bad* and *bared* [beːᵊd]. A very different shift is made by a middle-aged Jewish woman with a lower-middle-class background. Her basic pronunciation of *bad* as [beːᵊd]

gives way to a low tense vowel at the level of *bat* [bæːd], respond-
ing to the overt social stigma placed on the higher pronunciation.
Both of these shifts—towards the newer vernacular norm and towards the corrected prestige norm—can be distinguished from the
regular pattern of the speaker's original preadolescent vernacular
by two characteristics.[18] First of all, the shift is irregular; we observe a sudden break between one distribution and another, with a
completely irregular disruption of word classes. Thus one speaker
shows *land* as [leːənd] but *man* as [mæːn]: a sudden disruption
of the prenasal class which does not recur as a pattern for this or
any other speaker. Secondly, both kinds of shifting are proportion-
al to the amount of attention paid to speech, and maximized in the
formal reading of word lists or minimal pairs. Although we can observe traces of these shifts in casual and careful conversation, the
pattern is much stronger in the more formal styles.

We can use these criteria to distinguish the original vernacular of
any speaker from a superposed shift towards other norms. But for
some speakers the shift is so great that we have very little material
left as evidence of the state of the basic vernacular of his early
years. To study the internal evolution of a complex pattern of
phonological conditioning, it is therefore best to compare development through age levels of speakers who show minimal shift towards other norms. The following discussion will therefore be based
upon the speech of working-class New Yorkers who give us the
best evidence on the mainstream of this speech community.[19]

The data we will examine here on the raising of short *a* is drawn
from spectrographic measurements of the first and second formants of the connected speech[20] of eleven men and ten women,
all working-class informants (Lower East Side survey, Labov 1966).
The entire vowel system of each informant is studied through with
75 to 85 measurements for each informant.[21] The position of the
nucleus for each vowel is measured at the point of local maximum
for the first formant,[22] and plotted on a two-formant grid. The
positions of the upgliding /iy/ and /ey/ vowels give us relatively
stable locations from which we can establish the high, mid, and low
ranges for each speaker. In our overall study we are concerned with
the movements of all the long and ingliding vowels, including the
chain shift of /ah/ → /oh/ → /uh/ in the back vowels, and conse-

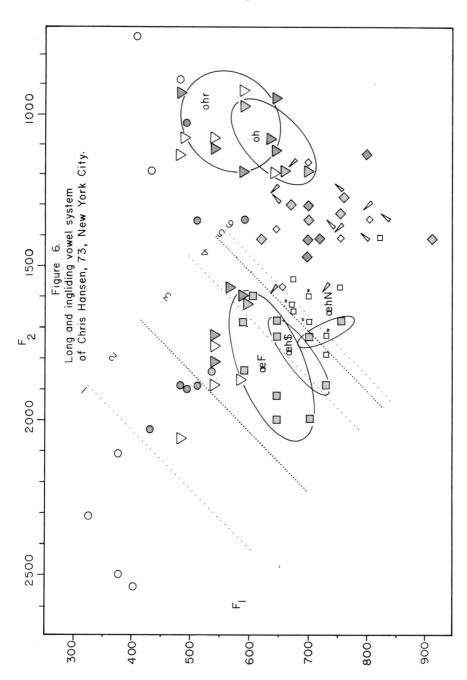

Figure 6.
Long and ingliding vowel system
of Chris Hansen, 73, New York City.

quent movements of /ay/, /oy/, and /aw/. Here we isolate the first step in this series, the raising of /æ/ to the level of /eh/ and /ih/. Fig. 6 shows the vowel system of the oldest New Yorker in our series, Chris Hansen, 73 years.[23]

In these vowel charts, high vowels are represented by circles, mid vowels by triangles, low vowels by squares (front /æ/ and /æh/) and diamonds (back /a/ and /ah/). The open symbols represent the upgliding, originally tense vowels /iy/ and /ey/, /uw/ and /ow/. Shaded and hatched symbols represent the new tense series, the long and ingliding vowels which are the chief focus of attention here. The shaded symbols are vowels before /r/; horizontal hatching shows long and ingliding vowels not before /r/—/ih/ in *idea,* /eh/ in *yeah,* /oh/ in *law, caught,* etc., /ah/ in broad *a* words *father, pajamas,* etc. The only short vowels shown are unraised /æ/ and /a/ (short *o* before voiceless finals in *stop, not,* etc.), both given as smaller symbols than the others. High and mid short vowels are not shown, nor are low upgliding diphthongs /ay/, /aw/, and /oy/. The subject of discussion, /æh/, is shown as the larger squares. The three chief subclasses are designated by the direction of the hatching: horizontal for /æhN/, vertical for /æh$/, and diagonal for /æhF/. Some of the short /æ/ symbols are weak words, which are indicated by a small *w* below the symbol.

These descriptions of the word classes obviously refer to the underlying vowels and consonants present in the dictionary entries. On the other hand, the symbols used within slashes represent the kind of broad phonetics developed in the tradition of Bloomfield, Bloch, and Trager-Smith. The reason for using this lower level notation is that it shows the phonetic position of the vowels in the system from which the sound changes depart. At this stage in middle-Atlantic states English, the long vowels now represented as $[\mathrm{I}^i]$ or $[\mathrm{i}{:}]$ and $[\mathrm{e}^I]$ or $[\epsilon^I]$ are relatively stable. The raising of the new series of tense vowels $[\mathrm{ɔ}{:}]$ and $[\mathrm{æ}{:}]$ and accompanying movements of the low nucleus of $[\mathrm{a}^I]$ and $[\mathrm{a}^o]$ are processes now under way in a great many regions of the United States. Such movements often reflect the original membership of the words involved in their most abstract morphophonemic classes, in ways that we will report at a later date, and it is therefore necessary to identify word classes on this basis. On the other hand, the sound changes now in progress

can only be understood on the basis of the point (or region) in phonetic space from which the change departs. We therefore will refer
to the class of short *a* affected by the raising rule as /æh/, meaning
those short *a* vowels which are relatively fronted, tense, and ingliding as compared to the subclass /æ/, and we will describe their interaction with /ihr/ and /ehr/, vowels in word classes which originally show long ēr and ār, respectively. The fact that in New York
City ār has now become a long mid vowel followed by a centering
glide [e:ə] is represented by the notation /ehr/. If this original ār
did not occupy this position in the present system, it would not
participate in the raising process which ultimately leads to merger
with /ihr/ and /æh/.[24] This notation is thus well suited to trace the
progress of sound change in the phonological space determined by
the current phonetics of American English.

The assignment of words to the /æh/ class represents the general
consensus of New York City speakers, as reflected in descriptions
from Trager to Cohen. There are several areas of divergence and
even indeterminacy (for details see Cohen 1970), but these are of
concern to us here only insofar as the lexical items involved appear
on our spectrographic charts. Two such areas, cited above in our
discussion of models of sound change, surround the voiced fricatives and weak words. Monosyllables ending in voiced fricatives
(*jazz, razz*) are rare in our materials, but *avenue* is common. In this
word, a vowel follows the *v* directly, and the æ should be lax as
with *savage,* but it is a well-established lexical exception and is
shown here as a member of the /æh/ class. The raising rule in New
York City does not apply to weak words, like auxiliary *can, an,* or
and, and all of these are shown as members of the /æ/ class. However, one will occasionally find in our charts a weak word in high
position; this is not a mistake of the speaker or of the measurer,
but rather reflects the fact that ongoing linguistic change is affecting the word classes selected as well as the height of the vowel.
Throughout this dialect area weak words ending in nasals are at
the leading edge of the change, and some younger speakers will
raise such weak words.

Fig. 6 also shows diagonal lines separating the high, mid, and low
vowels in the front region. These lines are drawn perpendicular to
the distribution of vowels in phonological space; they cut at right

angles the path which vowels must follow in moving from low to high. Their actual position is based on the location of the /iy/ and /ey/ vowels. Each third is also divided into halves, based on the distribution of /iy/ vs. /ihr/; /ey/ vs. /ehr/; and /æ/ vs. /æh/ in the earliest stages, giving us six "phonetic" regions. The upper half of the low vowel section is emptied in the course of this evolution, and remains blank.

It would be possible to base the divisions of height on first formant position alone, and draw horizontal divisions between high, mid, and low. Such a decision does not affect the form of the rules which we will present, since the internal development will show the same relations. But using first formant position alone leads to very odd results with some speakers, whose path from /æ/ to /iy/ is almost horizontal, and who differentiate /ihr/ from /ehr/ entirely through second formant position. Our divisions of "height" are based on the overall configurations which we actually find for each speaker, rather than on the abstract two-formant grid.

If we now examine the factual content of Fig. 6, we see that the /æh/ words appear as both low and mid vowels. The three vowels in mid position are all examples of /æh/ before voiceless fricatives— the /æhF/ class. Three mid vowels are also found in relatively low position: two cases of /ehr/ where consonantal [r] was pronounced, and one case of *yeah*. As a whole the /ehr/ vowels are more central than /æh/. (Note that if we used horizontal divisions of height, registering only F_1 position, we would still find three /æhF/ vowels in mid position.) We thus find a very clear separation of /æh/ allophones, in which vowels before fricatives are highest, those before voiced stops are next, and before nasals lowest. (In the following discussion, these three subclasses will be abbreviated as /æhF/, /æh$/, and /æhN/.) The same distribution appears in the vowel system of Michael Duffy, also 73 years old, who represents the important stratum of second-generation New York City Irish.

RULES FOR THE RAISING OF SHORT A

Our first inclination would be to write a single rule for the processes outlined above which would produce the right result for Hansen and Duffy, and which could be adjusted minimally to reflect the further evolution of the system. In our data there are three

major subclasses affected by the rule: /æh/ before voiceless fricatives, voiced stops, and front nasals.* We now see that these subclasses are not all affected by the rule in the same way and to the
same degree. If we write a variable rule, raising low front vowels

$$(13)\ [-\text{back}] \rightarrow <-\text{low}> / \begin{bmatrix} \\ -\text{W} \\ \ \end{bmatrix} \begin{bmatrix} C \\ \vdots \\ \vdots \\ \vdots \end{bmatrix}$$

we will have to indicate variable constraints such as <+nasal,- back>,
<+continuant, +tense>, and <- continuant, - tense>. We could then
order these constraints vertically to describe the system of Hansen
shown in Fig. 6. But such variable constraints in our present framework would necessarily allow the possibility of some /æ/ being
raised before voiceless stops and liquids in *bat* or *pal,* and these are
categorically out of the question in the New York City dialect.

As noted above, there are loose edges to the rule: We find some
weak words ending in nasals being raised by some speakers; voiced
fricatives in *jazz* and *razz* are lexically unpredictable; and there is
much subtle variation in the effect of a nasal or liquid after the
first consonant, as in *family,* or *magnet.* However, this kind of variation is quite different from variation in the actual degree of raising seen in Fig. 6. It concerns individual lexical items and it differs
from one individual to another. Furthermore, it does not affect the
outline of the major classes which we find in the records of normal
conversation. In our data, there are no cases of *bat, back,* or *pal*
being raised. To write a single rule reflecting both kinds of facts
would be very difficult. We would have to assert that constraints
such as <+cont, +tense> act in two different ways at once: categorically selecting vowels to be affected by the rule, then variably
affecting the extent to which the rule operates on them.

It is obviously simpler to write a single rule which converts certain classes of /æ/ vowels to /æh/—that is, makes them longer and
tenser. These vowels will then receive a single label, and a simple
raising rule will apply to them. One might assign a feature such as
[+long], since length is obviously involved, but we have not yet
been able to establish any simple correlation. We might choose
[+peripheral], implying extreme fronting, since high second for-

---

*In the rules below, [+W] indicates a diacritic common to all segments of
weak words, and [-W] the class of nonweak words.

mant position is characteristic of this /æh/ series. Furthermore, this would fit in with the general principle of chain shifting which we have established: That in chain shifts, vowels rise along the periphery, while vowels along a less peripheral track fall. However, this raising of /æh/ is not a chain shift, and eventually involves vowels that do not show extreme fronting. It therefore seems best to use a single cover term, [+tense], which may have no simple phonetic correlate.

To call this first selectional rule a tensing rule is attractive for a number of reasons. Historically, such raising operations do affect the general class of tense vowels more than lax vowels, even in isolated shifts. Secondly, we find that vowels which are phonetically "tense" are more emphatic and longer—they will rise further than other vowels. Thirdly, we note that other vowels such as /ehr/, which develop a tense nucleus followed by a lax glide [e:ə], become involved in the rule, while the originally tense vowels /iy/ and /ey/ do not. At this level of the phonetic output they appear as lax nuclei followed by tense glides—e.g., [ɛ:ʲ], and further developments in chain shifting justify this view. Therefore a tensing rule will set up the conditions for a simple raising rule to apply to a wide range of word classes.

$$(14) \quad [+voc] \rightarrow [+tense] \; / \; \begin{bmatrix} \underline{\quad} \\ -W \\ -back \end{bmatrix} \left\{ \begin{matrix} \begin{bmatrix} +cons \\ \alpha \, cont \\ \alpha \, tense \end{bmatrix} \\ \begin{bmatrix} +nas \\ -back \end{bmatrix} \end{matrix} \right\} \quad {\sim}V$$

This is a simplified version of the facts as presented in Cohen 1970, but it covers all the data in our spectrographic plots to be presented here, except the single (and unaccountable) item *avenue*. There are many difficult problems involved in adjusting this rule to show the relations with adjoining dialects, and the directions of change within the rule,[25] but it will give us a sound footing on which to proceed.

The raising rule for Duffy and Hansen then takes on the form

$$(15) \quad [+tense] \rightarrow \text{<-low>} \; / \; \begin{bmatrix} \underline{\quad} \\ -back \end{bmatrix} \begin{matrix} \text{<-nas>} \\ \text{<+tense>} \end{matrix}$$

This variable rule orders the three major subclasses as F-$-N. We select [-nas] as the most important constraint, since in all developments, differences between N and the other two classes appear to be greater than differences between F and $. We no longer need to refer to weak words or the following environment, since the only relevant question for rule (15) is whether the vowel is front and tense;[26] if so, it is variably raised to mid position. This early stage of the rule seems to have gone to completion by the first decade of this century. Hansen and Duffy were born in 1890, and learned to speak English on the streets of New York between 1890 and 1905. But speakers ten or fifteen years younger, raised between 1910 and 1920, do not have this low range of /æh/ vowels in the 5th level of Fig. 6. Fig. 7 shows an example in the vowel system of Henry Resnick, 60 years old, a conservative Jewish working-class speaker. All of his /æh/ vowels are at mid position, equal to or higher than /ey/, but lower than /ehr/, which is concentrated at the upper mid level. Furthermore, the advantage of the fricative environment has disappeared; all vowels are mid, no lower than /æhF/. It seems that a similar process to the one observed in Martha's Vineyard has taken place: The phonetic differentiation of the change in progress was replaced by a simpler rule as it went to completion. We might reconstruct an intermediate stage such as

$$(15') \: [\text{+tense}] \rightarrow \: <\text{-low}>/ \left[\overline{} \atop \text{-back} \right] \: <*[\text{-nas}]>$$

in which the rule goes to completion for the non-nasal environments while it is still variable for nasals. Here the asterisk notation indicates a rule schema in which a categorical subrule applies for /æhN/. Without the asterisk notation (see p. 117), we would have no way of combining these two rules into a single schema despite their obvious similarity. There is no need to enter the feature <+tense> since F and $ are no longer discriminated. In the next stage, the N environment becomes categorical, and the variable constraints are eliminated. Since all variability has now disappeared, we have a rule without any angled brackets:

$$(16) \: [\text{+tense}] \rightarrow [\text{-low}] \: / \left[\overline{} \atop \text{-back} \right]$$

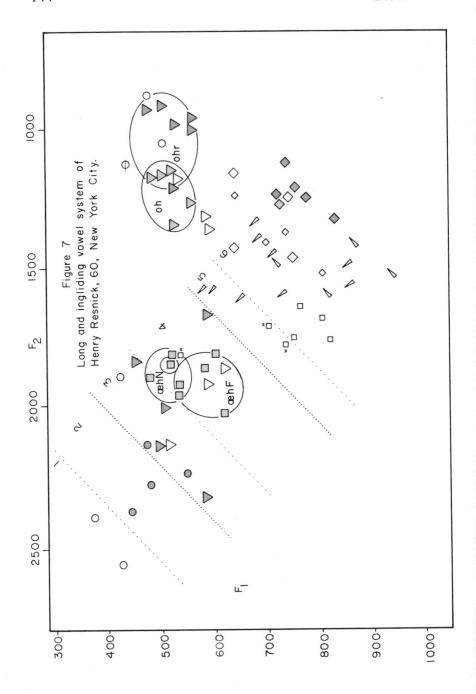

Figure 7
Long and ingliding vowel system of
Henry Resnick, 60, New York City.

We are fortunate in having an extraordinarily reliable observation of this process made at an earlier point in real time by E. S. Babbitt. Babbitt was a Columbia professor who informally noted the speech of working-class New Yorkers and reported a number of linguistically sophisticated observations in a brief article in *Dialect Notes* in 1896 (see Labov 1966 for further details). In regard to /æh/ Babbitt writes

> Among the older New Yorkers this very high vowel is used in all the set of words pronounced in New England with the broad vowel (*ask, half, pass,* etc.), and is really higher in these words than in *man, cab,* etc. But this distinction is now lost and the general vowel has quite overtaken the special one (*hend,* hand, *keb.* cab, *dens,* dance, *helf pest,* half past).

My original recollection of Babbitt's evidence was governed by his use of the "broad *a*" category. It was not until after we had discovered the patterns shown in the spectrographic records of Duffy's and Hansen's speech that I realized that Babbitt had accurately described the movement from (14) to (16). Although Babbitt does not explicitly distinguish the short *a* words which are never raised, all his examples are indeed /æh/ words as we have outlined them. The "broad vowels" he gives are before voiceless fricatives; when he compares them with vowels before nasals which are *not* broad *a*, his final examples include *dance* in a way that leaves open whether it is to be included in the broad class of special vowels. In any case, the raising of /æh$/ and /æhN/ to join the others is precisely the process which we have documented from our observations in apparent time. Babbitt's evidence indicates, however, that the process was completed earlier than we have suggested.

The process of raising /æh/ continued past the mid point and the momentum of the nasal environment continued. All our male informants who are younger than Resnick show that following nasals favor the rules more than stops or fricatives. Resnick himself shows a definite leaning towards the N class within the narrow distribution of Fig. 7. The class of /æhN/ is slightly higher than /æhF/, so we find *stand* and *family* relatively high, *bad* a little lower, and *bath* and *last* in the lowest position, all within the mid range. Fig. 8 shows the vowel system of Jacob Schissel, 57, with /æhN/ moving out of mid position into the upper edge of the mid vowels and be-

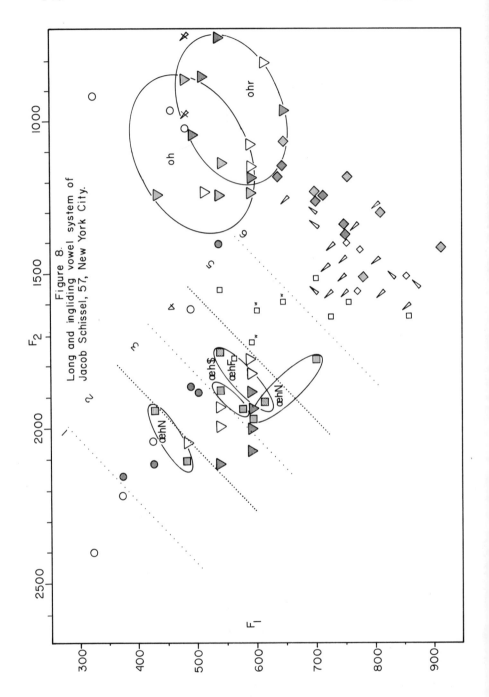

Figure 8.
Long and ingliding vowel system of
Jacob Schissel, 57, New York City.

yond, overlapping some /ihr/ vowels, while the stops are in the middle and the fricatives lag behind. We can thus write:

(17) $[\text{+voc}] \rightarrow <\text{+high}> / \left[\overline{-\text{back}}\right] <\text{+nas}>$

This is plainly a variable rule, for we do not find any absolute separation of subclasses: Some nasals are mid. It can be observed that Schissel has one corrected /æhN/ in low position, an occasional tendency in his casual speech which becomes a regular pattern in his reading style. It is significant that when /æhN/ becomes the most favored type for the raising rule, it also becomes the one most likely to be corrected to low position. This is the phonetic correlate of the general observation made in Labov 1966: The more a speaker tends to use a socially stigmatized form in casual speech, the more likely he is to stigmatize it in the speech of others.

If we move to the next generation of Jewish male working-class speakers, we see a gradual movement in the same direction, with the same ordering of the environmental constraints. The vowel system of Chester Wallach, 23, is shown in Fig. 9. Again, /æhN/ shifts towards high position, with stops and fricatives lagging behind. The chief difference between Wallach and Schissel is in the position of /ehr/, which has moved up considerably from the low mid position in Schissel's system and changed places with /ey/. Furthermore, we observe that the parallel raising of /ohr/ and /oh/ in the back has proceeded further in the younger speaker's system; as Fig. 9 shows, /ohr/ is now at high position for Wallach. In this analysis, however, we will confine our attention to the front vowels.

In the formal representation of the events displayed on Figs. 6–9, we observe the transformation of rule (15) into its inverse. A more detailed view of this evolution can be seen in Table 6, which shows the distribution of /æh/ words for eleven male working-class speakers, ranging in age from 73 to 13 years old. The actual consonant following each vowel is entered under the phonetic sublevel where the vowel is found, and ordering by height within each sublevel is indicated by the order of the symbols.

There are several stylistic shifts in this data which obscure the pattern slightly. One of the older speakers, Michael Duffy, has his vernacular mode at 5, but he also shows a second mode for /æh/ in high position, a reflection of the norm for younger speakers, which

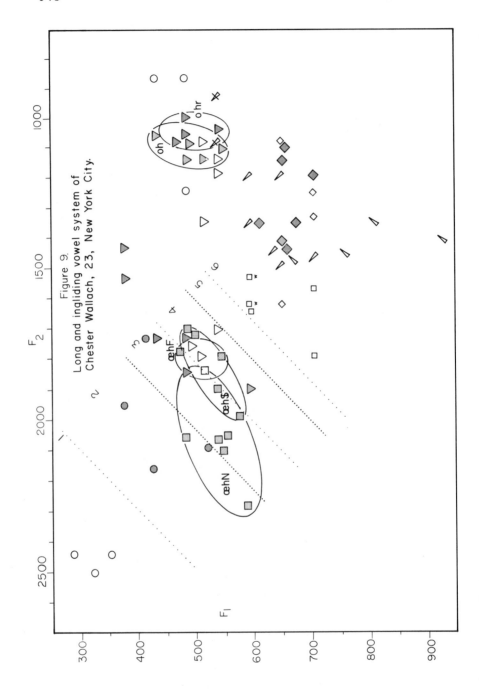

Figure 9.
Long and ingliding vowel system of
Chester Wallach, 23, New York City.

Table 6

Distribution of /æh/ by Following Consonant
for Eleven Working-Class New York City Men

| | | | phonetic level | | | |
| | | low | | mid | | high | |
Name	Age	6	5	4	3	2	1
Hansen	73	n	nbdsf	ssvff			
Duffy	73	n	nn	ssfsdb	n	ffnf	
Resnick	60			ssθndsn	m		
Schissel	57			ffnbd		nn	
Orann	56		ns	d	nn	mnnn	
Greenfield	46	f	vm	bsbv	ffnff		
Lazinsky	39		n	ndn	ndns	dn	
Le Count	31		sd	ss	dsnnn		
Wallach	23			ndsgz	nfnmv	nn	
Carlino	19			nfn		nn	
Resnick	13	n	d	snsb	f	sm	n

is shown further down on the table. Speakers of Duffy's age and position seldom show the linguistic insecurity which leads to correction under overt social pressure, but we do find occasional examples of such an upward shift toward the younger vernacular norm, which becomes even more pronounced in reading. Hypercorrection to prestige forms is plainly present in several instances among younger speakers. Again, we find that these movements reflect the overall attitudes of the speakers towards correctness, which are expressed in formal discussion about language. Greenfield shows this tendency quite strongly, and so does the youngest speaker in the series, Joel Resnick, Henry Resnick's son. Both Greenfield and Joel Resnick show the strongest pattern of upward social aspiration among these working-class speakers.

Table 7 organizes the ordering of the variable constraints for these eleven speakers. With due allowance for these shifts, and for the fragmentary nature of some of the data, one can observe an orderly progression from the oldest speakers, with an F-$-N ordering, to the middle group with N-$-F, to the youngest with N-F-$. The reversal of the nasal constraint is quite clear, whereas the ordering of

Table 7

Ordering of Variable Constraints on Raising of
/æh/ for Eleven Male New York City Speakers

| | | Order of Phonetic Subclasses | | | |
Name	Age	F $ N	N $ F	N $ F	N F $
Hansen	73	x			
Duffy	73	x			
Resnick	60		x		
Schissel	57		x		
Orann	56		x		
Greenfield	46				x
Lazinsky	39			x	
Le Count	31			x	
Wallach	23				x
Carlino	19			x	
Resnick	13				x

the stop and fricative subclass is based on much finer differences. In each case, we can easily distinguish /æhN/ from the others, while the differences between /æh$/ and /æhF/ are much smaller. Our original formulation showed the stops and fricatives behaving as a unit as against the nasals, and there is considerable support for this in Table 7. Of the six possible permutations of order:

```
1  2  3  4  5  6
F  F  $  $  N  N
$  N  F  N  $  F
N  $  N  F  F  $
```

only 1, 5, and 6 occur in our data. The reversal of the variable constraint <−nasal> to <+nasal> is equivalent to moving from case 1 to case 6. In the notation of (15), with the first constraint being *nasal*, cases 2 and 4 are not possible. The class described in the original tensing rule (14), [α tense, α continuant], therefore has some claim to be considered a natural class.

The progression from the oldest to the middle generation of speakers may thus be shown as a movement from (15) to (18) in which both variable constraints are reversed:

$$(18)\ [\text{+tense}] \rightarrow <\text{+high}> / \left[\overline{\text{–back}}\right] \begin{array}{c} <\text{+nasal}> \\ <\text{–tense}> \end{array}$$

In later developments, we see that the tense feature reverts to its original value, and fricatives are favored over stops once again. Whether this second reordering represents a regular and reproducible trend is difficult to say from the limited data we have assembled so far. But the differentiation of voiced stops and voiceless fricatives can be observed in other dialects, and Table 7 reveals age differences which deserve further investigation.

For the further development of the raising rule, we must look to female speakers. Their treatment of /æh/ is regularly more advanced than that of the men. Furthermore, women seem to show a greater tendency to adopt the norms of younger speakers. In our series these are four working-class Italian women, of second and third generation. All show a highly developed state of the raising rule. Fig. 10 shows the pattern of Rose Barisse, 42 years old. We observe a great gap between the low /æ/ vowels and the tense vowels involved in the raising rule. All the /æh/ words have risen beyond /ey/ to upper mid or high position. Furthermore, we find that /ehr/ has moved to the high level, and covers the same range as /ihr/. When we first examined this display, we could not find any clear evidence for the differentiation of the variable constraints. We therefore searched the interview for other evidence, but even with twenty /æh/ words, there is still no clear differentiation of /æhN, æh$, æhF/. For Rose Barisse, and the other Italian working-class women, the constraints have merged to produce the same effect. Even where the vowels have not all reached high position, we have

$$(19)\ [\text{+tense}] \rightarrow <\text{+high}> / \left[\overline{\text{–back}}\right]$$

in which the environments of (15) are all variable, but of equal effect. The end result of this evolution, in which all vowels are high, has been reached only by a small number of younger speakers, so we cannot yet write a categorical rule [+tense] → [+high].

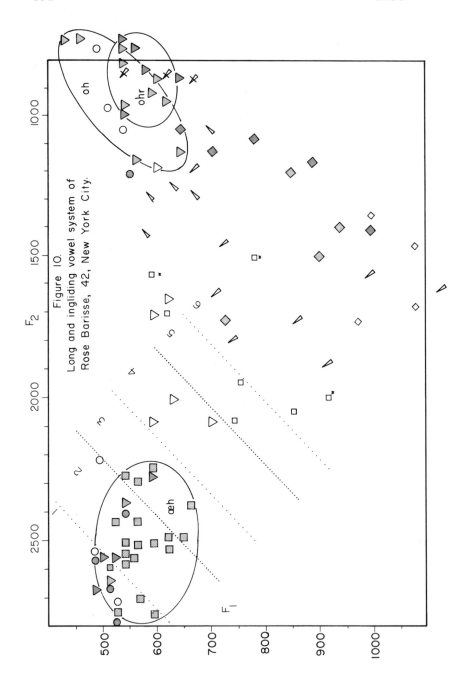

Figure 10.
Long and ingliding vowel system of
Rose Barisse, 42, New York City.

Not all women speakers fail to show a difference between these constraints, however. Half of them distinguish /æhN/ from the other constraints, and again, we find that the three oldest show fricatives favoring the rule more than nasals, and the two youngest reverse the pattern, with nasals predominating. The available evidence for women speakers therefore confirms the pattern we observed among men.

REVISION OF THE RAISING RULE

There are a number of difficulties which appear as we attempt to write formal rules within the discrete framework of ± high, ± low. One obvious problem is that we cannot combine (15) and (18) into a single rule with an alpha-switching symbol, because the former converts vowels to [-low], the latter to [+high] —though they are plainly two forms of the same process. The switching of the nasal constraint from − to + does not actually coincide with the rule change from (15) to (18), moreover. Table 6 shows that there are speakers in their fifties who still show some /æh/ as low vowels, but who have switched to the ordering in which nasals predominate. This being the case, we have to see the reversal of constraints as a process within a general raising rule, moving /æh/ from a low vowel to a high one. Our parallel studies of chain shifts in this dialect and elsewhere reinforce the impression that we are dealing with a single rule, not a pair of rules. These investigations have led us to the conclusion that chain shifts take place within a single dimension of height (or conversely, of "openness"), which ranges from [a] to [i]. A chain shift rule within this framework takes the form

(20) [x open] → <x-δ open>

The paired x's indicate that whatever differences in the openness of vowels existed before the rule are preserved after the rule applies. The symbol δ represents the amount of rotation, which varies with time, and is therefore a function of age. A rule of this sort will not produce mergers; all distinctions will be maintained. But the raising of /æh/ is a sound change of a different sort. The end result of this process is the total or partial merger of three major classes, /æh/, /ehr/, and /ihr/, as well as the minor classes /eh/ and /ih/ in *yeah* and *idea*. [27] It is similar to the general fronting and raising which has led to the modern Greek merger of so many vowels in [i]. A rule of this sort can be represented as

(21) $[+\text{tense}] \rightarrow <\text{x-}\delta\text{ open}> / \left[\overline{-\text{back}}\right] \cdot \cdot$

where there are two variable symbols, x and δ, which determine the degree of openness. The first symbol, x, may be taken as the primary function of age (in apparent time, synchronically; of real time, diachronically). It represents the central or modal position of /æh/. For the moment, we will consider x a discrete function with the six values given in the vowel charts, so that $6 \leqslant x \leqslant 1$. The oldest speakers will have higher values of x; the correspondence, according to Table 5, is roughly

Age level	x
70s	5
50s	4
30s	3

The situation is actually more complex than this. We have simplified the situation by focusing on the most uniform group of Jewish working-class men. But we find that the modal basic position of the vowel is also determined by sex (women more advanced than men), by social class (lower-class and upper-middle-class speakers being less advanced than working-class and lower-middle-class), and by ethnic group (Italians being more advanced than Jews or most other groups). We can then write

(21') x = f (Age, sex, social class, ethnic group)

or in other words by the relevant social characteristics of the speaker. The second determinant, δ, is a function of stylistic context. We have observed that more emphatic, more carefully formed utterances in the vernacular tend to be higher; while laxer, less stressed vowels tend to be slightly lower. On the other hand, there are occasionally very low vowels which seem to carry extra emphasis without necessarily being a response to social correction. For example, Paul Cohen reports that a friend who is a natural, uncorrected New York City speaker in his 20s with an /æh/ mode at 3, once turned on his heel and said quite naturally, "You [bæ·stɨd]!'' There may also be a probabilistic aspect to δ, since we cannot claim that every utterance in the course of a sound change is absolutely determinate. In any case, we can assert that δ is a direct function of style. It is inversely related to formality, so that the less formal the situation, the greater the decrement to the basic function x, and the higher the vowel will rise. We can conceptualize δ as somehow related to the force which lies behind the steady upward movement of the tense vowels, while x represents the level achieved by the rule for any one generation.[28]

Given the general form of rule (21), it would be attractive to specify a series of four rules to cover the actual developments in New York City: (22) for older generation speakers with F-\$-N ordering of the constraints, (23) for intermediate speakers with equally weighted constraints, (24) for younger speakers with N-\$-F order, and (25) for the smaller number of most advanced speakers who have carried the process almost to completion.

$$(22)\ [+\text{tense}] \rightarrow <5\text{-}\delta\ \text{open}> / \begin{bmatrix} \underline{\quad} \\ -\text{back} \end{bmatrix} \begin{array}{l} <-\text{nas}> \\ <+\text{tense}> \end{array}$$

$$(23)\ [+\text{tense}] \rightarrow <4\text{-}\delta\ \text{open}> / \begin{bmatrix} \underline{\quad} \\ -\text{back} \end{bmatrix}$$

$$(24)\ [+\text{tense}] \rightarrow <3\text{-}\delta\ \text{open}> / \begin{bmatrix} \underline{\quad} \\ -\text{back} \end{bmatrix} \begin{array}{l} <+\text{nas}> \\ <-\text{tense}> \end{array}$$

$$(25)\ [+\text{tense}] \rightarrow <2\text{-}\delta\ \text{open}> / \begin{bmatrix} \underline{\quad} \\ -\text{back} \end{bmatrix}$$

As regular and attractive as this model is, it fails to fit the observed facts in two respects. In our data, speakers with rule (24) actually show x at 4, those with rule (25) at 3. And despite Babbitt's statements, we do not have any really solid evidence of intermediate speakers with rule (23). Now that we have broken away from the high-mid-low framework, all the cases which approximate (23) could be assigned without too much trouble to (22) or (24). We can therefore write the series:

$$(22)\ [+\text{tense}] \rightarrow <5\text{-}\delta\ \text{open}> / \begin{bmatrix} \underline{\quad} \\ -\text{back} \end{bmatrix} \begin{array}{l} <-\text{nas}> \\ <+\text{tense}> \end{array}$$

$$(24')\ [+\text{tense}] \rightarrow <4\text{-}\delta\ \text{open}> / \begin{bmatrix} \underline{\quad} \\ -\text{back} \end{bmatrix} \begin{array}{l} <+\text{nas}> \\ <-\text{tense}> \end{array}$$

$$(25')\ [+\text{tense}] \rightarrow <3\text{-}\delta\ \text{open}> / \begin{bmatrix} \underline{\quad} \\ -\text{back} \end{bmatrix}$$

It is now obvious that these three rules can be collapsed to a single schema:

$$(26)\ [\text{+tense}] \rightarrow <\text{x-}\delta\ \text{open}> / \begin{bmatrix} \underline{} \\ -\text{back} \end{bmatrix} \begin{pmatrix} <-\alpha\ \text{nas}> \\ <\alpha\ \text{tense}> \end{pmatrix}$$

This rule combines all the possibilities open to speakers of New York City English. The α condition indicates that either direction of the constraints is possible, but that in any case, the nasal constraint is the most important. The parentheses around these constraints indicate that they are optional—that there is a version in which the rule operates in the same way for all phonetic contexts. And finally, the use of the x symbol states that *any* value of openness is possible in the pronunciation of tense low front vowels for New York City speakers.[29] They are equally prepared to interpret [æ:n], [ɛ:ᵊn], or [ɪ:ᵊn] as the name *Ann*. We have, for example, anecdotal evidence from Riverdale, in upper Manhattan, that some children recently complained to a father and mother that they had given their son a girl's name, [i:ᵊn] ! This certainly offers *a posteriori* proof that *Ann* and *Ian* can be considered homonymous in one current phase of the dialect.

The degree of opening is thus irrelevant to the identification of short *a* as the vowel of *man, past,* or *bad;* though as tense ingliding vowels these will still be opposed to *main, paced,* and *bead.* Rule (26) must not disguise the fact that the phonetic location of these new tense vowels does carry a great deal of expressive information. Working-class New Yorkers seem to be more sensitive to the quality of the short *a* vowel than any other element of pronunciation. They will occasionally mention this vowel as a bad mark of New York City speech and ridicule it in the speech of others. Almost every working-class informant will correct (irregularly) his vernacular form to a low [æ:] in reading lists of words. But the selectional rule (14) is not thereby reversed: The corrected form [æ:] is still tense; it is long, fronted, and usually quite distinct from short /æ/. This original tensing rule (14) seems to be operating at a higher level, not subject to direct observation and social correction. The subtle variations in rule (14) have no direct correlation with the social factors of (21'). Within the general framework of (26), we can still recognize that δ provides the interpreter with expressive information on the degree of formality and emphasis, and the attitude of the speaker towards him, while the value of x contains information on the social characteristics of the speaker.[30] But there is an important sense in which we need an abstraction such as (26) in order to represent the use of the /æh/ vowel in identifying words on the basis of their denotative content. Thus (26) carries out the intention of Bloomfield's fundamental postulate of linguistics, saying that *some utterances are the same,* despite wide variation in their phonetic realization. A competent speaker of the New York City dialect knows that [æ:n], [ɛ:ᵊn], and [ɪ:ᵊn] are the *same* in some important sense captured by (26). The confusion of the Riverdale children was caused by their ignorance of the lexical item *Ian,* although they did know that if such a word existed, it would be homonymous with their pronunciation of *Ann.*

Rule (26) does seem to capture the kind of general synchronic condition which we expressed in the broadest version of the consonant cluster rule (6). At first glance, these rules might seem to differ greatly in their generality; (6) was suggested as a very general condition on consonant cluster deletion which might apply to a wide range of languages, while (26) merely represents the general condition for the New York City dialect. But now that we have separated the raising rule from the selectional rule (14) and generalized it to (26), the special New York City flavor of this rule seems to have dissipated. Rule (26) applies generally to a wide variety of American dialects. Wherever we have the raising of low front /æ/, as in Boston, Detroit, or Chicago as well as in New York or Philadelphia, we find that the nasal constraint is the most important and we often find stops separated from fricatives as a minor constraint. Of course the tensing rule which selects from short /æ/ varies widely. In some areas, as in southern Connecticut, it affects only the nasal vowels; in other areas, particularly the northern cities from Buffalo to Chicago, we find all short *a* vowels affected (and involved in a chain shift in which short open *o* is fronted to [a] or even [æ] after short *a* is raised). Our original impression of these dialects was that there was no phonetic differentiation in the raising rule, but our recent studies of Detroit and Chicago show us that this is not always the case. Fig. 11 shows a speaker from Detroit, A.H., with a fine range of phonetic differentiation. The raising rule used here is equivalent to (24), with nasals in the lead, stops in the middle, and fricatives well behind.[31]

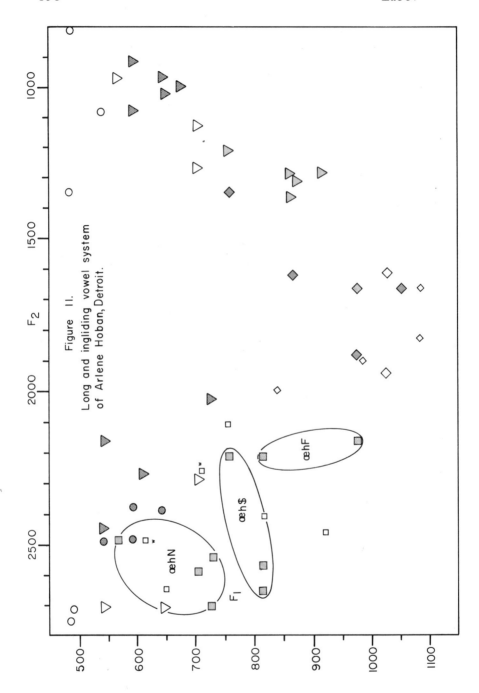

Figure 11.

Long and ingliding vowel system
of Arlene Hoban, Detroit.

The expressive information on age, social characteristics, and formality conveyed by x and δ are not constant from one speech community to another, although they will show some common characteristics.[32] This type of expressive information is often peculiar to a dialect, the product of the historical events—immigration, migration, social mobility—which operated to produce that particular community. In fact, we may profitably define a speech community as a group of people who share a common set of norms about language—norms directly related to the expressive values of such functions as δ and x in (21') (Labov 1966).

We can now return to the way rules (14) and (22-26) reflect the process of sound change in New York City. As far as the basic models of sound change are concerned, we will have to assign the tensing rule (14) to Model A—"regular" change. As I have noted at several points, there are subtle variations in this rule which are not considered here. Some reflect model C, "uniform decomposition," as in the uniform tensing of the lexical item *avenue* by almost every New Yorker. Other variations show model D, "ordered decomposition," as in the tendency of weak nasal words like *am* or *can* to be raised by younger speakers, or the tendency of polysyllabic forms with /š/—*fashion, passionate*—to be tensed. Finally, we find some variations which are defiantly Model E', "random decomposition," as in the fluctuations of *jazz* and *razz*. But despite these problems, discussed in some detail in Cohen 1970, the basic model for tensing found in (14) is "regular" change—and a categorical example of it. All our speakers tense the vowel before voiced stops, voiceless fricatives, and front nasals, yet it would be illusory to take this as a demonstration of the neogrammarian regularity of sound change *in progress*. In New York City and in other dialects studied, the tensing rule seems to represent a change that has gone to completion—or is approaching completion asymptotically. The activity which led to the formation of (14) seems to have taken place in the nineteenth century; we have inherited a fairly dormant form of that change. There are still occasional rumbles, and the geographic distribution proves that it was once an extraordinarily active process, but in the main the tensing rule has reached a plateau.[33] Why and how such rule changes pass from an active to a dormant state is a major puzzle, which we have not begun to solve—the "actuation riddle" (Weinreich, Labov, and Herzog 1968).

Our main concern is of course with the raising rule, as represented either by (26) or the series (22), (24'), (25'). The generalized form (26) tells us nothing about the sound change itself, which is represented either as the age function of x in (21') or as the distribution of (22), (24'), and (25') throughout the population. Insofar as the three major subclasses /æhN/, /æh$/, and /æhF/ behave as units, we have a good representation of the intact wave, model B', in its variable form. Here the variability appears as the degree of opening rather than the frequency with which the rule applies—for some degree of raising is used in any case.

What we now have to understand is why and how the relative ordering of the subclasses was reversed—in the terms of rule (26), why the alpha-switching applied to the environments, changing the rule from version (22) to version (24). In this case, the combination of the separate subrules into a single schema offers nothing in the way of explanation. Such explanations will differ according to whether we adopt a discrete or a continuous model of change. The question as to whether this sound change is discrete or continuous is still unresolved in our data, although we hope eventually to reach a conclusion on this difficult point. If the sound change is continuous, then in switching we must pass through a stage (23) with no variable constraints. Considerations of simplicity would argue that (23) is a stable state, produced by the generalization of rule (22). What reason would there be for the nasal constraint to re-emerge for younger speakers in the reverse direction? On the other hand, if the change is a discrete switching and (22) is succeeded abruptly by (24'), we can then argue for an alpha-switching meta-rule which reverses the direction of the nasality constraint. In the formalization of (22) and (24'), this switch coincides with the movement of x from low to mid position, thus restoring the possibility of operating with rules like (15) and (16). But the fit shown here is the result of segregating certain observed variation under δ, an abstraction which does not as yet have strong empirical confirmation. Although we must leave this possibility of discrete switching open, the data we now have favors the steady movement of the /æhN/ class from low to high, quite independently of the parallel movements of /æh$/ and /æhF/. The nasal subclass starts lower than the others, and ends up higher. It thus seems to be running on a faster track.

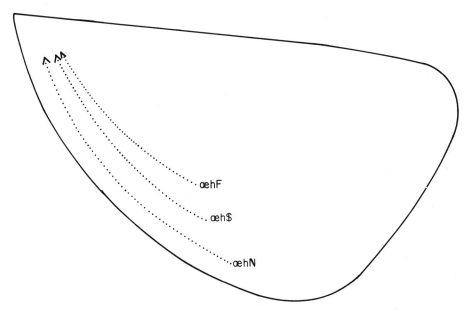

Fig. 12. Paths of /æh/ subclasses
in tensing and raising of short a

This impression is supported by the additional phonetic detail provided by Figs. 8-11. For all but the two oldest speakers—Hansen and Resnick—we observe that the nasal subclass is more fronted, with higher second formants than the stops and fricatives. There is a regular distribution at each phonetic sublevel, at right angles to the main path of the raising process, with nasals occupying the left-hand position. Our studies of chain shifts in other dialects confirm the notion that this outside track is a faster one, frequently occupied by nasal subclasses. The initial movement of /æhN/ under the tensing rule was to the left and downward, as indicated by the direction of the dotted lines. There appear to be acoustic explanations for this peculiar behavior of prenasal vowels, although we will not carry speculation further at this point. Accepting the model of phonological space indicated in Figs. 6-11, we see that the movements of the subclasses can be sketched as shown in Fig. 12. It appears that the /æhN/ class has a greater distance to travel under the raising rule, and it moves faster. It is therefore inevitable that the dialect pass through a stage in which /æhN/ and other subclasses occupy the same degree of height; but this is a true coincidence only if we abstract from the dimension of fronting. Our impressionistic phonetics stresses height rather than fronting or backing, but the spectrographic displays, which are quite sensitive to second formant position, show that /æhN/ follows an independent course in its path from low to high.

It will be necessary to enrich our current data on older speakers, if we are to confirm or disconfirm this view of the process. The relations between apparent and real time are naturally more difficult to establish as we go further back in the age range, but we have by no means exhausted the available empirical data. The results so far, however, suggest that explanations of sound change are not likely to be found by assembling subrules into complex schema, and searching for evidence of simplification. The behavior of these phonetic subclasses seems to be determined by phonetic considerations—the organization of vowels in a phonological space closely connected to acoustic and articulatory facts.

Many of the problems raised by Cohen in his treatment of the tensing rule reflect the same kind of argument—that the nasal subclass evolves on a parallel but separate route from the others. For example, the fact that the [-W] constraint may be relaxed for the /æhN/ class is difficult to register within a single schema, especially when combined with many other special conditions for nasals.

It is therefore possible that "internal evolution" is a misnomer. On the one hand, it is obvious that we are dealing with the internal evolution of a system of vowels, and we cannot escape evidence of a generalizing force active in this linguistic change. In this view of the New York City system, we have attended only to one front vowel; but it is certainly not accidental that a parallel process occurs in the back. This raising of /oh/ and /ohr/ shows somewhat the same relation to the raising of /æh/ as /æhN/ does to /æhF/. It starts later, and passes the earlier change for most speakers, reaching the [+high] position first.[34] If we were to write a rule combining both front and back raisings, it is not likely that we could accommodate the mechanisms that are specific to each. In the back vowels, we have a complex set of relations between /oh/, /ohr/, /ah/, and /ahr/, which are only roughly parallel to the relations of /ehr/, /eh/, and /æh/ (there being no /æhr/ in this dialect). We may easily construct a general rule

(27) [+tense] → $<$x-δ open$>$

but it remains to be seen if we can write significant constraints which will reflect the transition mechanism for such a rule diachronically, or synchronically, the distribution of various forms through the subsections of the population.

A very general paradox seems to be emerging from these considerations. The primary exercise of linguistic insight is to see two processes as "the same," and to combine them into a single description. But the structural economy thus achieved is not all gain. The parallels are not exact in most cases, and in such gross rule schema we find more and more vagueness as to detail, which moves us farther and farther away from the articulatory, acoustic, and distributional facts in which explanation may lie. The paradox is that the deeper we exercise our talent for linguistically significant generalization, the more we lose the formal detail on which linguistic generalizations are based. There is always the hope that in synchronic description, the correct generalization will suddenly emerge to describe all the facts with great accuracy, but in the discussion of sound change, it seems difficult to combine both kinds of explanatory force into a single rule.

This paradox may be partly resolved by the realization that the structural parallels observed in the most general rule schema are weak forces in linguistic evolution. We have observed that the generalization of a rule from front to back can take as long as thirty to fifty years. These parallels seem to be weakly felt by the native speaker. Over a long period of time, they may act with compelling force. But such weak constraints are not likely to give us the full solutions to the various problems which cluster about the facts of language change. The transition, embedding, and actuation problems demand the kind of precision which we have been attempting to supply here, and this may in turn always require the close examination of individual rules and subrules involved in the change.

6. *Summary*

In our pursuit of decisive solutions to the questions of sound change, we have been greatly encouraged by the data given to us by the spectrograph. No one should underestimate the value of the perceptions and intuitions of a trained phonetician, but impressionistic phonetics gives us no way of knowing how right or wrong we are. After many decades of listening to vowels, we still do not know exactly what we know, or how well we know it. As a result, the data of impressionistic phonetics do not give a firm enough base for us to build further conclusions, and we have turned to acoustic data for intersubjective knowledge about sound systems.

The work done at Haskins Laboratory and elsewhere has given us a sizeable body of information about the critical features of the sound spectrum; and steady improvements in the technical performance of the instrument has brought us to the point that the spectrograph can reliably confirm and pass beyond the data offered by impressionistic phonetics.[35] In this area of research, the spectrograph offers a splendid opportunity to bring precise empirical data to bear on broad issues of linguistic theory. With only a small amount of sociolinguistic sophistication, and with some confidence in the regularity of language behavior, we are all in a position to make significant additions to the theory of language change.

This paper has been concerned with the formal representation of the transition from one linguistic state to another. In our initial approach, it was seen that of the many models for the evolution of word classes, "regular sound change" is the one with no immediate application to the data we find. Study of the actual process of change necessarily involves the concept of rule-governed variation. The notion of "rule of language" was specified to distinguish categorical, semi-categorical, and variable rules, which reflect the difference between strict co-occurrence relations and a more general kind of co-variation.

Empirical data on three cases of linguistic change in progress were presented. None of these bodies of information could be seen as relevant to formal linguistic description if we were confined to the two options of categorical rule and free variation. It therefore appears that the formal construct of a variable rule is essential to the description of linguistic change. The transition from one rule form to another appears to take place through changes within a variable rule in the order and form of variable constraints upon the rule.

The development of consonant cluster simplification with age appears to be a characteristic shift within nonstandard Negro English; in this age-grading the relative order of phonological and grammatical constraints are reversed. The development of centralization of /aw/ on Martha's Vineyard was presented in a variable rule in which the tenseness of the following consonant gradually increased in importance to become the predominating factor in the categorical rule of the youngest generation. The raising of short *a* in New York City showed a reversal in the direction of constraints as the nasal environment became increasingly dominant with younger speakers. The stage at which the nasal subclass /æhN/ equaled the other constraints could have been represented by a simpler rule, but there was no reason to believe that the simplicity of such a rule was associated with a stability which retarded the further development of raising. The raising of short *a* appears to be one of many sound changes which takes place along a single dimension of openness, ranging from [a] to [i], in which phonetic subclasses move along paths determined by their specific articulatory and acoustic character.

NOTES

1. This case is particularly strong because the usual explanation drawing on analogy is impossible: There was no available model for distinguishing singular from plural by -o vs. -a.

2. For more data on the Philadelphia situation, see Ferguson 1968. In the raising of short *a* in New York City, we also find grammatical conditioning in the lax auxiliary *can* compared to the verb *can*, which has a tense vowel. But an argument from analogy can be applied by saying that speakers use the unstressed form of the auxiliary, necessarily with a lax vowel, as a model. No such model can be argued for the Philadelphia lax *ran, swam, began* vs. tense *man, fan, stand,* which appears in the speech of a few New Yorkers as well.

3. For decisive examples of this inability to interpret violations of the Negative Attraction rule, see the repetition tests of Labov et al. 1968: 3.9.

4. The violation quoted above is by my daughter, age 9. We find that constraints on *any* are changing rapidly in the dialects of the midwest, where it is acceptable to say *We go there anymore,* meaning "nowadays." A recent caption in *Life* read: "This is what lady authors look like anymore."

5. There are two basic routes for generalizing the consonant cluster simplification in English. In Labov et al. 1968: 3.2, we treated the *-sp, -st, -sk* clusters with a separate rule; by that option, (3) must specify [-cont, -anterior, -coronal]. The rule would then apply to *-nt,* and *-lt* in *dent* and *belt.* The other approach, introduced by Wolfram 1969, is to exclude *-nt* and *-lt* along with *-mp,* *-ŋk,* etc., as heterovoiced; rule (3) would then have in the environment [__ α tense, α tense]. At present the issue is unresolved, although the second alternative seems preferable. Note that forms such as *cinch* and *singe* may be excluded, even when a stop is present after the nasal, since there is a final continuant.

6. As pointed out to me by Fred Householder.

7. In the earliest version of these conventions in Labov et al. 1968: 3.4, there was considerable overestimation of the degree of order which could be imposed on these variable constraints. The more moderate statement in Labov 1969 suggests that three degrees—a geometric tree with six ordered subclasses at the output—is probably as fine an ordering as can be established at present.

8. Words in *-sps, -sts, -sks* are categorically simplified by NNE speakers. Depending on the ordering of the epenthesis rule (Labov 1969) one will have *lists* as [lIs] or [lIsɨz].

9. As in the case of *wasps, lists, desks* cited above. See Labov 1969 for further examples of the operation of this *feature.

10. The Yankee community at Chilmark was extremely self-contained. Many are direct descendants (11th generation) of the Thomas Mayhew who settled the island in 1642. The pattern of intermarriage became dangerously narrow, concentrating a recessive deaf-mute gene; it is said that at the turn of the century there were 35 deaf-mutes in a village of 200 inhabitants.

11. See the discussion of phonetic constraints on /ay/ in Labov 1963: 290.

12. The original tense vowel ū did not undergo the Great Vowel Shift in words like *stoop, tomb, shove,* and *double* with labial finals. We are also short of many examples before liquids, so that it is difficult to determine the relative positions of the *-r* and *-l* environments as against the nasal continuants.

13. The use of Greek letters to indicate the ordering of constraints can be confused with their paired use to indicate "same" or "different" values of two features. But we will not use *paired* Greek letters to indicate "same" ordering and any pairing present in the rules will therefore indicate "same" value of the paired feature: either + or − for both.

14. I am indebted to Bruce Fraser for suggestions and criticisms which led to the simplified and generalized version of the notation, as reflected throughout this discussion. Note that when all features in a segment are variable constraints, neither brackets nor braces are needed to group them.

15. The data and results cited here are drawn from "A Quantitative Study of Sound Change in Progress," supported by the National Science Foundation. I am greatly indebted to my co-workers on this project, Benji Wald and Virginia Hashii, for their many contributions to this analysis and specific suggestions which appear in this paper.

16. Spectrograms of /aw/ are measured on narrow band spectrograms, with additional data for locating measurement points drawn from simultaneous broad band spectrograms. Measurements of /aw/ are made at the point of relative maximum of the first formant, further specified by the relative minimum of the second formant where possible.

17. One might assume that any gaps in the data could be filled by giving the informants a list of words with /aw/ in all possible environments. Although a reading, "After the high winds . . ." was used in the original work, we do not rely on such formal speech styles for the study of sound change in progress. The tendency to shift to other norms—either socially approved ones or those of younger speakers—is strongest when attention is paid to speech. One of the most striking examples of this phenomenon occurred with an eighty-year-old farmer and ex-iron worker from Duncannon, Pa. In reading a list of words, he asserted that *cot* and *caught, hock* and *hawk, Don* and *dawn* were identical, and pronounced them so. But in his own natural speech, the two word classes were widely separated in every instance, throughout several hours of conversation. His reaction to minimal pairs was to reproduce the style of speech that he heard from younger people around him. Many similar examples can be drawn from New York City records.

18. We specify "preadolescent" since current evidence indicates that the vernacular is learned in its most systematic form between the ages of 4 and 13. See Labov 1966 for evidence that speakers who spend less than half of this time in the dialect area do not acquire the fundamental productive or interpretive pattern.

19. See Labov 1966 for evidence that working-class speakers give us the best representation of the main stream of linguistic evolution in New York City, as opposed to lower-class or upper-middle-class speakers.

20. In *connected speech,* we include Styles A and B, the "casual" and "careful" speech of the interviews reported in Labov 1966. Styles A and B differ mainly in the frequency of corrected forms, which is minimal for A. There are some speakers who show a distribution of phonetic position of uncorrected forms corresponding to A vs. B, but studies so far show that this is not a regular pattern. Our basic spectrographic studies were of Style A alone, but we found that corrected forms from Style B could easily be distinguished, and the large body of data added from Style B enabled us to carry the analysis to this level of detail.

21. The number of examples taken from each vowel varied with their frequency and their involvement in processes of change—which in turn governed their dispersion. In the examples given here, all available stressed syllables with /æh/ in connected speech were measured and plotted.

22. For the long and ingliding vowels which are studied here, there is usually a lengthy steady state for both first and second formants, so that the point of measurement is usually not difficult to establish.

23. Chris Hansen was a third generation New Yorker of Norwegian background. He spent his entire youth in New York City, though as a seaman and labor organizer he has done considerable traveling outside the city since then.

24. There are many unresolved problems concerning the route taken by /ehr/ in this evolution, the point at which it became involved in the tensing rule, and whether it ever merged with /æh/. The present discussion will consider only the development of /æh/.

25. The ~V notation (not a vowel) conceals a host of problems. An *r* or *l* in this position usually yields a lax /æ/, as in *fabric* or *athletic.* The latter shows that the original formulation of "open syllable" vs. "closed syllable" is not quite accurate; we also find considerable variation when a nasal occupies this position. But the ~V condition, which includes inflectional boundaries # but not derivational boundaries +, will suffice for all the examples in our conversational data. It should be noted that some weak nasal words with following nasals are sometimes raised by some of our informants.

26. At this stage in the historical development of the rule, it seems that it may not have applied at all to back vowels; for Duffy, at least, there is no trace of the raising of /oh/ and /ohr/ from a low position. But for all but the oldest speakers, we find parallel raising of this vowel. Since there was no mid ingliding vowel in the back, perhaps there was less interference with raising than in the front, and the process proceeded more rapidly. In our charts, we show /oh/ and /ohr/ with mid vowel symbols but they were originally low, parallel to /æh/—i.e., /ɔh/ and /ɔhr/. In the discussion to follow, no effort is made to collapse this raising of the back vowels with the front vowels, since all the phonetic conditions are not yet determined—and it is not clear, in any case, if this can be done without obscuring the phenomena we are studying here.

27. The mergers we are speaking of are "partial" in that the distributional range of /æh/ always extends downward below that of /ihr/. However, the merger is firm enough to be heard as "the same" for many speakers in minimal pairs, wherever social correction does not intervene.

28. The task of formalizing δ is a difficult one if we are to include hypercorrection of the vowel to very low levels as part of its function. If we assume that /æh/ was normally raised slightly as compared to /æ/, occupying level 5 of height, we find that it is no longer possible for a New Yorker to correct a stigmatized raised vowel to this position. As noted above, it is an empty slot. The only available reference point is the low level of /æ/–level 6, and for this reason I refer to low tense vowels at this level as "hypercorrect." It is relatively simple for Δ to represent stylistic fluctuation upward from the x level, which seems to be continuous, but correction downward will require some recognition of this discrete constraint. It is still an open question as to whether such behavior should be accounted for by a systematic rule.

29. Note that this would not be true for /ehr/ words. Most /ehr/ words receive support from morphophonemic alternations which show that they could not be low vowels of the /æh/ class; though *bared* can equal *bad* as [beːəd], it is plainly based on *bare,* an /ehr/ word. However, the word *scarcely* has no such alternant, and it is never corrected to *scassly* [skæsli]. If the /ehr/ tensing and raising is added to rule (26), some addition must be made to the interpretation of x to avoid the possibility of lowering /ehr/ words.

30. Perhaps we should not consider *age* to be an expressive characteristic, since it is not likely that listeners are aware of age differences in this particular variable (as opposed to their awareness of generational differences in lexical items like *icebox,* etc.). It is possible that age differences act as simple noise in this kind of communication, though we should not underestimate the speakers' unconscious knowledge in any case.

31. A.H. is one of two speakers from the series of interviews carried out in Detroit under the direction of Roger Shuy (Shuy, Wolfram, and Riley, 1967). Both are middle-aged lower-middle-class women but of different ethnic backgrounds, and both show the clear-cut ordering of the phonetic subclasses N-$-F. I am indebted to Roger Shuy for supplying me with these important materials.

32. For example, we find that the raising of tense vowels is most advanced with lower-middle-class women in many cities. Ralph Fasold has some evidence that this is the case in the raising of /æh/ in Detroit. We find that Jewish speakers in Chicago, as well as New York, show higher /ohr/ than other members of the community.

33. We find many fossil remnants of this active change as we pass from New York to Philadelphia. Perhaps the most extraordinary example of change frozen in mid-passage is the fixed word class in Philadelphia: *mad, bad, glad,* the only cases of /æh$/ in the dialect, as noted in section 2.

34. There is also a close parallel in the development of centralization on Martha's Vineyard. The first vowel affected was /ay/; the back upglide /aw/ followed, but passed /ay/ for most younger speakers, and became the predominant sound change. The oscillation evident in these three parallels suggest that there is a common principle involved here, which may go beyond the internal evolution of the rule system. In Labov 1965 it was proposed that the mechanism of linguistic change typically involves such oscillations because in

the course of a change new groups entering the speech community reevaluate the status of the changes then in progress. In each of the cases cited above, that part of the change which was secondary became primary, and in turn led to an associated series of changes. If we think of each phase of the change as taking place along an S-shaped curve, it follows that a secondary or associated raising may be accelerating more rapidly than the original change as the latter nears completion. The fluctuations of the secondary change in progress may carry more social affect, and one can imagine how such a switch in orientation takes place. The explanation for the reversal of the nasal constraint may lie— at least in part—in this more or less arbitrary social identification, which stems from the desire of the incoming group to use the vernacular in the most native-like way.

35. The spectrograph used in this research is the Kaye Sonograph 6061B. I am deeply indebted to Kaye Electric for supplying this paragon of instruments, which has produced over 3,000 spectrographs with no more mechanical difficulty than the usual base line drift.

REFERENCES

Bloomfield, Leonard. 1933. *Language.* New York: Henry Holt.

Cohen, Paul. 1970. The tensing and raising of short *a* in the metropolitan area of New York City. Unpublished Columbia University master's essay.

Eckert, Penelope. 1969. Grammatical constraints in phonological change: The unstressed vowels of southern France. Unpublished Columbia University master's essay.

Ferguson, C. F. 1968. "Short *a*" in Philadelphia English. Mimeographed.

Fishman, Joshua, Robert L. Cooper, Roxana Ma, et al. 1968. *Bilingualism in the Barrio.* Washington, D.C.: Final Report on OEC-1-7-062817-0297, Office of Education.

Gauchat, Louis. 1905. L'unité phonétique dans le patois d'une commune. *Aus Romanischen Sprachen und Literaturen: Festschrift Heinrich Morf,* pp. 175-232. Halle: Niemeyer.

Goidanich, P. G. 1926. Saggio critico sullo studio de L. Gauchat. *Archivio Glottologico Italiano* XX: 60-71.

Halle, Morris. 1962. Phonology in generative grammar. *Word* 18: 54-72.

Hockett, Charles F. 1958. *A Course in Modern Linguistics.* New York: Macmillan.

House, Arthur S. 1961. On vowel duration in English. *JASA* 33: 1174-78.

King, Robert. 1969. *Historical Linguistics and Generative Grammar.* New York: Holt, Rinehart and Winston.

Labov, William. 1963. The social motivation of a sound change. *Word* 19: 273-309.

——. 1965. On the mechanism of linguistic change. Georgetown Monograph on Languages and Linguistics No. 18, pp. 91-114. Washington, D.C.: Georgetown University Press.

——. 1966. *The Social Stratification of English in New York City.* Washington, D.C.: Center for Applied Linguistics.

——. 1969. Contraction, deletion, and inherent variability of the English copula. *Language* 45: 715-62.

Labov, William, P. Cohen, C. Robins, and J. Lewis. 1968. *A Study of the Non-Standard English of Negro and Puerto Rican Speakers in New York City.* Cooperative Research Report No. 3288. New York: Columbia University.

Martinet, André. 1955. *Économie des changements phonétiques.* Berne: Franke.

——. 1955. *Phonology as Functional Phonetics.* London: Basil Blackwell.

Moulton, William G. 1967. Types of phonemic change. *To Honor Roman Jakobson,* pp. 1393-1407. The Hague: Mouton.

Peterson, G. E., and H. L. Barney. 1952. Control methods used in a study of the vowels. *JASA* 22:175-84.

Postal, Paul M. 1968. *Aspects of Phonological Theory.* New York: Harper and Row.

Shuy, Roger, Walt Wolfram, and William K. Riley. 1967. Linguistic correlates of social stratification in Detroit speech. Final Report, Cooperative Research Project No. 6-1347. East Lansing: Michigan State University, mimeographed.

Trager, George L. 1942. One phonemic entity becomes two: the case of "short A." *American Speech* 17: 30-41.

Weinreich, Uriel, William Labov, and Marvin Herzog. 1968. Empirical foundations for a theory of language change. *Directions for Historical Linguistics,* W. Lehmann and Y. Malkiel, eds. Austin: University of Texas Press.

Wolfram, Walter A. 1969. *A Sociolinguistic Description of Detroit Negro Speech.* Washington, D.C.: Center for Applied Linguistics.

6.

Another Look at Drift

Robin Lakoff,
University of Michigan

Until a short time ago, it was assumed that grammars consisted of a sequence of rules that applied one at a time at some fixed point in a derivation. Some recent work suggests that this is not the case. Given an intermediate derivation and a rule which may or may not apply in the environment, there are cases where one must know what the deep structure of that derivation was, what rules will apply later, and what the final output will be—all this in addition, of course, to knowing whether or not the intermediate derivation meets the structural description of the rule. That is, there are constraints on synchronic derivations that involve the total grammar, not just the structural descriptions of individual rules.[1]

These constraints also work to control the possible outputs of the grammar as a whole. It has been intuitively recognized that a given language will prefer certain types of superficial forms to others. These constraints will channel the wide variety of possible derivational histories into a relatively small number of permissible surface structures by stating in effect that if a certain deep structure undergoes rules of a certain form, it must also undergo other sorts of rules to produce the desired superficial shapes for the language in question. To explain these "targets" as well, then, the linguist must be aware of constraints on the grammar as a whole; knowing individual rules will not help him account for the fact that certain derivations occur and others do not.

172

It has been tacitly assumed that what little work has been done in diachronic syntax was done in rather the same way as in synchronic syntax: To find out what had happened between two periods in the history of a language, the diachronic syntactician had to make a survey of the two grammars, rule by rule. At stage A, say, rule 36 applied; at stage B, it has been replaced by 36'; and by stage C, it was perhaps no longer in evidence. These differences were considered sufficient to describe the change that had taken place between stages A, B, and C in that particular part of the syntax.

In some cases, perhaps even most, this comparison may well be sufficient. But there are other cases, some of the most interesting and most discussed aspects of syntactic change, which this sort of rule-by-rule examination will not account for. Just as in the cases of synchronic derivational constraints, it appears that one must look at the grammar as a whole, to see why the changes took place, and just what they were. There are "targets" diachronically too: The language changes toward a certain direction, not haphazardly, so that at the end the shape of the language is quite different from its earlier form. One can point to individual rule changes, of course, just as, synchronically, one might point to the application of specific rules to account for the facts. But if one does, one misses a generalization. In all these cases something is happening to the language as a whole; it is not just that the rules change, but rather, there is some principle, outside our present concept of grammar, governing the forms the rules are to take. If we do not interpret at least some syntactic changes this way, we must assume that there were a set of truly staggering coincidences within and between the histories of all the Indo-European languages; that the same set of changes occurred, more or less, in all of them, but at different times and in different ways. The responsible linguist cannot believe in such a set of coincidences.

This paper is intended as a preliminary examination of cases of this kind in diachronic syntax, particularly in the development between Latin and the Romance languages. No explanation of the facts will be offered; it should be noted that there is no mechanism within the present theory of transformational grammar that would allow an explanation. But the historical syntactician should be aware that such things exist, and that it is the duty of his field to search for an explanation.

Let me begin by considering a list of some of the changes that come under this heading, changes that occur in many or all of the Indo-European languages, clearly not as a result of one being influenced by another. They are well known, and are often discussed separately. I should like to consider them together, and will give reasons why they should be so treated.

(1) The nominal system.

    (a) The obligatory use of anaphoric, nonemphatic, subject pronouns.

        This feature is absent in most of the older Indo-European languages, but present in probably a majority of the modern ones. Even in those in which it is not now obligatory, the tendency toward the use of these pronouns is stronger now than it was in the past. (Compare Spanish and Latin in this respect.)

    (b) The use of articles, definite and indefinite.

        In the earliest stages of most languages of this family, there were no articles (though demonstratives did exist, and the morphological shapes of the articles developed from them). In some of the languages only the definite article developed; in others, both. In one or two, like Russian, neither has developed. But the trend is to a system containing both a definite and an indefinite article.

    (c) The use of prepositions instead of case endings.

        The older IE languages expressed grammatical relationships in nouns through the use of case endings: morphologically dependent forms attached to a noun-stem that had no independent existence (that is, was a "bound" form). Later languages have tended to develop, instead, an invariable independent noun without endings (except for plural) and a set of prepositions, also morphologically independent, to fulfill the functions previously performed by case endings. In some of the modern languages cases still remain, though in the majority (e.g., Germanic and Greek) they are in vestigial form, and prepositions are becoming more and more essential. In most modern languages, cases (i.e., surface case markers) have vanished entirely, except for a few vestigial forms in the pronominal system.

(2) The verbal system

(a) The development of periphrastic causatives, inchoatives, etc. In the early languages, particularly Greek and Sanskrit, there were special endings that could be added to most verbs to give causative, inchoative, frequentative, or other meanings. These suffixes were generally productive. Within the history of the ancient languages, we can trace the loss of these productive processes. The number of verbal roots that can take these suffixes is more and more restricted, until it becomes an exception rather than a regularity for a verb to have these special forms. (Cf. English fall–fell, rise–raise, as examples of remnants of a formerly productive system.) To replace them there arose a group of independent verbs already in the language, which came to be used to carry the meanings formerly carried by the special endings; they took as complements the verbs that formerly had the suffixes added to them. In the modern languages, this is the usual way of forming expressions of this type.

(b) The development of periphrastic auxiliaries.

In the older languages, the tenses were expressed almost exclusively as endings on verbs, not as morphologically independent elements. There is a tendency, less strong than some of those previously mentioned but nevertheless quite noticeable, for these endings to be replaced by independent verbs, generally verbs that also occur independently. Thus, compare Latin *amavi* with Spanish *he amado;* Latin *amabo* with English *I will love.*

(c) The development of adverbs and comparatives.

In Latin, the adverb was formed by adding an unanalyzable ending (*-e* or *-iter*) to the root of the adjective (e.g., *rapidus rapide*). In early Romance this ending went out of existence in favor of a corresponding noun phrase: *mens,* "mind," in the ablative, with the adjective, of course, agreeing in number, gender, and case (for example, *rapida mente,* which became *rápidamente* in Spanish, where the feminine form of the adjective occurs). Modern speakers feel this form is a synthetic one, but it was not synthetic originally. Similarly, the comparative ending in various Indo-European languages is becoming less used, or is practically obsolete. In Romance, the -yo- comparative of Latin is gone completely, except for a few irregular forms; in English, *more* is appearing in environments where previously only -er was found.

These, then, are the changes that I wish to examine. I have called them examples of "drift," a term borrowed from Sapir. He seems to have been feeling his way towards an understanding of these problems, as is evident in the chapter on drift in *Language*, 1949. There he makes some rather interesting points, though he does not explore the question fully.

Sapir begins by discussing dialectal variations. He points out that, in general, there is a leveling influence at work within language, constantly ironing out dialectal differences and bringing variations back to the norm. If individual variations alone were the only means of change within a language, he feels, "we should be at a loss to explain why and how dialects arise, why it is that a linguistic prototype gradually breaks up into a number of mutually unintelligible languages." His explanation for this is that

> Language is not merely something that is spread out in space, as it were— a series of reflections in individual minds of one and the same timeless picture. Language moves down time in a current of its own making. It has a drift. [p. 150]

That is, there are factors embedded in a language, as it were, that force it to develop in certain directions. Sapir never quite states what he considers this "drift" to be; how it is related to the synchronic rules of a language; how much of it is universal, or even Indo-European; why it exists and how it can be defined. But the idea of there being something outside the individual rules of a language (Sapir does not quite state it this way, but this is what he apparently means) that causes changes in a given direction is looking in the right direction. Later in the chapter Sapir defines drift somewhat more precisely.

> We must return to the concept of "drift" in language. If the historical changes that take place in a language, if the vast accumulation of minute modifications which in time results in the complete remodeling of the

language, are not in essence identical with the individual variations that we note on every hand about us, . . . are we not imputing to this history a certain mystical quality? Are we not giving language a power to change of its own accord over and above the involuntary tendency of individuals to vary the norm? And if this drift of language is not merely the familiar set of individual variations seen in vertical perspective, that is historically, instead of horizontally, that is in daily experience, what is it? Language exists only insofar as it is actually used—spoken and heard, written and read. What significant changes take place must exist, to begin with, as individual variations. This is perfectly true, and yet, it by no means follows that the general drift of language can be understood from an exhaustive descriptive study of these variations alone. They themselves are random phenomena, like the waves of the sea, moving backward and forward in purposeless flux. The linguistic drift has direction. In other words, only those individual variations embody it or carry it which move in a certain direction, just as only certain wave movements in the bay outline the tide. The drift of a language is constituted by the unconscious selection on the part of its speakers of those individual variations that are cumulative in some special direction. This direction may be inferred, in the main, from the past history of the language. [pp. 154-55]

Sapir's point here is clear: that language moves in certain directions, despite the randomness of individual variations in language learning.[2] This direction is not discoverable from inspection of the synchronic language itself, but only from looking at the historical changes in the syntax over a period of time. He gives three examples of drifts, as he calls them, within the history of English. I would prefer to call all his examples subclasses of my (1c) above, rather than separate and isolated drifts. Moreover, judging from his terminology (he speaks of drifts in the plural), Sapir would consider the types of changes that I am discussing independently motivated and not necessarily related; while my point in discussing them is that they are, in fact, all part of the same phenomenon. But Sapir is correct in identifying his examples as cases in which the languages change because of something outside the individual rules themselves.

His three drifts are: the loss of case endings, the stabilization of word order, and the rise of the invariable word. But it seems apparent that all three are the same: One leads to another, and, in fact, implies another. This will be discussed later at greater length in connection with my item (1c). But Sapir fails to discuss any other types of drift, and fails as well to propose any generalization as to why all these things happen or whether they are connected. He also fails to discuss the rather astonishing fact that these mysterious drifts, strange and inexplicable as they are within the history of English, still more strangely and inexplicably occur again and again, independently, in the related Indo-European languages.

In the remainder of this paper I shall present evidence in justification of my claim that the drifts Sapir spoke of, as well as the others I have noted earlier, constitute a single phenomenon.

This phenomenon, it seems to me, cannot be described by talking about individual changes in transformational rules, in the phrase structure component, in the lexicon, or indeed, in any part of the grammar. Rather, it must be described as a metacondition on the way the grammar of a language *as a whole* will change.

This metacondition dictates where in the grammar the various changes will take place, over time; in which of the transformational rules, and in what way; in which parts of the lexicon, and again, in what way. (I know of no examples of change that are necessarily to be ascribed to the phrase structure component.[3]) Changes of the type I will discuss in this paper, in these accessible parts of the grammar, must be viewed as initiated elsewhere, in some aspect of language that is not evident to us on inspection of the synchronic data. But the fact that we do not understand what is happening should not blind us to the existence of this metacondition; rather, we should ask, as I shall now, what is meant by "metacondition on the way the grammar of a language as a whole can change"?

The existence of the metacondition on change is Sapir's stabilizing factor. It ensures that the drift of the language will go in a certain direction only, no matter what happens in individual synchronic idiolects. It determines, at least in part, the direction of change in the grammar as a whole. It is, simply stated, a tendency found in all the Indo-European languages and becoming stronger in time. The metacondition may be thought of as saying something like, "If there is a choice between a rule and a lexical item to produce a surface structure containing independent segments, as opposed to one containing morphologically bound forms, pick the former." Speaking metaphorically, it instructs the language to segmentalize where possible. In a wide variety of ways, every one of the phenomena I have identified as being drift-related is a change in the direction of greater segmentation, or, as Sapir put it, in the direction of the independent word.

I do not at present see any way of characterizing this metacondition formally. Nor can I imagine how it could be considered as part of a synchronic description of a language: I cannot imagine how it could have been learned by a speaker, if it is part of his linguistic knowledge at all. I merely wish to point out that many apparently disparate changes are part of a single general scheme.

Other things, too, remain unclear. I have no idea why this metacondition exists. The suggestion is sometimes made that an independent segment is easier to perceive in some sense than a bound form; but if this is true, why are languages outside the Indo-European family still highly synthetic? If there is no reason, then why did the condition arise in Proto-Indo-European? (It seems not to have been there from the earliest times, at least not if the traditional views of the development and shape of the proto-language are correct. It is generally assumed that case endings and verb endings were originally independent elements themselves, which coalesced in time with noun and verb roots to become dependent. This analysis raises some very troublesome problems if it is taken seriously, yet there is a reasonable amount of evidence in support of it.) It is also not clear what sort of thing this metacondition is; how it allows nonsegments to remain for long periods of time, and sometimes even reverse the direction of drift here and there; why it takes some forms in some languages, others in others, and operates in different parts of the grammar at different times in different languages.

Linguists investigating other language families have reported to me that in the languages on which they are working, in the period of history with which they are familiar, the drift seems to be operating in the other direction, toward greater syntheticity. Others have said that in languages on which they are working, there is a period of segmentalization followed by a period when change goes in the other direction. From these confusing facts, perhaps a few interesting points for those interested in pursuing this problem can be extracted. First, drift—defined here very freely as historical fluctuation between syntheticity and analyticity—is an extremely widespread phenomenon among the languages of the world; and second, there is apparently no reason to suppose that either total syntheticity or total analyticity is the most "desirable" state for a language, or the state in which a language is most stable, since many languages swing back and forth from one to the other. Further, since there is this great discrepancy among languages as to the direction of drift, it seems unlikely that one can assume any psychological motivation for languages to work toward one state or the other. So drift acts as a sort of linguistic pendulum—but why should language have such a pendulum built in? It appears not to be accidental, but a very real part of human linguistic ability.

Since we are so far from understanding why drift exists, let us at least see how much can be said about how and where it operates.

First let us consider the case of the overt appearance of subject nonemphatic pronouns. They are mandatory in English, French, and German, but not in Spanish or Latin. We can confine our examination here to Latin and French, and ask what has changed in the history of these languages, and how that change can be described. But first, of course, it is necessary to ask how pronoun formation occurs synchronically.[4] This is discussed by Postal (1966), whose description of the process of forming pronouns (assuming, of course, that the conditions under which nonemphatic pronominalization occurs are met) can be summarized in this way. Postal assumes, under these conditions, a series of rules, which apply in the order given, to the noun phrase to be pronominalized. The first rule, Pronominalization, inserts the feature [+pro] into the matrix of the noun phrase. The next, Definitization, adds two more features to the matrix: [+definite] (since a pronoun always refers to a noun that is presupposed or previously mentioned, it must be definite) and [−demonstrative]. The latter indicates that the form will not be emphatically demonstrative, like *this* or *that*. It does not point to the object mentioned by the noun, but merely is used to show that the object has been mentioned previously, or is known to exist by speaker and hearer. The next rule, called Segmentalization by Postal, takes several features from the matrix of the noun phrase and copies them as an independent matrix, which will ultimately become an independent word—a pronoun or definite article, as will be explained later, depending on the application of various later rules. Segmentalization copies the features [+definite] [−demonstrative] and the markings of person, gender, and number from the noun phrase. In languages like Spanish, it is clear that articles as well as pronouns must have indications of number and gender; in English, only pronouns have these overt markings.

How is the situation in Latin to be distinguished from that of French, or Modern English? One possible description of the change is that, in Latin, the rule of segmentalization did not apply in subject-position anaphoric pronouns. In this case, the features would remain features of the noun phrase itself. This is a poor solution for several reasons. First, there are situations in Latin in which segmentalization does in fact take place; for example, if the pronoun is emphatic, that is, stressed. These stressed pronouns clearly have a great deal in common with the nonstressed anaphoric pronouns. But this treatment would deal with the two in different ways. The generalization that both stressed and unstressed anaphoric pronouns are produced by segmentalization—a generalization that Postal makes for English—would not be possible for Latin. Secondly, if Latin and Spanish, which is like Latin in this respect, are treated this way, and French works as English does, there will be a considerable difference in the rules for pronominalization in French and in Spanish. While it is perfectly conceivable that in some respects the grammars of French and Spanish are quite different, if one has to choose between two otherwise equivalent solutions, the better one is probably the one that assumes the least difference between the transformational components of the two languages. Finally, and most significantly, consider Latin sentences where subject-raising has occurred; for example, with the personal passive, as in *Creditur esse bonus,* from (*Aliquis*) *credit eum esse bonum.* The pronoun subject of the lower sentence, an accusative, must appear as a nominative subject of the higher sentence when passivization and subject-raising occur. But if segmentalization did not take place, and if at no stage in the derivation of this sentence did an overt form of the pronoun *is* occur, the rule of subject-raising could not be stated, and this sentence could not be produced.

The natural solution is to let the segmentalization rule apply in Latin exactly where it does in French and English—in all environments where the structural description is met. But in Latin a later rule applies, deleting all subject pronoun segments that are not to receive stress. Noun-verb agreement and putting the person-number endings on verbs will of course have applied previously in all cases, so that there is no danger of non-recoverability, which is apparently avoided whenever possible in Indo-European languages, though not universally.[5] The difference between Latin and French here, then, is that the former has an extra rule, which is absent in the latter; its effect is to suppress an independent segment that has been produced by another rule.

Latin is more complicated by one rule, which French discards; but this is not merely what has been called "simplification" of the transformational component. It is simplification for a purpose: The loss of the rule allows another independent segment to exist in the superficial structure of the language.[6] This is a somewhat roundabout way of creating new segments in a language. The simpler, more direct, and more frequent method is to introduce new rules in a language to create new segments; here, however, the new rule suppresses the original segments. This is a case in which segmentalization is effected by indirect means, rather than direct, and therefore it shows particularly clearly that there is an overall constraint on the superficial forms of derivations operating, which influences the addition and deletion of rules diachronically. Spanish seems to be in an intermediate stage between Latin and French; the rule deleting the segment has gone from an originally obligatory state to one in which it is optional for some dialects, so that it is possible, though not usual, to use nonemphatic subject pronouns.[7]

The next case is that of the articles. They are generally treated as unrelated to the pronouns despite the very close morphological similarity, in many Indo-European languages, of the definite article and the personal pronoun. Postal (1966) gives some persuasive evidence for deriving the personal pronouns and the definite article from the same underlying source. The indefinite article has a different source, but its coming into existence results from the general trend toward the overt occurrence of segments. (See the discussion of the indefinite article in Perlmutter, 1970.)

Postal assumes that pronouns arise when the noun phrase in question is an empty form, with a meaning like "one(s)," and is, in addition, anaphoric. Otherwise, the superficial form is that of the article. (A morphological distinction between pronoun and definite article is found in English, but not in German, and in rather weaker

form in the Romance languages.) The difference between the behavior of the subject pronoun and the definite article in Latin is
that the pronoun, as was noted earlier, occurs superficially when
stressed; but the definite article never occurs superficially in ordinary usage in the Classical language, though it shows up in Vulgar
Latin, probably as early as Plautus (c. 200 B.C.), and certainly by
the time of Petronius (c. 100 A.D.). (The indefinite article does
not appear at all until much later.[8]) Here again there is a choice between two interpretations of the facts: Either, as with the pronouns,
the articles became overtly realized because the rule deleting segments, which was operative in Latin, was suppressed; or (and I know
of no strong arguments against this interpretation) the segmentalization rule did not apply in Latin, but became applicable in Romance. But the chronology of the development of the definite
article coincides closely with that of the pronoun in Romance; and,
of course, they are derived from the same word, *ille*. This fact may
be an argument in favor of the first interpretation for the pronouns
as well as the definite article, but aside from this chronological information, there is no evidence in favor of either.

The history of the indefinite article requires a different interpretation. There is, as far as I know, no evidence of *unus* used as the
indefinite article until the Vulgar language had already split up into separate dialects. Just as *ille* could previously be plugged into a
matrix only when the feature [+demonstrative] was present, but
later could be plugged in also if the feature were [–demonstrative]
(when personal pronouns and definite articles received overt forms,
and *ille* additionally replaced *is* as the unmarked demonstrative pronoun), *unus*, in the Classical language, was found only if specific
reference to number was being emphasized, but later was used elsewhere as well. Perlmutter (1970) proposed that in English, *a(n)*
is derived from *one,* the latter changing to the former when unstressed. It can also be said for Romance that the indefinite article
and the numeral are the same, with much the same sort of evidence
as Perlmutter brings forth for English. But in Latin, unstressed *one*
had no overt superficial form. How is this change to be described?

Perlmutter presents evidence that the indefinite article is derived
not from a deep structure source similar to that of the definite
article and the pronoun, but rather from a structure containing a

quantifier, the numeral *one*. Therefore, there can be no article segmentalization rule involved. In English, as in the Romance languages
and in other languages containing an indefinite article, when *one* is
unstressed, a segment remains: The indefinite article is still an independent word. But in a language like Latin, this rule operates in
a different way: If *one* is unstressed, it is deleted entirely. Thus the
superficial result of the behavior of the definite and indefinite noun
phrases is the same in Latin; in both cases nothing is present at the
superficial level. This superficial similarity is brought about in two
different ways: With the definite article, either Latin contains an
extra segment-deleting rule, or the article-segmentalization rule does
not apply; with the indefinite article, a rule reducing unstressed *one*
must apply, but in Latin its effect is to remove the segment completely. In Romance and English, it leaves a segment. It is not surprising that these two changes should occur independently of each
other. They involve different processes, although both are the result of the tendency to segmentalize.

The last of the nominal-system drift-related changes to be discussed is the change from the use of cases to express nominal relations to the exclusive use of prepositions. Here, too, I would
like to use Latin and Spanish as the basis of the discussion. It is not
really correct to call Latin a case-language, though it is often done.
A true case-language is one in which relations are expressed purely
by case endings. Latin, however, makes considerable use of prepositions as well, increasingly so in the course of time. But Latin can
be considered a case-language since the noun has no existence without a case ending; there is no such thing as an invariable noun. This
change between Latin and Romance is a very clear instance of one
of Sapir's drifts: the tendency to the invariable word. There is
some indication that the tendency advanced faster in Greek, which
had only four cases and consequently made more use of prepositions, than in Latin, which retained its five cases quite late in its
history.

To return to the question of case versus preposition in Latin and
Romance, it should be noted that the change from case-language to
preposition-language did not happen all at once in Latin. Rather,
even in the Classical language, as noted above, the accusative and
ablative cases were accompanied by a preposition in many of their

uses. (The other cases never occurred with prepositions, however.) The case ending by itself was quite ambiguous; an added preposition greatly reduced the range of possible meanings that could be assigned, in a given sentence, to a particular case ending.

If Latin itself were totally prepositionless (as Sanskrit very nearly is), the change between it and Spanish could be described as a replacement of cases by prepositions—an obvious instance of the trend toward greater segmentalization. But this is not an accurate description of the change. Latin had a well-developed set of prepositions along with its five cases; in Spanish, the prepositions remain and increase in the range of environments in which they must occur, while the cases vanish. This cannot be called movement toward segmentalization, since here—unlike the types of change discussed previously—no new types of segments are introduced into the language. Rather, nonsegmental forms are lost—forms that previously carried meaning and served to disambiguate sentences, forms without which sentences would be uninterpretable. When Latin made use of both prepositions and case endings, they shared the burden of carrying the meaning-load of the relationship between the noun to which they were attached and the rest of the sentence. When one of the two is lost, the whole weight of the meaning-load falls on the other, which therefore becomes more crucial in the sentence. Thus, there is an increased semantic load on the independent segments, and they become more prominent semantically. In this way, the change can be considered as one in favor of segmentation, as it increases the importance in the sentence of the independent segment. Here again, the tendency toward segmentalization is reinforced not by the addition or deletion of a rule so much as by changes in other parts of the grammar. It has often been noted that the loss of cases coincides roughly in time with the phonologically governed loss of endings in the form of falling-together of vowels and loss of final consonants, leading to a lack of distinctiveness among case endings. There has been discussion in the past as to how to interpret the interaction of these changes, one purely syntactic, the other purely phonological. The question is usually raised, Which came first? Did the loss of distinctiveness in endings force the Romans to abandon their beloved case system? Or, conversely, did the decline and fall of the case system and consequent growth of prepositions enable the decadent Romans to slough off the endings, which were so hard to pronounce? These arguments are as ridiculous as they sound. Clearly, the two changes took place simultaneously; neither was caused by the other. Rather, each depended on the other. The phonological changes could not have occurred, with preservation of intelligibility, unless prepositions had developed beyond their functions in Classical Latin; and the syntactic changes in the case system would not have flourished had not changes in the phonology rendered them essential. Thus, to explain the change from case- to preposition-language, one needs to look simultaneously at two levels of grammar: the syntactic and the phonological components. This process, too, is analogous to synchronic derivational constraints.

Another change occurred in various members of the Indo-European language family along with the change from case- to preposition-language—the imposition of restrictions on word order, in the form of the loss of a scrambling rule, such as was described by Ross 1967b. It is true that the older Indo-European languages varied in the amount of scrambling each tolerated, but they all tolerated much more than do any of their modern descendants. Since this change is an invariable concomitant of the drift-related changes already noted, it would seem to be related to them. The usual explanation is that if scrambling is permitted, and the language is not a case-language, one would be unable to distinguish subjects from direct objects. This difficulty could be avoided by a language bent on retaining scrambling by adopting a direct-object preposition (as has Spanish, which has fewer constraints on scrambling than many other modern Indo-European languages). But most languages appear not to have adopted this expedient, but to have abandoned scrambling instead. Why this should have happened is a question that deserves investigation. Drift-influenced change also occurs in the verbal system. As was noted above, earlier Indo-European languages had special endings added to verbal stems, which gave those stems causative, inchoative, frequentative, or similar meanings. This process was originally quite productive. Thus in the early stages of Sanskrit (cf. Whitney 1896: 378), virtually every verb could form a causative. This was regularly done by adding the suffix -aya- after the verbal root on which one of several phonological changes might be performed, for example:

vid, "know," formed the causative *vedaya,* "inform."
pa, "drink" forms *pāya-* "give to drink, water."
sr, "flow," forms *saraya,* "follow."
klp, "be in order," forms *kalpaya-,* "appoint, ordain."
dṛc, "see," forms *darcaya-,* "show."

In Latin, however, only a few isolated causative forms remain. Far more frequently, the causative is formed periphrastically. In early Latin, too, frequentatives and desideratives were quite frequent, but in the Classical period, the remaining frequentatives and inchoatives were very few. A trend was developing toward periphrasis in the verbal system. In English, too, there were a few relics of an earlier stage in the language, causatives formed by ablaut: *rise-raise;* and frequentatives formed by suffixation: *gleam-glisten.* But only the historical linguist is aware of these relationships anymore. To most speakers of modern English, *raise* does not seem to be derived from *rise.* Some insight into one possible way in which these changes took place can be seen in Sanskrit, where the obsolescence of the causative can be gained by looking at the sequence of changes. At first the causative suffix could be added to any verb. At this stage of Sanskrit there was an abstract verb of causation, which can be represented as [cause], below which any verb could be embedded. There were no restrictions on what could occur inside the complement. A rule then operated on the lower verb, plugging it in under the matrix of features of the higher, abstract verb [cause].[9] According to this rule, a real verb with phonological and morphological feature markings is first written out. Then the abstract verb is represented as an ending on this real verb. (In English, the suffixes *-ize, -en* sometimes work this way.) At a later period in Sanskrit, the causative suffix, and the rules that went along with the plugging-in rule that produced it, could only occur if the real verb was intransitive.[10] If the verb was transitive, a real verb meaning *cause* had to be used instead, with the transitive verb embedded in it as its complement, parallel to English "I made Bill hit John."

The interpretation given to this change may depend on which of two opposing positions one takes on the insertion of lexical items in derivations.[11] A lexicalist might ascribe the change to a change in redundancy rules in the lexicon, a transformationalist to a change in the restrictions on the applicability of the rule that plugs the real

verb in below the causative abstract verb. But it really is not relevant for this issue which of the two positions one adopts. What is
interesting is that this change, like the others mentioned, cannot
be described in any satisfying way simply by looking at changes
in the application of individual rules. One can identify such changes,
true—either as additional restrictions in the lexicon, or as additions
to the structural description of a rule—but they are merely results
of the changes already described. A good theory, one which cap-
tures generalizations and tries to show *why* things change as well
as the fact that they *do* change, must note that the change in lexicon or rule is motivated from outside the grammar as a whole.

A similar, though not identical, situation is found in Latin with
inchoatives, frequentatives, and desideratives. At an earlier stage
they were fairly productive. It is impossible to tell now whether
the native speaker of Plautus' time or slightly earlier could form
these verbs with any verb, or only with the ones that are attested.
But in any case, the possibilities become steadily narrower; it is
well known that by later Vulgar Latin (i.e., Petronius) the frequentatives often no longer had frequentative meaning, but were
thought of as synonymous by-forms of the simple verbs, eventually replacing some of them entirely. It is perhaps best, given the
scanty evidence we have, to assume that the plugging-in rule in
these cases was probably governed not by semantic class but (as
with the English passive) by individual verbs. In time, these lexical markings changed. Verbs able to be plugged in under the frequentative abstract verb became more and more exceptional, as
fewer and fewer verbs fell into that category. If a verb were not subject to this rule, a periphrastic form would of course have to be
used instead. In this case, then, a growing tendency toward segmentalization in this part of the grammar is definitely the result
of changes in the lexicon itself: the loss of markings on verbs. The
phasing-out of rules occurs outside of drift, too. So, for example,
canto, cantare, in Classical Latin, a frequentative of *cano, canere*
"sing," in Vulgar Latin, was used as a synonym of *cano,* and in
Romance (French *chanter,* Spanish *cantar,* Italian *cantare*) has replaced it altogether. A rule, at first regular, gradually passes out of
existence; or the opposite takes place, when a rule formerly confined to a few forms extends its domain to include most, or all, of

the appropriate forms in the language. This is an example, then, of how otherwise extant types of syntactic change may also occur in drift.

In both the Latin and the Sanskrit examples, it is impossible to formulate these changes in any intuitively satisfying and non ad hoc way without invoking abstract verbs. Causatives, frequentatives, and the like are not parts of the phrase structure auxiliary even in those theories that contain phrase structure auxiliaries. There is no way of introducing a causative or frequentative ending transformationally in such a way as to restrict its occurrence later and replace it in any natural way by its periphrastic equivalent. The only way to describe the change in such a theory is to assume a complete break between the grammars of the two different stages in Sanskrit, or the innumerable different stages in Latin, one stage having a phrase structure rule that introduces a special optional causative ending everywhere (or optional frequentative ending in the environment of any verb on a particular list), then restrict this rule in Sanskrit and gradually reduce the list in Latin, at the same time having a completely unrelated periphrastic form come into wider use. This formulation is possible, since the theory does not specifically prevent it, but it does not seem to describe what is actually going on, or give any reason why the change should take place. Of course, with more recent theories of the form of the base, this kind of formulation is expressly ruled out.

Next, there is the question of the development of periphrastic tenses. Except for the passive system, Latin had totally synthetic tenses. In some of these tenses the Romance languages developed analytic forms. The question is how this came about, and why.

It is necessary to ask first what the tenses are in the underlying structure. It had of course been assumed until recently, and still is assumed by many transformational grammarians, that tenses and modals are introduced as tenses and modals, different from main verbs, as part of an auxiliary constituent. There is a good deal of strong evidence now that unless modals (certainly), and perhaps tenses as well, are treated as independent real verbs that take the so-called real verbs as their complements, it becomes impossible to state many generalizations.[12] On the assumption (since it would take too long to present the evidence here) that Ross's analysis is correct, how is the Latin tense system to be represented, and how are we to describe the change between it and the system found in Romance? This change can be described in a satisfactory way only if we adopt the analysis of tenses as main verbs.

If the tenses are to be dealt with as the causative was, each tense is a verb that takes the "main" verb as its complement. This tense verb can be either a real verb with phonological form, or an abstract verb that is subject to plugging-in. In Spanish, for example, the preterite is formed from an abstract verb and the perfect from a real verb, *haber*, just as the corresponding tenses are in English. In Latin, on the other hand, both are formed with abstract verbs; in fact, they reduce to the same superficial form, just as the different deep structures underlying the superficial form of a modal in English emerge identical on the surface. Why this should happen is not clear, but it is also not particularly relevant here. The perfect tense, then, goes from synthetic to analytic between Latin and Romance. The future tense works in a rather strange way. In Latin, there were two means of forming the future tense, governed by the conjugation class (a completely morphologically governed category) of the main verb. If the main verb was first or second conjugation, the future was formed by adding the suffix -*b*- to the verb stem, followed by endings resembling those of the third conjugation of real verbs. If the main verb was third or fourth conjugation, a different set of endings, somewhat resembling the forms of the subjunctive, were added. Both were synthetic.[13] In Romance, both methods are discarded, and in the early stages of pre-Romance we find evidence of a future of *amo* formed by using *habere* (have) preceded (never, curiously, followed—the usual position of a complement in Latin) by the main verb as its complement, with an infinitive ending. That is, instead of *amabo* we find *amare habeo,* which became *amar he* by regular phonological changes. It is still analytic, as evidenced by the occasional insertion of adverbs between the main verb and *haber.* But in present-day Spanish the form is *amaré,* synthetic again. (It must be considered synthetic, and a single lexical item, despite the special stress, because nothing can be inserted between *amar* and *e,* as adverbs, for instance, can be inserted between *he* and *amado* in the perfect.) There is, then, a progression from synthetic to analytic back to synthetic again in the course of 2000 years. Leaving this problem aside for the moment, the changes in the perfect and future can be accounted for just as the changes in causatives and frequentatives were, except that the mechanism must be slightly different: There, the change was either in the semantic classes of verbs (transitive vs. intransitive) governing a rule, or in the markings of individual verbs. Here, the changes do not appear to have taken place verb by verb, or class by class. At first the speakers of proto-Romance appear to have had a choice for all verbs of using the synthetic or analytic forms, and later no choice, but only the analytic form available. The change can be described without assuming a change in the base component; plugging-in, with these tense-verbs, was first obligatory, then optional for all verbs, then nonapplicable. This, too, is a frequent type of syntactic change, and here again the metacondition makes use of this means of change to create another segment where previously there was none. When plugging-in did not apply, as with the cases mentioned above, a real verb had to be substituted. This real verb apparently was picked out of a pool of "empty" verbs—verbs of general meaning. Why a particular verb is picked—e.g., for the future, "have" in Romance, "will" in English, "become" in German—cannot even be guessed at now.

Finally, let us discuss the drift-induced change in adverbial phrases, in particular the history from Latin to Modern Romance of adverb endings and comparatives. The first one, the change from the unanalyzable Latin -e or -iter to the Romance -mente, has already been discussed in sufficient detail. The comparative suffix on adjectives (and adverbs) was always synthetic in Latin, with the exception of a very few irregular adjectives and adverbs which, generally for phonological reasons (e.g., pius) could not take the comparative ending and, when comparison was unavoidable, formed their comparatives with plus or magis. These two adverbs are used in Italian, French, and Spanish (as piu, plus, and más) as the only means of forming the comparative. At the same time, the superlative ending is lost in most of its uses, replaced by this adverb of comparison plus the definite article. In English there appears to be a trend, not pronounced perhaps but visible, away from the -er, -est comparative and superlative endings toward more, most. All adjectives can be used with more and most; those of more than two

syllables cannot take *-er, -est,* and those of two syllables now seem
more and more to prefer the analytic form. Here, too, we must
wait for synchronic transformational theory to provide acceptable
deep structures and derivations for both adverbs and comparatives.[14]
In any Indo-European language the grammar may have one of two
types of rules for adverb or comparative endings. One type attaches
the ending to the stem, and one keeps the forms independent. For
comparatives, the tendency seems to be in favor of the latter in the
course of the history of most Indo-European languages. We are
dealing here with a change in the choice between two transformational rules. In the case of the English comparative and superlative,
one of two optional rules is prevented from applying in certain environments for phonological reasons—number of syllables, and perhaps position of stress—to a greater and greater extent. This is another example of a diachronic derivational constraint. The effect
of the rules, plus the constraint, is to encourage the spread of
analytic forms at the expense of synthetic.

In this paper I have presented a number of instances of changes
that cannot be understood by examination of the rules of the
synchronic grammar alone. Since they are presumably not universal,
they also cannot be explained by recourse to concepts of greater
intelligibility or other psychologically relevant notions.[15] It is not at
all clear where this metacondition exists: neither as part of a grammar nor as a universal condition on the forms of grammars. It is not
clear how a constraint on change within one language family, a constraint that is not absolute but which is nevertheless influential, is
to be thought of. But there is no other way to think of these things:
Either there is such a metacondition, whatever it is, or all the Indo-
European languages have been subject to an overwhelming series of
coincidences. Nothing in present transformational theory allows us
to characterize the metacondition, or to justify it. If we accept the
facts as given, either another explanation must be postulated, which
seems unlikely, or we must accept the idea that in order to understand syntactic change we must come to a fuller understanding of
synchronically oriented syntactic theory.[16]

NOTES

1. For a discussion of the need for and nature of derivational constraints in
synchronic analyses, cf. Lakoff (to appear).

2. As pointed out by Klima 1964.

3. This claim is contrary to that made by Traugott (1969), who gives examples of change she considers to be located in the phrase-structure rules. In the theory under which she is working (essentially, that of *Aspects of the Theory of Syntax*), this would indeed be the correct place to pinpoint the changes involved. But in the post-*Aspects* theory that I shall be assuming, the location of all these changes is elsewhere: either in the lexicon or in the transformational component. While I believe that the arguments for the post-*Aspects* type of theory are compelling, it should be noted that under any other view of transformational grammar, the claim made in the text cannot be supported. Hence, argument on this point is empty unless the participants in the argument hold the same views of linguistic theory.

4. I am assuming here that, prior to the rules I am considering, and Postal was considering in his paper, the rules which determine where pronouns occur in the sentence have applied. I am considering only the rules which determine the forms of the pronouns.

Because of space limitations and because everything is in print elsewhere, I shall not attempt to justify here the synchronic analyses on which the assumptions of this paper are based. I find them convincing; the skeptical reader may judge for himself upon examining the references cited.

5. For example, in Japanese much more ambiguity as to person and number is tolerated than in any of the Indo-European languages.

6. When the historical linguist talks, as some have, about "simplification" and "elaboration" of rules or parts of the grammar as a mechanism of syntactic change (cf. in particular Traugott 1969), he is missing the point if he views the naming of these phenomena as an end in itself. Neither the fact that a rule (or component) has been simplified nor the fact that it has been elaborated is interesting in itself unless we know other facts about these processes (as noted by David Perlmutter in an oral comment at this conference): whether there are reasons for the simplification or elaboration (such as I shall discuss for some cases); whether there are constraints on what can be simplified or elaborated, and whether there is a limit in the grammar as to how much of either of these processes can be tolerated; whether these terms can be more strictly defined, as they ought to be; and under what conditions each tends to arise. Until these questions have been explored, historical linguists would do well to treat these terms as words of no more explanatory power or significance than the word "change" itself.

7. These pronominalization phenomena in Spanish, French, and Latin are related by Perlmutter (1970) to certain other facts about the grammars of these languages. Perlmutter divides languages into two groups: In one, anaphoric subject pronouns are obligatorily present, there is a rule of *there*-insertion, an expletive *it* is found (as in, *It is cold in Boston*), and subjects cannot move out of indirect questions. In the other type, the opposite of each of these facts is true. English and French are examples of the first type, Spanish and Latin of the second. Many of these phenomena can be viewed as being related to the metacondition we are discussing. But it is of especial interest to

note that two languages derived from Latin fall into different groups in this respect; it is not clear how this historical change in group affiliation in French can be described.

8. Even in Plautus, *ille* is sometimes used in a way that is very close to the way in which a definite article would be used; that is, in the lexicon of a speaker of Plautine Latin, *ille* may or may not be marked as [+demonstrative]. The tendency to drop the [+demonstrative] marking is still stronger for the speakers in Petronius' *Cena Trimalchionis;* and, of course, in modern Romance it is dropped completely for the form descended from *ille,* now unequivocally the definite article. But there is no trace of *unus* being used in "unemphatic" position in Latin, Classical or Vulgar; in fact, this use of *unus* is not documented, as far as I can find, until Latin has broken down into the various dialects of proto-Romance. Occasionally the pronoun *quidam,* "certain," is used with a meaning close to that of some uses of the English indefinite article, but it is always emphatic, and in any case this use did not survive into Romance.

With respect to the definite article, it is wrong to believe that the definite/indefinite distinction (if any existed) could not be perceived by speakers of Classical Latin. It is true that no *overt* distinction was possible, but certainly these speakers could distinguish between definite and indefinite uses of nouns. Thus, in philosophical writing, when a Roman wished to make perfectly clear that he was using a definite noun, he sometimes had recourse to the Greek definite article. If he were unaware of the distinction, he would not have been able to do so.

9. For a discussion of abstract verbs and the rule of plugging-in, cf. G. Lakoff 1965 or R. Lakoff 1968.

10. This Sanskrit example was brought to my attention by Paul Kiparsky.

11. For a discussion of these two theories, cf. Chomsky 1969 and G. Lakoff 1965, for explanations of the lexicalist and transformationalist positions, respectively.

12. The only discussion of this topic currently in print is in Ross 1967a.

13. There is some reason for suggesting, as I have done informally (in lectures, Linguistic Institute, summer 1968) that in Latin the *b-o, b-i-s,* etc., endings of the future and the *b-a-m, b-a-s,* etc., endings of the imperfect are interestingly viewed as the reflexes of plugged-in abstract verbs of tense, the *i* (from *e*) and *a* representing the third and first conjugation endings of real verbs, respectively. I further hypothesized that the *-e-* future of the third and fourth conjugations was derived also from an abstract verb, but in this case by complementation, like the subjunctive, since it shares with the subjunctive certain morphological similarities, well known to traditional Indo-Europeanists. If this tentative analysis is in fact correct then the synchronic English analysis based on other evidence (e.g., the statement of *do*-support) and this independent analysis based on verbal endings coincide.

14. Cf. G. Lakoff 1969, Hale 1969, and Ross 1964 for discussions of the structure and analysis of adverbs, comparatives, and superlatives, respectively.

15. Thus, for example, Kiparsky 1968 suggests psychological motivation for the existence of certain types of phonological change, but not for others.

16. Answers to the questions raised in this paper—in fact, the complete understanding of the questions—will not be possible until a great deal of progress has been made in the field of synchronic transformational theory. In particular, the relationship of these cross-family changes, and the existence of a metacondition such as I have suggested, appear to be related in an interesting way to the kinds of synchronic universals of language that have been discussed by Greenberg (1961). If Greenberg's correlations are due to factors beyond mere chance—as they certainly must be—then they appear to provide evidence that the metacondition I have been discussing is, perhaps, part of an even larger phenomenon in the Indo-European languages, and perhaps in other language families as well. The data with which I am concerned involve the correlations Greenberg found between the dominant word order of a language and other properties it has, which as far as anyone can tell at present, appear to be unrelated (though they undoubtedly are not).

Examining proto-Indo-European as it is reconstructed, and the ancient Indo-European languages as they appear in documents (both admittedly rather unsatisfactory sources for speculation), we find that these languages have properties that, according to Greenberg, occur with more than chance frequency in languages whose dominant word order is subject–object–verb. In fact, in the attested languages, we find this word order most frequent. (This fact alone need not force us to consider them SOV languages, for stylistic preferences might be operative.) Besides this superficial predominance of SOV order, the other reasons for believing early Indo-European languages to have basic SOV order are the following:

(1) Adjectives most often follow their nouns, as do genitives. This is true of SOV languages. (Greenberg's Universal 5.)
(2) Postpositions occur, particularly in Sanskrit, where there are virtually no prepositions, and in Homeric Greek as alternate forms of certain prepositions, generally for metrical reasons (anastrophe). Perhaps cases can be looked at as deriving from postpositions, though there are reasons to doubt this analysis. (Greenberg's Universal 4.)
(3) Periphrastic tenses, when they occur in Greek and Sanskrit, are generally in the form verb+auxiliary. Greek lelumménoi eisín, and Sanskrit corayàm asa are examples. (Greenberg's Universal 16.)
(4) Relative clauses may either precede or follow their noun phrases. (Greenberg's Universal 24.)

However, in later languages (it was already apparent in Classical Latin, and was becoming quite definite in Romance and the other modern Indo-European languages) we find correlations, according to Greenberg's results, with languages whose dominant order is either subject–object–verb, or, even more strongly, verb–subject–object. (For arguments for English—and, by extension, most other modern Indo-European languages—as an underlying verb–subject–object language, see McCawley 1968.)

(1) The correlations true of SOV have all vanished. Adjectives precede nouns; prepositions, never postpositions, occur; periphrastic tenses are always auxiliary-verb (but see note below); relative clauses invariably follow their noun phrases.

(2) The modern languages are exclusively prepositional, like all VSO languages. (Greenberg's Universal 23.)

(3) These languages all have SVO as a possible (generally, in fact, the only possible) superficial order. (Greenberg's Universal 6.)

(4) Where question particles were frequent (cf. Latin *-ne*) in the ancient languages, they have been dropped in the modern languages. (Universal 10.)

(5) The modern languages always or, at least virtually always, put a question-word first in the sentence. The ancient languages, though they generally did this, did not do it quite so invariably. (Universal 12.)

(6) As stated above, the auxiliary in the modern languages always preceded the main verb. (Universal 16.)

(Note, however, that the placement of adjectives regularly before the noun violates Universal 17 if the languages are VSO; however, this is not an invariable universal, according to Greenberg, but merely a greater than chance correlation.)

Universal 16 is of especial interest with regard to the problem of the development of the Romance future and perfect tenses, discussed in the body of the paper. Ross 1967a analyzed auxiliaries as main verbs, and the "main" verb in the sentence as derived from a complement of the auxiliary-verb containing sentence. Thus, in this interpretation, the sentence, *John has gone* has the underlying structure:

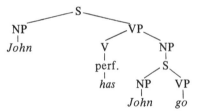

That is, *John* is the subject of the highest sentence, *has* is the verb, and *go,* or *gone,* is the superficial reflex of the underlying direct object. In terms of basic word-order types such as Greenberg discusses, *John has gone* has the order SVO. But *John gone has,* with the order verb+auxiliary, is SOV. As Ross points out, this is perfectly reasonable, since this is reducible to an order SOV. It is notable that in the ancient languages, where periphrastic tenses occurred, they tended to be in the verb+auxiliary order, as noted above. But in the development from Latin to Spanish, two things happened: Either the auxiliary changed its place—from *amatum habeo* of Vulgar Latin to Spanish *he amado,* as would be expected if the language as a whole changed from SOV to SVO or

VSO; or the auxiliary stayed where it had been. But the latter was apparently not permissible, so coalescence occurred: *amare habeo* became *amarhe*, then *amaré*. Or perhaps the way to view the different development of perfect and future tenses between Latin and Spanish is this: The language, at some point in its development, was faced with two choices, in changing from SOV to SVO (VSO):

(1) The auxiliary and the verb could coalesce, keeping the same order, or (2) Auxiliary and verb could invert. The first choice was apparently the "simpler" thing for the language to do: The change occurred at a lower level, and was less drastic in some sense. But coalescence was possible only under certain phonological conditions, which the future met and the perfect did not. So the preferred choice (1) was open to the future; only (2) was left for the perfect, which it underwent.

This is not a complete explanation of the change, by any means, but if we consider the possibility that many of the changes discussed were, ultimately, due to a shift from underlying SOV to SVO order, we can begin to see the motivation for all these things. Of course, the question is still open as to why the language did make this change in order. But the changes induced by the metacondition can then be looked at as the products of this change. It would be useful to look at other language families in which "drift" in one direction or both is known to have occurred to see if there are also arguments for changes in the underlying order.

This is perhaps a plausible viewpoint, which overlooks the question of the motivating force behind it all. But if we find it sufficiently persuasive and of sufficient explanatory power to be adopted, we are faced with a serious dilemma if we also adopt the view of linguistic theory as propounded by George Lakoff, McCawley, Ross, and Postal. It is their belief that the form of the base component is universal, and the only difference lies in the order of the elements; that is, for example, whether the initial rewrite rule is S→ NP VP or S→ VP NP, as in Japanese. The order of these constituents can automatically be determined by looking at the shape of transformational rules in the languages in question. Since, in Latin and in English, these rules are the same, and both differ from those in Japanese in a way in which one would expect according to the universal base hypothesis, English being VSO or SVO and Japanese OSV, one would conclude on that basis that English and Latin shared the same underlying word order—but we have just suggested, perhaps they do not. If we do adopt the view that the order has changed, many if not all of the arguments given by the universal base theorists must be abandoned. This is an unattractive prospect, especially since their theory is what has enabled us to formulate our arguments for an SOV → SVO change in the first place. Thus, we must leave the question unanswered, but it is crucial if we are ever to understand anything about the mechanisms of syntactic change, or if we are ever to understand what motivates linguistic change—assuming as we must that change is seldom if ever really spontaneous, though it often seems to be.

REFERENCES

Chomsky, N. 1969. Remarks on nominalization. *Readings in English Transformational Grammar,* R. Jacobs and P. S. Rosenbaum, eds. Boston: Ginn-Blaisdell.

Greenberg, J. 1961. Some universals of grammar. *Universals of Language,* J. Greenberg, ed. Cambridge: The M.I.T. Press.

Hale, A. 1969. Quantification and the English comparative. *Readings in English Transformational Grammar,* R. Jacobs and P. S. Rosenbaum, eds. Boston: Ginn-Blaisdell.

Kiparsky, P. 1968. Universals of change. *Universals of Linguistic Theory,* E. Bach and R. Harms, eds. New York: Holt, Rinehart and Winston.

Klima, E. 1964. Relatedness between grammatical systems. *Language* 40:1-20.

Lakoff, G. 1965. *On the nature of syntactic irregularity.* The Computation Laboratory of Harvard University, Mathematical Linguistics and Automatic Translation, Report # NSF-16. Cambridge, Mass.

———. 1969. Pronominalization and the analysis of adverbs. *Readings in English Transformational Grammar,* R. Jacobs and P. S. Rosenbaum, eds. Boston: Ginn-Blaisdell.

———. Forthcoming. On syntax and semantics. *Semantics: An Interdisciplinary Reader.* L. Jakobovits and D. Steinberg, eds. Urbana: University of Illinois Press.

Lakoff, R. 1968. *Abstract Syntax and Latin Complementation.* Cambridge: The M.I.T. Press.

McCawley, J. D. 1968. English as a verb-initial language. Paper read at the Linguistics Society of America Annual Meeting, New York, December 1968.

Perlmutter, D. M. 1967. The two verbs "begin." Brandeis University, dittoed.

———. 1968. Deep and surface structure constraints in syntax. Unpublished M.I.T. doctoral dissertation.

———. 1970. On the article in English. *Recent Developments in Linguistics,* M. Bierwisch and K. E. Heidolph, eds. The Hague: Mouton.

Postal, P. 1966. On so-called "pronouns" in English. *Report of the Seventeenth Round Table Meetings on Linguistics and Language Studies,* F. Dinneen, ed. Washington, D.C.: Georgetown University Press.

Ross, J. R. 1964. A partial grammar of English superlatives. Unpublished University of Pennsylvania master's thesis.

———. 1967a. Auxiliaries as main verbs. M.I.T., dittoed.

———. 1967b. Constraints on variables in syntax. Unpublished M.I.T. doctoral dissertation.

Sapir, E. 1949. *Language.* New York: Harcourt, Brace and World.

Traugott, E. C. 1969. Toward a grammar of syntactic change. *Lingua* 23: 1-27.

Whitney, W. D. 1896. *Sanskrit Grammar,* 3rd ed. Boston: Ginn and Co.

7.

Natural Rules in Phonology

Sanford A. Schane,
University of California, San Diego

As in many other concepts in linguistics, it is difficult to give any simple definition of a natural rule. Yet I believe that anyone who has worked in phonology has a fairly clear, intuitive notion of what is a natural rule and what is an unnatural one. Therefore, at the outset, I shall have to rely on the reader's intuitions for distinguishing between the two types. The following are pairs of rules which have some features in common. The first member of each pair is the natural rule, the second the unnatural one.

(a) $V \rightarrow$ [+ nasal] / ___ $\begin{bmatrix} C \\ + \text{nasal} \end{bmatrix}$

   $V \rightarrow$ [+ nasal] / ___ #

(b) $C \rightarrow \emptyset$ / ___ C

   $C \rightarrow \emptyset$ / ___ V

(c) $\begin{bmatrix} V \\ + \text{high} \end{bmatrix} \rightarrow$ glide / ___ V

   $V \rightarrow$ glide / ___ V

(d) [+ obstruent] $\rightarrow$ [α voiced] / $\begin{bmatrix} + \text{obstruent} \\ \alpha \text{ voiced} \end{bmatrix}$ ___

   [+ obstruent] $\rightarrow$ [$-\alpha$ voiced] / $\begin{bmatrix} + \text{obstruent} \\ \alpha \text{ voiced} \end{bmatrix}$ ___

(e) [+ obstruent] $\rightarrow$ [− voiced] / ___ #

   [+ obstruent] $\rightarrow$ [+ voiced] / ___ #

The natural rules exemplify phonological processes recurring in language. Although unnatural rules may not have this kind of universality of expectancy, nonetheless, they do occur as phonological processes in particular languages. In fact, every one of the unnatural rules which I have given could conceivably be a rule in some language or other. In the first part of this paper I shall cite examples of both natural and unnatural rules occurring within the phonology of a single language, and we shall see how they interact. I shall then suggest some contingencies between the two types of rules. The second section of this paper is devoted to characterizing the "naturalness" of natural rules. I shall maintain that many of the rules fall into one of three categories. In the third part of the paper I shall show the relevance of these categories within a general theory of phonology, and discuss the kinds of internal linguistic constraints to be imposed on natural processes. Also I shall consider the question of finding external explanations for the fact that some rules are natural. Finally, I shall establish some notational conventions for natural rules; I shall do so in the context of an evaluation metric which must give preference to natural rules over unnatural ones.

Let us examine some forms in five German dialects. I first encountered these data in a seminar given by T. Lightner at the Linguistic Institute in the summer of 1968. The data were reconstructed on the basis of some limited forms cited by Heffner in his *General Phonetics* (pp. 113-14). Some of the issues which I raise concerning these data were discussed by various participants in that seminar.

(1) Data:

	I	II	III	IV	V
"Sohn"	zo:n	zõ:n	zõ:	zõ:	zo:
"Sohne"	zo:nə	zõ:nə	zõ:nə	zõ:nə	zõ:nə
"Floh"	flo:	flo:	flo:	flõ:	flo:
"Flohe"	flo:ə	flo:ə	flo:ə	flo:ə	flo:ə

(2) Rules:

(A) $V \rightarrow [+ \text{nasal}] /$ ___ $\begin{bmatrix} C \\ + \text{nasal} \end{bmatrix}$

(B) $\begin{bmatrix} C \\ + \text{nasal} \end{bmatrix} \rightarrow \emptyset /$ ___#

(C) $\begin{bmatrix} V \\ + \text{stress} \end{bmatrix} \rightarrow [+ \text{nasal}] \ / \ \_\_\_ \#$

(D) $\begin{bmatrix} V \\ + \text{stress} \end{bmatrix} \rightarrow [- \text{nasal}] \ / \ \_\_\_ \#$

(B') $\begin{bmatrix} C \\ + \text{nasal} \end{bmatrix} \rightarrow \emptyset \ / \begin{bmatrix} V \\ + \text{nasal} \end{bmatrix} \_\_\_ \#$

(3) Rules used in each dialect:

I	II	III	IV	V
–	A	A	A	A
		B	B	B
			C	B
			D	

In column V: A, B or B, A

There are two ways of looking at these data. One could consider the problem to be a diachronic one; that is, what rules have applied in each dialect to derive its particular forms from a common ancestor? Alternatively, one could adopt the synchronic point of view: What rules are needed in each dialect to account for the phonological alternations exhibited there. Actually, for these data it is immaterial which approach is taken, since, as will be seen, the same rules happen to be involved in both cases. Therefore, I shall freely refer to both diachronic and synchronic considerations throughout the discussion.

Dialect I is Standard German. Dialect II differs from Dialect I in that vowels become nasalized whenever they precede a nasal consonant. Dialect III, like Dialect II, has vowel nasalization. In addition a final nasal consonant is deleted after vowel nasalization has taken place, exactly as in Modern French. Dialect IV is like Dialect III; however, it has the peculiarity that *flo:* has become *flõ:*, probably by analogy to *zõ:*. In Dialect V the analogy works the other way. Here the nasalized *zõ:* has become *zo:*, like *flo:*.

We shall assume that all dialects have the same underlying forms and that the different surface manifestations are due to particular rules which have been applied to these underlying forms. The underlying representations are equivalent to the forms cited in Dialect I.

In Dialect II the first two forms are obtained by applying Rule A to the underlying representations. According to Rule A a vowel becomes nasalized if it precedes a nasal consonant.

Dialect III has two rules: Rule A, the vowel nasalization rule, plus Rule B, which deletes a word-final nasal consonant. Note that these two rules must be applied in the order given. These two rules account for the first two forms listed in Dialect III.

Dialect IV also has Rules A and B, which again account for the first two forms. The third form *flõ:* is due to Rule C, which nasalizes a final stressed vowel. Note that it is not sufficient to say that a final vowel becomes nasalized, since the final schwa in *flo:ə* does not undergo nasalization. Hence, stress or some other condition is needed to assure that nasalization occurs only in the appropriate places.

Dialect V, like Dialects III and IV, has Rules A and B. In addition, it has Rule D, which denasalizes a final stressed vowel. The first form *zo:* is obtained by applying all three rules to the underlying *zo:n.* Rule A nasalizes the vowel, giving *zõ:n;* Rule B deletes the final nasal consonant, giving *zõ:,* with a final nasalized vowel; and Rule D denasalizes this final nasalized vowel, yielding *zo:.* Again, note that the three rules must be applied in the order given.

Rule D which denasalizes a final stressed vowel, is an unnatural rule. Interestingly enough, it is possible to describe Dialect V without having recourse to Rule D at all, if one assumes that in Dialect V there has been a reordering so that Rule B applies before Rule A. If Rule B applies first, then for the first form, underlying *zo:n,* the final nasal consonant will be deleted, yielding *zo:.* Rule A, which comes next, will not apply to derived *zo:* as the vowel is no longer followed by a nasal consonant. Hence, it will remain *zo:.* Rule A is still needed of course to get the nasalized vowel of the second form, *zõ:nə,* in Dialect V.

We see that there are two different sets of rules for deriving the forms of Dialect V. At first glance it would seem that the solution with reordering is to be preferred since fewer rules are involved and, as a bonus, we have managed to eliminate an unnatural rule. Furthermore, it has been fairly well established by now in generative studies that two dialects may differ in their rule ordering. However, I wish to claim that although the solution which involves reordering may look elegant it is not right. Rather, I shall show that the data of Dialect V must be derived by applying the three rules A, B, and D. I shall present three arguments, beginning with the weakest one.

First, if Rule D is unnatural then so is Rule C, which nasalizes a final stressed vowel. But whereas in Dialect V it was possible to eliminate Rule D through rule reordering, in Dialect IV it is not possible to get rid of Rule C. It is Rule C which converts underlying *flo:*, with an oral vowel, to *flõ:*, with a nasalized vowel. Without Rule C there would be no mechanism for converting a final oral vowel to a nasalized one. Now one might maintain that for Dialect IV the underlying form should be *flo:n*, with a final nasal consonant; then by Rules A and B we would obtain a final nasalized vowel. However, this position is untenable. The related form *flo:ə* gives no evidence of an underlying nasal consonant. Next, postulating an underlying nasal consonant would violate our original assumption that all dialects have the same underlying representations. Considering the historical development of the form it should be evident that *flõ:* could have only come from an earlier *flo:*. Hence, we have no choice but to recognize Rule C for Dialect IV. If for Dialect V we accept the solution with Rule D then the descriptions for Dialects IV and V are quite similar. Both dialects have Rules A and B and differ only in the third rule—Dialect IV containing Rule C, Dialect V containing Rule D. Rules C and D are very similar; they differ only in their structural changes, Rule C nasalizing the final vowel, Rule D denasalizing the final vowel. Earlier we described dialect IV by saying that *flo:* became *flõ:* by analogy to *zõ:* and similarly we described Dialect V by saying that *zõ:* became *zo:* by analogy to *flo:*. Rules C and D in conjunction with Rules A and B are the formal analogues of these analogizing processes. Thus, by adopting the solution with rule D for Dialect V we obtain a parallelism with Dialect IV, a symmetry which would be missed with the solution involving reordering.

A second argument for rejecting the solution with reordering is based on Kiparsky's notion of marked and unmarked rule order. Kiparsky (1968) has shown that when there is a reordering in the rules the tendency is for marked order to become unmarked order, where the unmarked order is that ordering in which the rules would have maximal applicability. Given the two rules A and B the unmarked order is A, B. In Dialect V the reordering solution requires that the order be B, A, which means that unmarked order has changed to marked order, a direct violation of Kiparsky's principle for the preference of unmarked rule order. If Kiparsky's observations are correct, then there is a serious counterexample to be explained. If, on the other hand, we adopt the solution with Rule D, there is no violation of the principle or marked-to-unmarked rule order.

The third reason for rejecting the reordering solution for Dialect V is based on the format of Rule B, one of the crucial rules in the reordering. Rules A and B reflect fairly normal phonological processes—what we are calling natural rules. But Rule B is a natural rule of the grammar only if it is preceded by Rule A. According to Rule A a nasal consonant causes a preceding vowel to become nasalized. Only then can the nasal consonant be deleted—that is, it seems that what is natural is that the nasal consonant is deletable only if it has left a vestige of itself in the preceding vowel. Hence, Rule B as presently stated is not natural. To make it a natural rule an additional environmental constraint is required—namely, that the deletion of a final nasal consonant is contingent on a preceding nasalized vowel. The natural rule is given above as Rule B'. Now if Rule B' replaces Rule B, then the reordering solution for dialect V is no longer possible. With the reordering, Rule B' would have to apply before Rule A. However, given underlying *flo:n* Rule B' could not delete the final nasal, since the preceding vowel is not nasalized. (Later I shall argue that natural rules are to be preferred to unnatural ones.) Since Dialects III and IV in their first two forms exemplify the natural nasalization processes, Rule B' must be the appropriate formulation for nasal consonant deletion. Once this fact is recognized, reordering becomes an impossible phonological phenomenon for Dialect V.

Let us compare Rule B with Rule B'. If we employ the evaluation measure of counting features, proposed by Halle (1962), we find that Rule B', the natural rule, is more complex than Rule B, the unnatural rule, since Rule B' has an additional environmental constraint. One would hope, of course, that natural rules would be more highly valued than unnatural ones, and that there would be some way for the notation to reflect this. Later I shall suggest that feature counting is in fact the appropriate metric for evaluating natural and unnatural rules, in spite of the fact that the two rules B and B' for the moment appear to be counterexamples.

Dialects IV and V demonstrate that both natural rules and unnatural rules occur as phonological processes. Let us compare these two types of rules. Consider Dialect IV and in particular Rules A and C, since they both involve vowel nasalization. As we have already noted, Rule A is the natural rule, since vowel nasalization takes place before a nasal consonant, whereas Rule C is the unnatural one, as vowel nasalization takes place at the end of the word. That Dialect C should have a rule like Rule A, a natural rule, is not unusual, providing that there is a linguistic explanation for such rules. Given a theory of natural rules it is then to be expected that languages will exhibit such rules. That Dialect IV should contain Rule C, an unnatural rule, is not so obvious, although it is a fact of life. How or why such rules get added to the grammar is an open question. Earlier I suggested that historically Rule C represents an analogizing process; that is, in Dialect IV *flo:* could become *flõ:* once forms such as *zõ:* were in the language. This analogy explanation for the unnatural rule C has some interesting consequences. It implies that Rule C can come into being only if Rule A is already present. Diachronically, this entails that there is first a normal vowel nasalization process. It is this natural process which brings nasalized vowels into the language. Once vowel nasalization operates as a phonological process it may be extended to new environments, and these new environments need not necessarily be natural ones. Thus, the unnatural process must be historically later than the natural one. If we approach the problem now as a synchronic one, the implication is that in the set of ordered phonological rules the natural rule must always precede the unnatural one. This is the order we have given for Dialect IV. However, a closer examination of Rules A and C will reveal that these two rules are not critically ordered with respect to each other—that is, C could precede or follow A without affecting the results in derivations. Hence, Dialect IV neither substantiates nor refutes the claim that synchronically the natural rule must precede the unnatural one. However, as we noted earlier, Dialect V does provide clear evidence for the appropriate ordering. In Dialect V Rule D is the unnatural rule. Rule D denasalizes the final vowels, which implies that nasalized vowels must already be in the system at the time Rule D applies. These nasalized vowels are due to Rule A. Thus, it is evident that Rule A, the natural rule, must precede Rule D, the unnatural rule.

It would be very nice if one could demonstrate that in a given language all unnatural rules are contingent on certain specific preceding natural rules. However, I doubt very much that Mother Nature is likely to be so kind to the phonologist. One can imagine unnatural phonological processes which would be difficult to conceive of as outgrowths of natural ones. As an example, in *Introduction to the Handbook of American Indian Languages* (p. 25) Boas cites a rule in Pawnee whereby "*tr* in a word changes to *h.*" Boas's data clearly indicate the necessity for such a rule, albeit an unnatural one. However, I am at a loss to speculate as to the nature of the natural rule Boas's rule would be contingent on. (Margaret Langdon has suggested to me that the explanation of *tr* becoming *h* may perhaps be due to cluster simplification, and she has cited some data from child language where *tr* was replaced by a fricative.) Although it is an attractive hypothesis that all unnatural rules are dependent on preceding natural rules, it is doubtless too strong a claim. Yet it is of interest that such dependencies do exist, and it ought to be a worthwhile line of investigation. I leave this then as a tantalizing problem.

Why are natural rules "natural"? So far I have been relying heavily on intuitive feelings for determining which rules are natural. It goes without saying that such intuitions exist. I would feel confident in asserting that a group of phonologists would agree fairly well as to which phonological processes are natural ones. We hopefully look for them in the languages we study. Natural rules, then, have a universality—we expect them as phonological phenomena in languages of diverse type. Why should such rules recur in language after language while other rules—that is, the unnatural ones—may have an extremely limited distribution? One would hope to find something in the structure of natural rules which would explain their universal popularity.

I find that natural rules fall into a small set of categories according to the function of the rule. In this section I shall discuss three of these categories, illustrating the function which the rules of each type perform. Believing that these categories have an interest other than the taxonomic one of classifying kinds of natural rules, I must then demonstrate that these particular categories of natural processes (as well as some others) have to be recognized within phonological theory. In the next section I shall turn to this question and consider the problem of determining the internal linguistic constraints to be imposed on each type of natural process. Such constraints are imperative if one is to claim that there is a theory of natural rules. I do not believe, however, that it is sufficient merely to come up with a set of constraints, even though it may account elegantly for which processes are natural ones and which are not. We would like to know, in addition, why those particular constraints are imposed on natural rules, rather than, say, opposite constraints. This requirement will lead us to search for external explanations for the internally motivated constraints.

Let us turn now to the three categories of natural rules with which we shall be concerned throughout most of the discussion. I shall refer to these types as *assimilative rules, preferred syllable structure rules,* and *rules for maximum differentiation.* All of these notions have been discussed separately in the phonology literature, but except for the first, not usually in reference to natural rules.

The assimilative rules are the easiest to illustrate. They correspond to the various kinds of assimilation which are well known in phonology. These types of rules involve two or more near-by segments. One of the segments becomes more similar to the other one or ones. There are many natural rules of the assimilative type: vowels are nasalized when adjacent to a nasal consonant; obstruents agree in voicing with a contiguous obstruent; obstruents become voiced between vowels since vowels are generally voiced; nasal consonants become homorganic to the following obstruent; velar consonants become palatal before palatal (front) vowels; vowels become umlauted (fronted) by a following front vowel; vowels agree in height, or in backness, or in rounding with other vowels (i.e., various instances of vowel harmony), etc. Rules of assimilation provide some of the clearest examples of natural rules. In all such rules the values for one or more features of a segment are changed so as to agree with the values for the same features in some other segment.

I shall introduce the second type of natural rule—the preferred syllable structure rules—by way of a French example. Words in French may terminate in a consonant in their underlying representations. For many words this final consonant is dropped if the following word also begins with a consonant. Thus, the word *petit* "little" will have different variants before the words *garçon* "boy" and *ami* "friend"—namely, [pəti garsõ] but [pətit ami]. As we have said the underlying representation of a word such as "little" must terminate in a consonant—i.e., [pətit]—and the form [pəti garsõ] is derived by a rule similar to the first rule under (B): A consonant is deleted before a consonant. We can ask why French has this rule instead of the second rule under (B): A consonant is deleted before a vowel. The second rule would give the forms *[pəti̇t garsõ] and *[pəti ami], which could conceivably be French (cf. [pətit fiy] *petite fille,* "little girl," and [žɔli ami] *joli ami* "nice friend"). Yet the language does not have this unnatural rule. Why not? When applied to the underlying forms, the first rule—the natural one—yields CVCV syllable structure between morphemes— e.g., [pəti garsõ], [pətit ami]. On the other hand, when the second rule—the unnatural one—is applied to the underlying forms the result is either clusters of consonants, e.g. *[pətit garsõ], or sequences of vowels, e.g., *[pəti ami]. A theory of syllable structure which claims that the CVCV pattern—that is, open syllable structure—is the preferred one allows an explanation for the naturalness of the first rule and the unnaturalness of the second. In fact, in French, the whole complex interplay of elision and liaison is intended to guarantee the CVCV pattern. Thus, rules which convert complex syllable structures to simpler ones constitute the second type of natural rules.

A theory of syllable structure makes some interesting claims concerning how phonological rules are to be applied. Consider the rule which converts a high vowel to a corresponding glide when the vowel is adjacent to another vowel. Assume we have a situation with three high vowels in a row, e.g., *i u i.* Which one or ones of these high vowels should become glides? A theory of preferred syllable structure would predict that given three high vowels in a row the gliding rule must be applied to the middle one only, e.g., *i w i,* for it is this environment which gives the preferred syllable structure where consonants and vowels alternate. On the other hand, if either the first or third vowel is glided we obtain CVV or VVC, either of which is a better syllable structure than VVV, but not the optimal preferred one, VCV.

Not all the natural rules for preferred syllable structure necessarily yield the optimal structure with consonant-vowel alternation. For example, if we have the sequence: consonant, high vowel, second vowel, and apply the gliding rule we obtain a new sequence: consonant, glide, vowel. That is, the structure CVV is converted into CCV, the latter of course not being the optimal syllable structure. This shows that if there must be clusters, consonant clusters will be more tolerable than vowel clusters. Hence, there is some kind of hierarchy of preferred syllable structure. Some indications of this hierarchy are presented in the marking conventions for syllable structure proposed by Chomsky and Halle (1968).

There is another interesting observation that is easily explained by reference to preferred syllable structure. It has been noted that in phonological rules a process which happens before consonants may also take place at the end of a phrase (or at a pause). So, for example, in French, the rule which deletes a consonant before a consonant also deletes the same consonant before a pause, e.g., [il ɛpəti] *il est petit,* "he is little." On the other hand, one does not (or at least rarely) find rules in which a vowel and a word boundary are alternate environments. But note that, as in the French case, deleting a consonant before another consonant or a pause creates an open syllable structure, that is, syllables of the type CV. This explains why a pause acts like a consonant in natural rules.

Two or more natural rules may be linked together to produce a particular desired result. Consider the dialects cited earlier in which *zo:n* becomes *zõ:* The underlying form *zo:n* has CVC structure. First the vowel becomes nasalized before the nasal consonant. This is an assimilative rule. Then after the vowel is nasalized the word-final nasal consonant is deleted. This is a preferred syllable structure rule. The original CVC structure has now become CV, open syllable structure. Incidentally, as we noted previously, the nasal consonant can be deleted only if the preceding vowel is nasalized. But this is not a sufficient condition, at least not for the natural case, for in addition the nasal consonant must be followed by a consonant or a word boundary. Thus, in the German examples we may have *zõ:nə,* with a nasalized vowel followed by *n,* but not *zõ:ə,* with the *n* deleted. The same observation holds for vowel nasalization in French, but not in Portuguese.

In addition to the preferred syllable structure rules already noted, other natural rules of this type include the deletion of vowels before vowels, the insertion of a vowel to break up certain consonant clusters or of a glide to break up vowel clusters, the conversion of post-vocalic liquids to glides, coalescence rules such as *ay* and *aw* becoming *e* and *o,* respectively, or the case where a consonant plus *h* becomes an aspirated consonant, which functions as a unit segment, a rule found in Korean, for example.

The third category of natural rules are those which provide for maximum differentiation, a notion discussed by Trubetzkoy (1939), Jakobson (1940), and Martinet (1955). It is also the basis for the Chomsky-Halle marking conventions. In maximum differentiation there is a tendency for segments to be kept perceptually as far apart from one another as possible. Thus, given a three-vowel system, *i a u* is more natural than, say, *e a o.* In the first case high vowels are opposed to the low one; in the second case mid vowels are opposed to the low one. The desirability of *i a u* is explained by maximum differentiation, as this is the only three-vowel system where the extreme corners of the vowel triangle are represented. Similarly, if there are two high vowels in a system they will be *i* and *u,* rather than, say, *i* and *ü,* since the former are opposed in two features, backness and rounding, whereas the latter are less differentiated, being opposed only in one feature, rounding.

Instances of neutralization, which are not due to assimilation, are characterized by rules of maximum differentiation. Thus, in Russian, there are five vowels in stressed position: *i e a o u.* In unstressed position there is neutralization in the mid vowels: *e* merges with *i,* while *o* merges with *a.* The result is the maximally opposed three-vowel system *i a u.* In English and German, except for schwa, there is neutralization between tense and lax vowels in a final open syllable, all vowels being tense. This eliminates lax vowels of intermediate quality between adjacent tense ones. In German obstruents are devoiced in word-final position. This is maximum differentiation in accordance with Jakobson's claim that the optimal consonant is voiceless.

Earlier I mentioned intervocalic obstruents. In cases of neutralization they are often voiced, unlike the initial or final neutralized obstruents, which tend to be voiceless. Both of these phenomena are natural processes, but they are due to different phonological principles. The voicing of intervocalic obstruents is a case of assimilation (because of the voicing in the surrounding vowels), whereas the devoicing of obstruents, either initially or finally, is a case of maximum differentiation. That is, I reject the explanation that considers devoicing as a kind of assimilation where word boundary or pause is treated as containing the feature, voiceless or silence. We have already noted that very often consonant and word boundary behave alike in phonological rules. One might maintain, therefore, that word boundary contains the feature, consonantal. But why should it contain this feature rather than some other one? Actually, as we saw, no distinguishing feature at all is needed to characterize word boundary once there is a theory of preferred syllable structure, for the theory automatically provides an explanation for the appearance of consonant and word boundary as alternate environments in the same rule. Thus, boundaries need never contain phonological features. Consequently, assimilation rules must only be those in which a segment picks up phonological features from some nearby segment.

Other natural rules for maximum differentiation include palatal and velar liquids becoming the corresponding glides *y* and *w*, respectively, palatal stops being converted to alveopalatal affricates, affricates becoming the corresponding fricatives, and various stops and fricative becoming glottal stop and *h,* respectively.

I have discussed three categories of natural rules: assimilative, preferred syllable structure, and maximum differentiation. It is of interest to note how the various kinds of rules permitted in phonology are partitioned within these three categories of natural rules. Five types of phonological processes have been explicitly recognized in generative phonology: rules which change or modify feature values, rules which delete segments, rules which insert segments, rules which coalesce or contract two or more segments into a single segment, and rules which interchange or metathesize two or more segments. Rules which delete or insert segments can only be of the syllable structure type. It should be apparent that if a segment is deleted or inserted the total syllable structure is changed. Coalescence rules must also be of the syllable structure type, since, again, if two segments are replaced by one, the syllable structure will no longer be the same.

Metathesis rules also are probably of the syllable structure type. The interchange of two segments of different major classes can lead to a change in syllable structure. Since convincing examples with metathesis as a general process are hard to find I am unable to cite instances. If metathesis should occur between segments of the same major class, the syllable structure would not be changed. In such cases the metathesis may simply be a prelude for some subsequent natural process. An example of this phenomenon might be the Hanunoo (Philippine Islands) data cited by Gleason in his *Workbook in Descriptive Linguistics* (p. 30). In this language the sequence glottal stop-consonant is converted to the sequence consonant-glottal stop. This change could induce a subsequent coalescence whereby the consonant-glottal stop sequence becomes a unit segment— namely, a glottalized consonant. This latter conversion would of course be of the syllable structure type. Whereas natural rules of insertion, deletion, coalescence, and probably metathesis all belong to the category of preferred syllable structure, the feature changing rules, on the other hand, are distributed throughout all three categories of natural rules. An example of maximum differentiation is the devoicing of final obstruents; an example of preferred syllable structure is the conversion of high vowels to glides when adjacent to a vowel; and an example of assimilation is the conversion of velar consonants to palatals before palatal vowels. Also it would seem to me that all natural alpha rules—that is, rules with variables—should be of the assimilative type.

Up to this point, I have shown that a significant number of natural rules can be classified into one of three categories, which I have called assimilation, preferred syllable structure, and maximum differentiation. A legitimate question to ask is why these particular process types have been chosen. Do they have linguistic significance other than the fact that they provide for a convenient taxonomy of natural rules? If notions like assimilation, preferred syllable structure, and maximum differentiation are to have any import within a theory of natural rules, then the properties underlying these processes need to be explicitly characterized. It will not do to say that assimilation, preferred syllable structure, and maximum differentiation are more or less general tendencies to which many natural rules happen to conform. Rather, one has to formulate precisely the conditions under which these processes can take place. Essentially, then, what needs to be developed are theories of assimilation, preferred syllable structure, and maximum differentiation. A theory of assimilation must specify which segment types are candidates for assimilation, which features of these segments can be assimilated, and the permitted directions of assimilation. A theory of preferred syllable structure must provide the appropriate hierarchy of syllable types, and stipulate the mechanics of syllabic simplification. Finally, a theory of maximum differentiation must provide a set of constraints under which nonassimilatory neutralizations can take place and an exact account of the directions of these neutralizations.

A rigorous specification of the constraints needed to characterize types of natural processes provides the necessary internal linguistic justification for the various categories of natural rules. These constraints determine what can qualify as a natural rule. A second, and more interesting, problem is an explanatory account of the nature of these constraints and of the functions which natural processes perform. For example, we have noted that assimilation is a process whereby segments are made more like each other, whereas in maximum differentiation they are made less like each other. Note that preferred syllable structure is a kind of differentiation also— the CVCV pattern leads to an alternation of maximally different major classes. We could adopt Saussure's terms and say that preferred syllable structure is syntagmatic differentiation, whereas the neutralization which yields maximum oppositions would be paradigmatic differentiation. On the surface it looks as though there are two conflicting tendencies at play: things being made more like each other, and things being made less like each other. Yet these tendencies are not in conflict if there are clear-cut external explanations for each type. As a first, and overly simple, approximation, one might claim that when segments become more alike there is a physiological explanation; that is, assimilation phenomena are a consequence of inherent properties of the articulatory mechanism. On the other hand, it does not seem unlikely that when segments are made less like each other—for example, the processes of preferred syllable structure and of maximum differentiation—the explanation to be sought would be a psychological one. There may be perceptual strategies for keeping different segment types maximally opposed. This of course does not exclude the possibility of there being both physical and psychological explanations for some or even all types of natural processes. For example, there may be both articulatory and perceptual explanations for constraints on permitted consonant clusters. What is being claimed here is that the processes, the particular processes themselves, and the constraints imposed on them will find ultimately their explanation outside of phonological theory per se.

In phonology, one can draw a useful analogy between a theory of natural rules and a theory of distinctive features. Just as there is a universal set of distinctive phonetic features or categories for characterizing all the phonological and phonetic segments found in language, so there will be a set of universal processes or categories—such as assimilation, preferred syllable structure, maximum differentiation, and doubtless others—for characterizing the kinds of natural rules found in language. Within a distinctive feature theory, there are constraints imposed, such as the co-occurrence restrictions on sets of features, the hierarchization of individual features, etc. By the same token, a theory of natural rules must state the conditions and constraints within each of the categories, as well as the interactions between one category type and others. The distinctive features provide a taxonomy of phonological segments, to be sure. Yet the features are more than just of classificatory interest, since there are also internal phonological considerations involved in the choice of a set of features. The features provide the appropriate natural classes on which the phonological rules can operate. Finally, one does not arrive at a set of distinctive features in an ad hoc manner, but instead demonstrates that the features have specific articulatory, acoustic, or perceptual correlates. In the same way, a set of natural processes or categories should have external physiological or psychological explanations.

At present, I obviously cannot lay out a full-fledged theory of natural rules based on the proposed categories, along with all the required internal constraints and external justifications. Research in natural rules has just begun, and it should be evident that there is a long haul ahead of us. But enough people are worried about this problem, as exemplified by several papers presented at this conference. Although there have been various proposals for dealing with natural rules, any one person has merely scratched the surface.

It might be instructive to enumerate some of the problems faced by one concerned with constructing a theory of natural rules. First, many more examples of such rules are needed. Like everything else in linguistics, there is no discovery procedure for determining which rules are natural. Often the naturalness of a rule is based on one's intuitions. To be sure, there is a certain amount of empirical corroboration of these intuitions, for as we have noted, natural rules tend to be those which recur in languages of diverse types. However, I believe that the distinction between natural and unnatural processes—or perhaps it would be more appropriate to say more natural and less natural processes, for there are degrees of naturalness—could be shown to exist through appropriate psychological experimentation.

I have suggested that there are only a limited small number of processes, or functions, which natural rules can perform. I have discussed three of these. There are other categories as well, and these will have to be determined. For example, vowel shift cannot be accommodated within any of my categories. It is not an instance of assimilation, it has nothing to do with preferred syllable structure as all the vowels stay intact, and it cannot be a case of maximum differentiation, because no neutralization is involved. Rather what is happening is that all the vowels are being shifted in the articulatory plane. Labov, in his paper, has proposed a set of constraints governing the direction of vowel shift: Tense vowels move upwards and toward the front, whereas lax vowels and diphthongs move downwards and to central position. Another category not accommodated within my framework would be natural rules of weakening—for example, lenition. Foley, in his paper, has some interesting suggestions concerning a hierarchy of strength of consonant types. Also I think that just as there are preferred syllable structures, there are preferred stress patterns, and I shall return to this topic later.

A theory of natural rules must also grapple with the problem of the relation between natural and unnatural rules, or degrees of naturalness. For example, we have seen that for high vowels to become glides when adjacent to another vowel is a natural rule. For mid vowels to become glides in the same environment is less natural, and for all vowels to become glides in that environment is less natural yet. Earlier it was suggested that perhaps many unnatural rules, or in any event less natural rules, can be considered as generalizations or extensions of a process to new environments. At this conference similar proposals have been suggested by Labov, Bach and Harms, and Venneman, and many of Foley's data can be interpreted in this way, although that is not to say that he would necessarily give them this interpretation.

What does one do with natural rules that are counterexamples to a proposed theory? For example, natural rules of dissimilation ought to be counterexamples to any theory of assimilation. Now it is true that good examples of dissimilation as a general phonological process are hard to come by. Dissimilation is of course attested frequently in historical linguistics. However, most of the time it is sporadic, affecting only individual lexical items. Or else it may be productive, but restricted to a particular morpheme. For example, in Latin words the final *l* of the derivational suffix *al* is dissimilated to *r* whenever the preceding morpheme terminates in *l* (cf. *final, regular*). I know of only one good example of a general—that is, productive—dissimilation that is not restricted to a particular morpheme, namely Grassman's law, where an initial aspirate is deaspirated if there is an aspirate beginning the next syllable. Hence I would surmise that there are few natural rules involving dissimilation. Do we then have the right to throw out dissimilation, and to say simply that Grassman's law is not a natural rule? After all, has anyone found Grassman's law operating in any language other than Indo-European? On the other hand, if Grassman's law is a natural rule, then it ought to be accommodated within a theory of natural rules. Actually, one can say very little about how dissimilation is to be handled until there are more solid examples of this phenomenon.

Counterexamples to preferred syllable structure are easier to find. Rules of apocope or syncope, in which final or unstressed vowels are deleted, would be of this type, causing consonant clusters to arise. French offers a fascinating problem in this area. We have seen that the purpose of the rules for elision and liaison is to provide for preferred syllable structure—that is, open syllables. Yet, in colloquial French there are schwa dropping rules which undo this neat pattern so that the result is the formation of complex syllabic structures. Consequently, rules of syncope work exactly counter to what is expected according to the concept of preferred syllable structure. Obviously there is something wrong with a theory of preferred syllable structure which allows both natural rules that yield preferred syllable structures and natural rules that yield less desirable ones. If there is to be a theory of preferred syllable structure, then it will not do to have natural rules of syncope or apocope as unexplained exceptions. It becomes imperative to account for such putative exceptions within the general framework.

Perhaps the theory of preferred syllable structure should be modified in such a way so as to accommodate directly cases of syncope. Now the natural conditions under which syncope takes place are straightforward: Syncope affects a vowel which is unstressed and lax (that is, schwa-like). One might then maintain that reduced or weak vowels do not contribute in any significant way to preferred syllable structure so that such syllable structures may become optional variants of syllable structures without the reduced vowels. This ploy would account for the free variation exhibited between CəC and CC in languages like Modern French. But this solution to the problem leaves much to be desired. It is nothing more than a fix-up procedure to accommodate syncope or apocope within a theory of preferred syllable structure. I believe that an account of natural rules of syncope is to be sought elsewhere, and not within the theory of preferred syllable structure. We have noted that syncope affects a vowel which is unstressed and lax. This means that syncope is a consequence of the stress dynamics. Processes involving stress would then constitute a separate category of natural rules. Just as there is a hierarchy of preferred syllable structure, it is not inconceivable that there is also a hierarchy of preferred stress placement.

Let me illustrate these stress dynamics within the history of French. In Latin, in words of three or more syllables, stress could appear in one of two places: on the penultimate vowel, if it was long or followed by a consonant cluster; or on the antepenultimate vowel. In the development from Latin to Old French, the penultimate vowel was syncopated in all forms with antepenultimate stress. Consequently, there was a regularization in the placement of stress: In all words of two or more syllables stress always occurred now on the penultimate vowel. A further development of such forms was the deletion of all final vowels, with the exception of *a,* which was reduced to schwa. As a result of this rule, stress could again appear in one of two places: The stress is on the final vowel unless that vowel is schwa, in which case the stress is on the penultimate vowel. A subsequent development in Modern French has been another round of apocope: The final schwa which follows the stressed vowel is deleted. This then leads to a system in which stress is uniquely on the final syllable.

What initially appeared as two opposing and contradictory phenomena—natural rules which lead to desirable syllable structures and natural rules which destroy such syllable structures—are due to vastly different natural processes, preferred syllable structure and stress dynamics. In the former, segments (both consonants and vowels) can be deleted according to the nature of adjacent segments, whereas the latter is restricted to lax vowels in unstressed position. The latter deletions often lead to a situation in which stress always occurs on the same syllable. Both processes affect the shape of syllables in some way. I suspect, therefore, that they are not totally independent phenomena but that there will be complex interactions between them (e.g., can stressed vowels be deleted before other vowels?). Later, when I discuss explanations of natural rules, I shall cite an example from French in which a schwa deletion rule of the preferred syllable structure type and one of the stress dynamics type interact, and I shall attempt to give an external explanation for this.

I shall now turn to the problem of determining the internal linguistic constraints governing natural rules. As an example, consider natural rules of assimilation. Not all features of a particular segment can assimilate to those of an adjacent segment. Whereas consonants may become palatalized before palatal vowels, palatal vowels do not assimilate to preceding consonants. Hence, we need to know which features can be assimilated and what the direction of assimilation is. In a recent unpublished paper, Paul Schachter (1969) has suggested some metatheoretical constraints on assimilation. He proposes two principles. The first is that the feature values of nonvowels assimilate to those of adjacent vowels. This principle handles phenomena such as the palatalization of consonants before front vowels, the labialization of consonants before rounded vowels, and the voicing of obstruents intervocalically. However, the principle does not account for phenomena such as a vowel becoming nasalized when adjacent to a nasal consonant, when the vowel is picking up features from the consonant. Schachter then proposes a second principle for such cases: Unmarked feature values assimilate to adjacent marked feature values. Since nasalization is considered a marked value, the direction of assimilation then is from unmarked to marked. Schachter's principles do account for the direction in which assimilations take place, but one still wonders why they should work that way rather than conversely; that is, are there explanations for these principles? Also his second principle appears to be intended primarily to handle counterexamples to the first one.

I believe that both of Schachter's principles can be subsumed under a single one, provided one recognizes the traditional phonetic distinction between primary modes of articulation and secondary modes of articulation. For vowels, the features of height, frontness, and rounding are primary. On the other hand, for consonants, features such as palatalization, velarization, pharyngealization, and rounding are secondary modes of articulation. Accepting the proposal in *Sound Pattern of English* that these four consonant features are vowel colorings imposed on the consonant would suggest as a principle that it is the primary features which are assimilated. Consider now the voicing of intervocalic obstruents. As vowels are inherently voiced, voicing is a primary, although to be sure a redundant, feature for vowels. Since the voicing for obstruents, on the other hand, can be variable, the primary voicing of the vowels will be assimilated by the consonant. This principle also accounts for vowel nasalization. The feature nasalization is considered to be primary for consonants, but secondary for vowels. Hence, vowels can assimilate that feature. I shall offer below an explanation for the constraint that primary features are assimilated.

Neither Schachter's two principles (as he points out) nor my single principle account for all cases of assimilation. For example, they do not explain voicing agreement in consonant clusters. Clusters may end up either voiced or voiceless, depending on which feature the assimilating consonant contains. Similarly, the cited principles will not account for nasals becoming homorganic to following stops. At present I am unable to suggest the principle which underlies these particular types of assimilation, although it is interesting to note that all the unexplained ones involve variables in the specification of the rules, whereas the kinds of assimilation which are handled by the proposed principles contain specific feature values. My proposals and those by Schachter constitute only the beginning of the kinds of constraints which need to be set up to account for assimilation. In the same way, there will be constraints for preferred syllable structure, maximum differentiation, stress dynamics, and other natural processes to be recognized. Here lies a virgin territory of phonological exploration.

Once there are internal linguistic constraints, such as the proposed principle that primary features become assimilated, we would then require that there be some extralinguistic explanation to account for this particular constraint rather than its opposite or some other one. It has been suggested that rules of assimilation may have their explanation in articulatory gestures. This observation is by no means novel; it is, in fact, the classic explanation for assimilation, usually going under the rubric of "ease of articulation." Obviously, notions such as "ease of articulation" need explicit characterization, which they have not received in the past. However, I believe we can expect to see such explanations coming from modern experimental phonetics; for example, the research being done at UCLA by Ladefoged, Fromkin, and Smith. I quote the following passage from a recent article by Fromkin (1968), which offers a partial explanation for the proposed principle that primary features are assimilated. "Work in experimental phonetics . . . reveals that in articulating consonantal sounds anticipation of the following segment occurs when such anticipation does not involve muscles antagonistic to the primary articulation. This is the case where palatalization occurs as a secondary articulation with labials, and where labialization occurs as a secondary articulation with velars" (p. 162). Thus, the direction of the assimilation and the features assimilated can be explained as due to the coordination of different tongue muscles.

Psychological factors would provide a different sort of external explanation of natural processes. I believe that some of the stress dynamics can be explained in this way. Earlier we noted the syncope rule which affected the posttonic penultimate vowel in the development from Latin to Early French. Whereas Latin could have either antepenultimate or penultimate stress, French in this very early period has only penultimate stress. Thus, the rule of syncope changed the system from one in which stress placement was partly variable (antepenultimate or penultimate) to one in which stress placement was invariable (penultimate only). What function does invariable stress now serve? It serves a demarcative function in that the limits of the word are clearly determinable. This would be a useful perceptual strategy (I borrow this term from Bever) in that it would allow one to segment the sentence easily into its component parts. This explanation of syncope is based on two assumptions. First, there is an advantage in having phonological signals of word divisions. Such signals can of course be implemented in various ways; for example, there may be different allophones for initial and final segments (e.g., many of the segments of English), or, as we have noted, stress may serve this function (e.g., the initial word stress in Hungarian). The demarcative function of stress implies a second assumption—that invariable stress is preferred to variable stress. I think both assumptions have a certain amount of empirical justification. Concerning the first assumption that word signals are an advantage, note that English speakers learning French experience difficulty in determining the component words of sentences, since Modern French has not only lost stress maxima on the individual words of phrases but has further obliterated word divisions through elision and liaison. On the other hand, English speakers learning German or Spanish appear to have considerably less difficulty in segmenting the sentence. There is some support for the fact that invariable stress is preferred to variable stress within English in the creation of new words. Whereas the pair *telegraph, telegraphy,* and even *telephone, telephony,* have different stress patterns, the word *allophony* for most linguists has the same stresses as *allophone.* If we assume there is a perceptual advantage in having clearly marked word divisions, then in a language with stress it would be a useful strategy to use stress demarcatively, but to be so used the stress must be invariable. One way to accomplish this would be to retract or advance the stress always to the same syllable. Another way, would be to keep the stress on the original vowel but to syncopate extraneous vowels.

Perceptual strategies might also explain various unnatural rules, for example, the history of the deletion of final schwa in French.

We noted that in the development from Latin to Old French the penultimate vowel was syncopated in all forms with antepenultimate stress leading to a system where all stresses were penultimate. A further development of such forms was the deletion of all final vowels, with the exception of *a*, which was reduced to schwa. As a result of this rule of apocope, stress could again appear in one of two places: on the final vowel, unless that vowel is schwa, in which case the stress is on the penult.

We are now at the stage where word-final schwas are pronounced; for example, the feminine adjective]pətitə] *petite* "little." Such schwas can appear in one of three environments: before a vowel (*petite amie*), before a pause (*elle est petite*), or before a consonant (*petite fille*). In Modern French all these word-final schwas are generally deleted. Historically, the deletions did not take place at the same time but occurred in stages: first prevocalic, then prepausal, and finally preconsonantal. Synchronically, there is still stylistic evidence for this ordering (Schane 1968a, 1968b). Songs, which represent the most conservative style, have only prevocalic schwa deletion. In classical poetry prevocalic and prepausal schwas do not count as syllables for metrical purposes, but preconsonantal schwas do.

From the earliest stages, French has the rule that a schwa is deleted before a following vowel. Hence, there are no vowel clusters of the form: schwa–second vowel. In this period then there is only one schwa deletion rule, a natural rule of the preferred syllable structure type.

Consider now prepausal position, which includes words in isolation or in phrase-final position. I assume, as in Modern French, that words not in prepausal position are no longer stressed, so that within the phrase, the only word which will bear stress is the prepausal one. Consequently, the deletion of prepausal schwas will involve precisely those which follow the stressed syllable. This too is a natural process due to stress dynamics. As a result of this rule stress appears uniquely on the final vowel. Thus, we see that the deletion of word-final schwa starts out as a natural phenomenon, in fact, two different natural processes: prevocalic schwa deletion, which yields preferred syllable structure, and prepausal schwa deletion, which leads to preferred stress placement.

The next schwa deletions are the preconsonantal ones. This deletion cannot be attributed to any natural process. It is not of the
preferred syllable structure type since the deletion, in fact, leads
to a more complex syllabic structure, nor is it due to stress dynamics as there is no stress on nonfinal words within the phrase.
Hence, the deletion of schwa in this environment cannot be a
natural one. Is there then an explanation for the origin of an unnatural rule that deletes preconsonantal schwa? I should like to
suggest the following hypothesis. Because of the two natural rules
of schwa deletion, we obtain an unbalanced system. Of the three
environments in which schwa originally occurs, it is deleted in two—
prevocalic and prepausal—but retained in the third—preconsonantal, so that forms of the same word no longer have the same surface
representation. Assume that there is the following perceptual strategy: a tendency to give the same surface representation to the same
forms. Such a strategy would then lead to word-final schwas being
dropped in preconsonantal position as well, even though this is not
a natural environment. But there may also be (as Douglas Walker
has pointed out to me) internal structural pressures for the deletion
of preconsonantal schwa. Note that as a synchronic rule, prepausal
schwa deletion need not make reference to a preceding stress since
the prepausal environment alone would be a sufficient specification
for the rule to operate. Previously, in the discussion of natural rules,
we noted that the prepausal and preconsonantal environments frequently are found as natural alternate environments in the statement of rules. Since these environments occur together, one might
expect that a rule which applies only before one of them would be
logically extended to the other one. If only the environments are
considered, then the generalization is a completely natural one. But
such a generalization in only part of the rule would then lead to an
unnatural situation elsewhere in the rule. All these proposals are,
needless to say, speculative, but, it is hoped, will suggest possible
explanations not only for natural processes but also for the relation
between natural and unnatural ones—in particular, a psychological
account of certain types of analogy.

That some phonological phenomena are more natural than others
is by no means a recent observation. What is recent is the new interest taken in characterizing natural phonological phenomena. The

marking conventions proposed in *Sound Pattern of English* illustrate one such attempt in this direction. However, these marking conventions are by and large limited to characterizing natural segment types—in particular, the naturalness of segments or syllable structures within lexical representations. Chomsky and Halle also propose that these marking conventions should be linked to the phonological rules. So, for example, if a velar stop becomes a palatal before a palatal vowel, the marking conventions will convert this new palatal stop to an alveopalatal affricate. Again what is being captured here is the naturalness of individual segment types. Nothing, however, is said about the particular rule which causes the palatalization, that this rule is natural in a way in which other rules are not. A theory of natural rules is therefore needed along with a theory of natural segment types. It is to be hoped that proposals in both areas would support each other, and in fact they would have to.

The three categories of natural rules which I have dwelled on are compatible with the marking conventions for segment types. For example, the unmarked obstruent is considered to be voiceless; however, it has been suggested that the unmarked value may depend on the particular context, so that the unmarked obstruent would be voiced in intervocalic position. As another example, consider the unmarked nasal, *n*. It seems plausible that when the nasal is followed by an obstruent, the unmarked value should be homorganic with that obstruent. What this implies, then, is that natural rules of assimilation, as phonological rules, may be identical to the context-sensitive marking conventions for the lexicon. Turning to the natural rules of preferred syllable structure, it would be expected that the required hierarchy would be compatible with that demanded by the marking conventions for characterizing syllable structure within lexical items. Finally, if we consider the rules for maximum differentiation, we see that they too have specific correlates in the marking conventions. Just as the marking conventions stipulate that the most natural underlying three-vowel system comprises *i, a,* and *u,* exactly the same conditions obtain on surface vowels resulting from the rules for maximum differentiation.

The similarities between marking conventions and natural rules suggest, then, that the deep structure and the surface structure are both governed by the same set of constraints. Why should this be the case? The constraints on the phonological representations of the individual lexical morphemes may be severely altered when these morphemes are strung together and where the sequences are now viewed in their totality. Phonological rules would then serve to bring the surface representations closer to underlying ones. If this observation concerning the functioning of natural rules is correct, it provides particularly strong evidence for the claim by Chomsky and Halle that the same set of distinctive features must be utilized at both the abstract and surface levels and for Postal's claim that there must be a naturalness condition imposed on underlying representations. Since the phonetic representations, after all the rules have applied, are "natural," and if it is true that many of the phonological rules serve to make phonetic representations conform to the constraints imposed on the abstract representations of individual lexical morphemes, then it follows that the abstract representations of these morphemes must be "natural."

The fact that deep and surface structures are governed by similar constraints also accounts for certain nonnatural phenomena. Earlier we considered the rules for deleting word-final schwa in French. We noted that of the three environments in which it occurs—prevocalic, prepausal, and preconsonantal—the deletions in the first two were natural processes of preferred syllable structure and stress dynamics, respectively, whereas the preconsonantal deletion was an unnatural one. We explained the historical appearance of the latter as due to an asymmetry in surface representations at the time when only the two natural rules were in the language. I suggested that the unnatural rule may arise from a perceptual strategy of having a consistent surface representation for the same form (cf. *allophone, allophony* cited earlier). But to have a consistent representation whenever possible is precisely the constraint imposed on underlying forms. What is being suggested then is that perceptual strategies are being invoked in dealing with surface forms so that they will conform more to the deep forms.

So long as I am free to speculate, allow me to conclude this section with just one final bit of heresy. What significance might all this have for a theory of language change? The constraints imposed on lexical representations are pivotal for all the phonology. These constraints are of two types: naturalness conditions and a uniqueness criterion. The naturalness conditions, embodied in marking conventions, determine what kinds of segments are allowed in lexical representations and what phonotactic restrictions are imposed on them. The uniqueness criterion is nothing other than the requirement that lexical morphemes have a single underlying representation. These constraints may break down when morphemes are concatenated to form words and phrases and where the phonological environments now go beyond individual morphemes. The phonological rules—I should emphasize *natural* phonological rules—can be viewed also as a set of naturalness conditions, which reimpose the original constraints on derived structures. Although natural rules guarantee that the surface or phonetic representations will conform to the naturalness conditions, they do so only at a high cost. As a consequence of trying to preserve naturalness, the second constraint—the uniqueness criterion—must be forgone, for what the natural rules do in altering the underlying forms is to produce phonological alternations or allomorphs of the original uniquely represented morphemes. To conserve uniqueness a set of "natural" strategies may then come into play, whose purpose is the leveling of allomorphs in the surface representations. The allomorph which triumphs is one of those resulting from an original natural rule. But this new unique surface representation now differs from the original unique underlying representation. At some subsequent stage restructuring inevitably takes place and the unique surface representation becomes the new underlying representation. The cycle is then ready to repeat itself.

If there are strategies for leveling surface alternations and if the products of these strategies are formulated as rules, such rules may, indeed, look very unnatural. Does this suggest, then, that attempting to treat the results of strategies as rules of language change has obscured our understanding of what superficially appears as unnatural processes? Is there any reason to believe that unnatural rules exist at all—at least as historical phenomena, or is language change nothing more than a never-ending series of interdependent natural processes and "natural" strategies?

Epilogue

I should now like to consider briefly the problem of establishing an evaluation metric for natural rules. Within generative phonology the development of an evaluation measure has been tied up with the form of notational conventions, the claim being that the more general the process, the less complex the notation. Thus, Halle has proposed that the more inclusive a natural class the fewer features needed to characterize that class. If we accept that more natural phenomena should have a simpler characterization, then we should expect natural rules to be simpler to state than unnatural ones. Consider, for example, the two rules given under (3) at the outset of this paper. According to the first one, high vowels become glides before other vowels, whereas in the second rule all vowels become glides before other vowels. The first rule is the natural one, yet it necessitates more feature specifications than the second. It appears then that the natural rule requires a more complex statement, which is counter to the proposed evaluation metric. We find the natural rule recurring in language after language, but always with the specifications that the vowel to the left of the arrow must be a high vowel and there must be some other vowel in the environment. If these two features always accompany the natural rule, and if these environmental constraints are universal, it should be unnecessary to state these restrictions in individual grammars. This means that the environmental restrictions on gliding should be stated once and for all in the metatheory and not restated each time in each particular language in which this natural rule occurs. Instead, what ought to be stated in each particular language is any deviency from the natural phonological process. What I propose then is that the natural rule be stated simply as: A vowel becomes a glide. The metatheory then supplies the additional information that the gliding vowel is a high vowel and that it is adjacent to some other vowel. Since the gliding rule is a preferred syllable structure rule the metatheory should also predict that the ideal case is the one in which the gliding vowel is found between two other vowels. If, on the other hand, there are only two vowels present, both of which could conceivably become glides—that is, given *iu* do we obtain *yu* or *uy*?—we need to indicate in the particular language whether the gliding takes place before or after the environment vowel, but we still do not need to indicate that the gliding vowel is a high one. However, if in some language, both *i* and *e* should become glides, then we would have to indicate in our language-particular rule that mid vowels may also become glides in this language. Continuing along these lines, if we find in a language that all front vowels become glides, then we would have to indicate that both mid and low vowels also become glides. Hence, as the rule becomes less natural in a particular language, more feature specifications are required in the statement of the rule.

As a second example, consider Rule B' on page 201. The natural environment for the deletion of a nasal consonant requires two environmental constraints: The nasal consonant is preceded by a nasalized vowel and is followed by either a consonant or a word boundary. Again the environmental constraints should be stated in the metatheory. Since the environments are predictable, the rule ought to read simply: A nasal consonant is deleted. This is how we ought to state the nasal consonant deletion rule in a language such as French. In a language such as Portuguese, in which some nasal consonants are also deleted before vowels, it would then be necessary to state the special prevocalic environment in the Portuguese rule, since this environment is not a natural one. This proposed evaluation metric has some interesting consequences. It implies that natural rules are context-free; all their environments are predictable, that is, the environments can be stated in the metatheory. Unnatural rules, or deviations from natural rules, are context-sensitive; their environments are not predictable since they are language-specific. In essence what it amounts to is this: Natural rules, which are context-free rules, are universal; unnatural rules, which are context-sensitive rules, are language-specific.

REFERENCES

Boas, F. 1911. Introduction to *Handbook of American Indian Languages*. Washington, D.C.: Georgetown University Press. Reprint (n.d.).

Chomsky, N., and M. Halle. 1968. *The Sound Pattern of English*. New York: Harper and Row.

Fromkin, V. 1968. The what and why of intrinsicalness. *Working Papers in Phonetics*, 10, UCLA.

Gleason, H. A. 1955. *Workbook in Descriptive Linguistics*. New York: Holt, Rinehart and Winston.

Halle, M. 1962. Phonology in generative grammar. *Word* 18: 54-72. Reprinted in *The Structure of Language*, J. A. Fodor and J. J. Katz, eds., pp. 334-52. Englewood Cliffs, N.J.: Prentice-Hall, 1964.

Heffner, R. M. S. 1950. *General Phonetics*. Madison: University of Wisconsin Press, reprinted 1964.

Jakobson, R. 1941. *Child Language, Aphasia and Phonological Universals,* translated from the German by A. Keiler. The Hague: Mouton and Co., 1968.

Kiparsky, P. 1968. Linguistic universals and linguistic change. *Universals in Linguistic Theory,* E. Bach and R. T. Harms, eds. New York: Holt, Rinehart and Winston.

Martinet, A. 1955. *Économie des changements phonétiques.* Berne: Francke.

Schachter. P. 1969. Natural assimilation rules in Akan. *IJAL* 35: 342-55.

Schane, S. A. 1968a. *French Phonology and Morphology.* Cambridge: M.I.T. Press.

——. 1968b. On the hierarchy for the deletion of the French "E Muet." Unpublished.

Troubetzkoy, N. S. 1939. *Principes de phonologie,* translated from the German by J. Cantineau. Paris: Librairie C. Klincksieck, 1949.

8.

Sound Change and Markedness Theory: On the History of the German Consonant System

Theo Vennemann,
University of California, Los Angeles

1. Markedness theory

While phonological *simplicity* has played an important role in all transformational work on phonology ever since Morris Halle introduced this concept,[1] discussion of phonological *naturalness* by transformationalists has only recently begun to appear in print.[2] This discussion attempts to combine knowledge about phonological universals[3] with the Praguian notion of "marked" and "unmarked" values of features.[4]

In the simplicity approach, features are either specified as + or −, with equal cost (viz. 1) attached to both specifications in the evaluation metric, or they are left blank (sometimes indicated by 0), in which case no such cost arises. Thus maximal simplicity is gained by leaving unspecified as many features as possible, utilizing universal and language-specific redundancy rules to supply the omitted values. In the new markedness approach, features can be specified as +, −, U, or M, while blanks do not occur.[5] U stands for "unmarked" and indicates that the specified feature assumes the value (in terms of + and −) that is "natural" in the given context; M stands for "marked" and indicates that the feature thus specified assumes the opposite value. For example, a dental spirant can be either [+ strident], i.e., [s]; or [− strident], i.e., [θ]. [s] is more natural than [θ]. Therefore, in terms of markedness, [s] is [U strident] and [θ], [M strident].[6] To give a second example, in which not only the segmental but also the sequential context is relevant: The natural values of the place of articulation features in nasals immediately followed by obstruents are identical with the actual values in the obstruents, irrespective of what the natural values in nasals may be in other contexts.[7] Thus, while in German both the [m] of *Ampel,* "traffic light," and the [n] of *Kante,* "edge," are [U coronal], the [m] of *Amt,* "office," is [M coronal].

In this system, the concept of simplicity is supplemented by that of minimal complexity, where phonological complexity is the total number of +, −, and M values, while U's do not contribute to the complexity of a grammar (Chomsky and Halle 1968: 402-404, 409). Since by definition U means "natural," lesser complexity, i.e., a greater number of U's, for example, in one segment as compared with another in the same context, is the formal correlate of the intuitive concept of "greater naturalness." In one of the above examples, [s] differs from [θ] only by being [U strident]. Its greater naturalness is thus reflected by the fact that the number of U's defining this segment in a language-independent way is greater by one, its complexity smaller by one. In the other example, both the [m] in *Ampel* and the [n] in *Kante* are the most natural nasals possible in their respective positions, and so is the [ŋ] in [baŋk] *Bank,* "bench." They are defined in the lexicon by identical distributions of M's and U's in their feature matrices. The [m] in *Amt,* on the other hand, is a less natural nasal to occur in that position. This is reflected by the fact that in the matrix defining this nasal, an M occurs with one feature, Coronality, where the previous nasals have a U.

Since one and the same segment can in a given context be described both in terms of + and − (the traditional description without blanks) and in terms of U and M (or M and blank, cf. note 5), we have to ask when the one description is to be used and when the other. In Chomsky and Halle 1968, the values M and U occur only in the lexicon and in certain universal conventions that change these values into + and − in a context-sensitive way. Convention (XXI), p. 406, to which I will have to return later, may serve as an example; see (1).

$$(1)\ [\text{U voice}] \rightarrow [-\text{voice}] \ / \begin{bmatrix} \rule{2cm}{0.4pt} \\ -\text{sonorant} \end{bmatrix}$$

It replaces [U voice] by [- voice] in segments previously specified as [- sonorant] by similar conventions and—this is implicit in the notation, cf. p. 403—[M voice] by [+ voice] in the same context. After all the marking conventions have applied in proper sequence, all M's and U's have disappeared, and all segments are now described exclusively in terms of + and - (p. 408). Therefore all phonological rules work exclusively in terms of + and -.

Chomsky and Halle (1968: 419-35) suggest that the marking conventions can also be used with respect to phonological rules in the following way: When a change, synchronic or diachronic, occurs, the marking conventions are checked in proper sequence if they apply to the result of the change (the features actually changed by the rule are exempted from this comparison). If such a check turns out positive for some feature G—in the sense that *all* segments resulting from the change are covered by some convention (p. 431) —this feature assumes the specification that is natural (U) according to the convention (p. 420). If, on the other hand, such automatic adjustment, called linking, is to be prevented, the + or - value for G that would be M according to the convention must be given in the structural change of the rule, which is thus complicated. To give a simple example, German has a rule changing [x] into [ç] after front vowels:

$$(2) \begin{bmatrix} + \text{ consonantal} \\ - \text{ coronal} \\ - \text{ anterior} \\ + \text{ continuant} \end{bmatrix} \rightarrow [- \text{ back}] \ / \ [- \text{ back}] \ \underline{\quad\quad}$$

(Cf. Vennemann 1968a: 47-50, 59.) The marking convention (XXIII) (Chomsky and Halle 1968: 406, 421), whose relevant part is reproduced here, applies to the output of this rule.

$$(3) \ [\text{U coronal}] \rightarrow [\alpha \text{ coronal}] \ / \ \begin{bmatrix} \overline{\quad\quad\quad} \\ - \alpha \text{ back} \\ - \text{anterior} \end{bmatrix}$$

[ç], deriving from [x] through application of (2), is a [- back, - anterior] obstruent. It should therefore automatically be further changed by (3) into a [+ coronal] segment. This segment would, through the application of a further marking convention, (XXVII), become strident, [š]. However, no such additional modification

occurs in the standard language. Therefore, according to Chomsky
and Halle's hypothesis, the rule should read as in (4),

(4) $\begin{bmatrix} + \text{ consonantal} \\ - \text{ coronal} \\ - \text{ anterior} \\ + \text{ continuant} \end{bmatrix} \rightarrow \begin{bmatrix} - \text{ back} \\ - \text{ coronal} \end{bmatrix} / [- \text{ back}]$ ——

thus indicating that the resulting segment does not switch to a more
natural feature composition.

Notice that this hypothesis fails to take into account the system
in which the rule operates. Thus in the example, it is certainly far
from irrelevant that there exists already an [š] at the stage in the
phonology where (3) operates. That merger should come about as
the result of an automatic adjustment is quite improbable (cf.
Harms 1967: 172). Therefore, the specification of marked features
in the structural change of a rule is probably superfluous in cases
in which linking would lead to merger.[8]

Postal 1968 also has the two-level interpretation of feature values
peculiar to the Chomsky-Hallean conception of markedness: "On
the deeper, or more abstract level, features have only two possible
values, M(arked) or U(nmarked) . . . . There is, in addition, a less abstract level of matrix representation in which every cell contains
either + or – marking" (pp. 166-67). In addition, however, Postal
discusses possibilities of using markedness not in linking, but directly in phonological rules (pp. 184-88). He observes, for example,
that in languages in which a Voice contrast is neutralized in word-
final obstruents, it is always the voiceless obstruents that appear in
this position, i.e., those obstruents that are unmarked for Voice
in this position.[9] Probably this would require a new format for
phonological rules in which specifications in terms of U values
would occur in the structural change, together with + and – where
these represent the marked values (p. 184).

More recently Schachter (1969) has likewise contended that
"markedness is relevant not merely to the *output* of the P-rules but
to the *functioning* of these rules as well" (p. 10). Like Postal, he
suggests that "P-rules be permitted to assign not only + and – feature
values but also certain metatheoretically-specified natural feature

values. More specifically, let us propose that certain P-rules have the general form

(5) $A \rightarrow Nf \,/\, X \,—\, Y$

where f is any feature, and N is the metatheoretically-specified natural value for that feature in the context $X—Y$" (pp. 12-13). The second of the two new universals that Schachter proposes earlier in his paper, which says that "unmarked feature values assimilate to adjacent marked feature values, rather than conversely" (p. 9), now assumes the form (6).

(6) "$[Nf] \rightarrow [mf] \,/\, [mf]$

where $m = \alpha$" (p. 13). This "universal naturalness convention . . . is to be interpreted as follows: the natural value of a feature is the marked value of that feature ($[mf]$) when an adjoining segment shows the marked value of the feature, and when, further, the marked value is the same for both segments" (p. 13).[10]

If I understand this proposal correctly, Schachter is proposing a third type of feature specification: In addition to the descriptive specifications +, – and the interpretive classification as M or U, he introduces an evaluational distinction between natural (N) and non-natural: "In assessing the relative simplicity of P-rules (which is the formal correlate of their relative predictability), specifications of natural feature values are not counted: that is, . . . a rule assigning the value N to a feature is simpler than an otherwise identical rule assigning the value + or – " (p. 13).

It seems to me that this proposal somehow underestimates the possibilities inherent in the markedness notation. "A major difference between the Praguian conception of markedness and our own is that in the former the marked coefficient of a feature was assumed always to be + and the unmarked coefficient always – " (Chomsky and Halle 1968: 404n). Chomsky and Halle overcame this deficiency of the older conception by making markedness context-sensitive, i.e., dependent in many of their conventions on both segmental and sequential conditions. For example, their convention (XXIV) says that while generally the optimal consonant is noncontinuant, the opposite is true morpheme-initially before a consonant (pp. 406, 412). Schachter seems to interpret the Chomsky-Hallean marking coefficients in a Praguian sense, namely in the sense that there is a unique correlation between +, – values and M, U values—in this case determined by the Chomsky-Hallean marking conventions—which remains constant in all environments not specified in the marking conventions as they stand. However, the conventions are intended by their authors only as a "sketch" (p. 400), as "a *tentative* statement of *some* marking conventions" (p. 404, italics mine). Ideally, a complete set of marking conventions states for each feature in every observed (or otherwise predictable) segmental and sequential environment which +, – specification is unmarked and which is marked, where the unmarked value designates the "natural" +, – specification. To say that in a certain environment the marked value (*m*) of a certain feature is natural (*N*) is, from this point of view, self-contradictory.

There remains, of course, the problem that Chomsky and Halle provide no tools to express the distinction that a certain change is more plausible than, say, the opposite change under the same conditions. This, however, is not a weakness of the Chomsky-Hallean conception of markedness itself but rather of the self-imposed limitation to use markedness only in the lexicon and in linking, but not in the interpretation of phonological rules. If this limitation is renounced, it should be possible to use "unmarked" synonymously with "natural" everywhere in a grammar.

I believe that at least until we reach a more comprehensive picture of what is natural in phonology—and perhaps even then—we should keep M's and U's out of phonological rules. I believe further that we should keep M's and U's out of the lexicon as well. In other words, M's and U's, in my opinion, have no place whatsoever in phonological descriptions. They belong to a different level of representation. Like Chomsky and Halle 1968 and Postal 1968, I propose that two different levels of representation be distinguished. However, in my view these levels should not occur at two different stages in the grammar, but they should be parallel in the sense that at each stage in a derivation both levels of representation are available. These are a *descriptive level,* on which features are specified for what they are materially, independent of the context in which they occur, and an *interpretive level,* on which such material specifications are characterized as more or less predictable (more or less natural) in their segmental and sequential contexts. The descriptive specifications are exclusively in terms of + and –, and of integers where features allow for more than binary specification. The interpretive characterizations are, at our present level of understanding, in terms of U (unmarked, natural, optimal) and M (marked, deviant from greatest naturalness or optimality). However, there is no reason to believe that our present binary characterizations are the last word on the subject. On the contrary, it seems quite obvious to me that there are many degrees of naturalness, ranging from complete predictability to mere factuality to total impossibility. It undoubtedly makes a difference whether an M occurs with the feature Voice or the feature Murmur (cf. note 10). It is at least conceivable that the degree of aspiration in obstruents is a factor in the evaluation of a grammar, and similarly with other detail rules (cf. Postal 1968: 65-69). In any event, the interpretive level plays an important, although perhaps not exclusive, role in the evaluation of phonological descriptions of both lexical items and rules. Descriptive specifications interpreted as U should not contribute to the complexity of a grammar either in the lexicon (Chomsky and Halle 1968: 403, 404; Postal 1968: 166) or in the structural changes of rules (Postal 1968: 187).[11] On the other hand, M's (or their more specifically quantified–e.g., numerical–counterparts) do contribute to the complexity of phonological descriptions at all stages in a grammar.

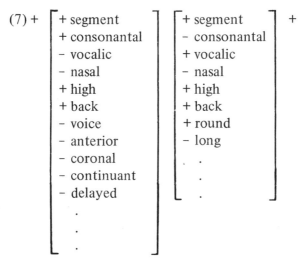

$$(7) + \begin{bmatrix} + \text{ segment} \\ + \text{ consonantal} \\ - \text{ vocalic} \\ - \text{ nasal} \\ + \text{ high} \\ + \text{ back} \\ - \text{ voice} \\ - \text{ anterior} \\ - \text{ coronal} \\ - \text{ continuant} \\ - \text{ delayed} \\ \cdot \\ \cdot \\ \cdot \end{bmatrix} \begin{bmatrix} + \text{ segment} \\ - \text{ consonantal} \\ + \text{ vocalic} \\ - \text{ nasal} \\ + \text{ high} \\ + \text{ back} \\ + \text{ round} \\ - \text{ long} \\ \cdot \\ \cdot \\ \cdot \end{bmatrix} +$$

Consider the preceding example (cf. Vennemann 1968a: 386n). The German word *Kuh* [ku:], "cow," is, in the framework just sketched, lexically represented as /ku/, i.e., as in (7). This is the phonological form with which the word is learned and stored in the lexicon. All features that are at all applicable to the segments occurring in (7) are specified in a complete description. There is absolutely no systematic value in leaving certain applicable features unspecified, because the evaluation of the lexicon does not operate on the descriptive level but on the interpretive level. At the interpretive level (7) is represented as in (8).[12]

(8) +

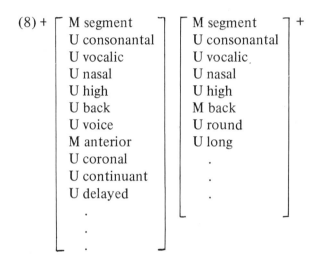

The number and position of the M's in this representation are obviously independent of the degree of specification at the descriptive level, and they alone matter in the evaluation of a lexicon.

For a second example, let us return to the point-of-articulation specification of nasals in pre-obstruent position. Again, in the framework proposed here, such nasals are, at the descriptive level, fully specified in the lexicon. For example, the nasals in *Ampel, Kante,* and *Bank* have differing but invariable representations, cf. (9), as indeed they do in all other positions; e.g., the [m] in *Amt* has the same specifications as that in *Ampel.* At the interpretive level, however, the first three have identical representations, while that of the [m] in *Amt* differs. This follows from the convention—which

(9)   [m]   [n]   [ŋ]

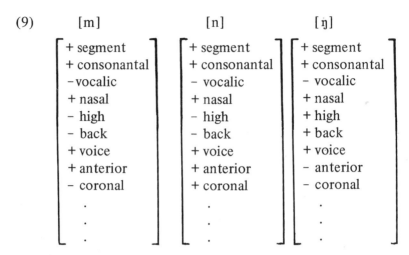

$$
\begin{bmatrix}
+ \text{segment} \\
+ \text{consonantal} \\
- \text{vocalic} \\
+ \text{nasal} \\
- \text{high} \\
- \text{back} \\
+ \text{voice} \\
+ \text{anterior} \\
- \text{coronal} \\
\cdot \\ \cdot \\ \cdot
\end{bmatrix}
\begin{bmatrix}
+ \text{segment} \\
+ \text{consonantal} \\
- \text{vocalic} \\
+ \text{nasal} \\
- \text{high} \\
- \text{back} \\
+ \text{voice} \\
+ \text{anterior} \\
+ \text{coronal} \\
\cdot \\ \cdot \\ \cdot
\end{bmatrix}
\begin{bmatrix}
+ \text{segment} \\
+ \text{consonantal} \\
- \text{vocalic} \\
+ \text{nasal} \\
+ \text{high} \\
+ \text{back} \\
+ \text{voice} \\
- \text{anterior} \\
- \text{coronal} \\
\cdot \\ \cdot \\ \cdot
\end{bmatrix}
$$

will probably go undisputed—that the optimal nasal in pre-obstruent position is the homorganic one, cf. (10).

(10)   [UF]
                             ⇑

$$
\begin{bmatrix}
\alpha\, F \\
+ \text{consonantal} \\
+ \text{nasal}
\end{bmatrix}
\begin{bmatrix}
\alpha F \\
- \text{sonorant}
\end{bmatrix}
$$

where F stands for any one of the features High, Back, Coronal, and Anterior. With this convention, the interpretive representations are as in (11).

(11)   [m] in *Ampel*   [m] in *Amt*
          [n] in *Kante*
          [ŋ] in *Bank*

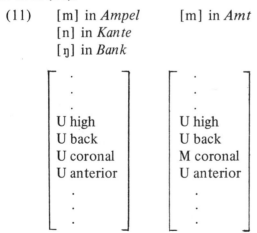

$$
\begin{bmatrix}
\cdot \\ \cdot \\ \cdot \\
\text{U high} \\
\text{U back} \\
\text{U coronal} \\
\text{U anterior} \\
\cdot \\ \cdot \\ \cdot
\end{bmatrix}
\begin{bmatrix}
\cdot \\ \cdot \\ \cdot \\
\text{U high} \\
\text{U back} \\
\text{M coronal} \\
\text{U anterior} \\
\cdot \\ \cdot \\ \cdot
\end{bmatrix}
$$

Clearly, interpretive conventions such as (10)—and the Chomsky-Hallean marking conventions interpreted in a parallel fashion—make the so-called universal lexical redundancy rules superfluous. All lexical redundancy rules are language-specific.

Changes of segments as well as individual segments can be represented at two different levels. Assume that in the context X—Y, a segment A^1, with the feature composition $[\alpha_1^1 F_1, \ldots, \alpha_n^1 F_n]$, is changed into A^2, with the feature composition $[\alpha_1^2 F_1, \ldots, \alpha_n^2 F_n]$, where the α's are either $+$ or $-$. Both A^1 and A^2 have in the context X—Y a representation on the interpretive level, say $M^1 = [\mu_1^1 F_1, \ldots, \mu_n^1 F_n]$ and $M^2 = [\mu_1^2 F_1, \ldots, \mu_n^2 F_n]$, where the μ's are naturalness coefficients (i.e., U or M—or more precisely speaking, 0 for U and 1 for M—in the binary interpretation, which is the only one presently available). Now the descriptive change

(12) $[\alpha_1^1 F_1, \ldots, \alpha_n^1 F_n] \rightarrow [\alpha_1^2 F_1, \ldots, \alpha_n^2 F_n] \; / \; X$—$Y$

is paralleled at the interpretive level by the change

(13) $[\mu_1^1 F_1, \ldots, \mu_n^1 F_n] \twoheadrightarrow [\mu_1^2 F_1, \ldots, \mu_n^2 F_n].$

If we combine this notation with that used in the interpretive convention (10), the formulas (12) and (13) can be brought together in a schema such as (14), where the above abbreviations are used.

(14) $M^1 \twoheadrightarrow M^2$
$\quad \Uparrow \qquad \Uparrow$
$A^1 \rightarrow A^2 \; / \; X$—$Y$

Given now an evaluation measure which assigns to A^1 and A^2 the complexity values c^1 and c^2 (e.g., $\sum_i \mu_i^1$ and $\sum_i \mu_i^2$), one can study a change from the point of view of whether it increases or decreases segmental complexity. An evaluation of the change would have to be based on a comparison of c^1 and c^2 (perhaps on $c^2 - c^1$), and would in addition depend on considerations of the system in which the change occurs, such as the typological soundness of both the original and the resulting systems, or the question of to what degree the change leads to merger.

While this is fairly straightforward, it is less obvious how a rule changing several segments is to be evaluated. Sometimes inclusion of more segments seems to make a rule more plausible, sometimes less so. For example, a rule palatalizing both /k/ and /g/ before non-low front vowels may be more plausible than one palatalizing only /k/ in the same environment. On the other hand, while a change of /p/ into /f/ may occur in a grammar,[13] a rule spirantizing all voiceless stops seems impossible, because it would result in a typologically impossible phonetic system.[14] It must also be considered that the change in complexity will not necessarily be identical in all the affected segments. Take, for example, the umlaut of long vowels in Literary German (inclusion of short vowels and diphthongs does not make the situation any clearer), i.e., the change of /a: o: u:/ into /ä: ö: ü:/. In the binary system of Chomsky and Halle 1968, /a:/ changes two U's into M's in the process, while /o:/ and /u:/ change only one each (cf. their table on p. 409). There is reason to believe that in a multi-value interpretation system such gradation of the individual complexity changes effected by a rule is the normal situation.

While the problems of detail are great and apparently well beyond the limits of our present understanding of phonological theory, the following generalization can be made. Call a rule that decreases the complexity of all affected segments a *D-rule*, one that increases the complexity of all affected segments an *I-rule*.

(15) D-rules, in particular D-rules not leading to merger, must be favored over I-rules by the evaluation metric.

D-rules seem to be essentially of two types: *assimilatory rules* (*A-rules*) and *typological adjustment rules* (*T-rules*). Both types characteristically proceed in the direction of typologically preferred structures. The difference is that for A-rules the sequential context is the motivating factor, while T-rules are motivated by a momentary imbalance in the segmental system.

Take the rule that unvoices word final obstruents. Since it decreases the complexity of all affected segments, it is a D-rule, cf. (16).

(16)   [M voice]   ⟹   [U voice]
              ⇑   ⇑
$$\begin{bmatrix} + \text{ voice} \\ - \text{ sonorant} \end{bmatrix} \rightarrow \quad [- \text{ voice}] \ / \ \text{—\#}$$

Notice that the inverse rule is an I-rule, cf. (17).

(17)   [U voice] $\rightarrowtail$ [M voice]

              $\Uparrow$ $\Uparrow$

$\begin{bmatrix} - \text{ voice} \\ - \text{ sonorant} \end{bmatrix}$ $\rightarrow$ [+ voice] /——#

The I-rule (17) does not occur. The D-rule (16), on the other hand, has been reported for several languages. The fact that it is not more popular than it actually is, e.g., a universal rule, must be attributed to its inescapable neutralization effect. Note that being sequentially motivated, (16) is an A-rule (cf. Schachter 1969: 27).

For a simple, although probably hypothetical, example of T-rules consider the interpretation of Grimm's Law in Greenberg 1966a: 63: "Once unvoiced stops had become fricatives, we would be left with such sets as b^h, b, f. The b with its marked feature of voicing having no partner p, was free to lose its mark and become p. Now given b^h, p, f, in similar fashion the b^h having no partner, b could lose its marked feature of aspiration, although it became a voiced fricative rather than a voiced stop in most environments."[15] The changes of the voiced stops into voiceless stops and of the so-called voiced aspirates into voiced stops and spirants, both of them obviously D-rules, are not sequentially conditioned. Rather they are conditioned by Roman Jakobson's famous universal of *unilateral foundation* (1939: 320; 1941: 360; cf. also 1958: 526), which in the terminology of markedness theory assumes the following form (Cf. also Lakoff 1968: 168):

(18) The existence in a phonological system of a series X of segments marked for a certain feature F presupposes the simultaneous existence of the series that differs from X only by being unmarked for the feature F.[16]

A system such as the above b^h, b, f, where each symbol stands for a series, is indeed characterized by principle (18) as typologically extremely unlikely if not impossible. Therefore, if through some historical accident such a system originates, or threatens to originate, a T-rule, or sequence of T-rules ($b \rightarrow p$, $b^h \rightarrow$ b, b̦), will restore a typological system that is in accordance with principle (18).

In this paper I will not concern myself with the question of how the universals I use have been ascertained. Postal (1968: 168-72) discusses how the following areas of phonological research can contribute evidence for universal preferences: neutralization, typology, relative frequency and differential predictability in particular languages, phonological change, dialect variation, physiological and perceptual investigations, first language learning and language pathology—the order is that in which the areas are discussed by Postal and is not intended to constitute a hierarchy of relevance. I have nothing to add to this list. The intention of this paper is not to suggest new universals; with the exception of a single one, all the universals employed below have been discussed in the literature (cf. note 3). Rather I want to show how the concept of a D-rule, based on those universals, in particular that of a T-rule, can serve in the interpretation of certain diachronic developments. I select as a testing ground the major changes in the German obstruent system from Pre-Old High German to Late Middle High German. These changes are sufficiently well known to supply a rich amount of connected data, while at the same time their motivation and the direction of their spread are a matter of dispute. Since all the predictions made by the hypothesis of the preferred status of the D-rules are borne out by the data where the evidence is conclusive, we can study the question of how the hypothesis can in turn contribute to a solution of the problematic issues.

2. The High German Consonant Shift and Its Consequences

Table (19) represents the reconstructed phonetic obstruent system of Proto-Germanic.[17]

(19)

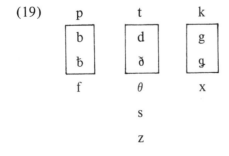

[z] either merged with /r/ or was lost in Pre-Old High German (Pre-OHG) times and need not concern us further here. The voiced stops and voiced spirants were in complementary distribution, the latter occurring essentially in positions after [+ vocalic] segments, with certain individual differences that remain without consequence for the present discussion (cf. Moulton 1954: 40).[18]

Two major changes occurred between the stage represented in (19) and the High German Consonant Shift (HG CS): the West Germanic Gemination, after which all stops were richly represented as geminates (the number of geminate spirants was only slightly increased); and the change of [ð] into [d], so that after the change /d/ was exclusively represented as [d] (cf., for the latter development, Braune/Mitzka 1967: §§82, 84). Although the change of [ð] into [d] probably occurred in Pre-OHG times (cf. also Moulton 1954: 21, 29, 33), I would like to discuss it here, as a first application of the method.

The question of whether the unmarked value of Voice in obstruents is the same in all positions is a matter of dispute. Chomsky and Halle (1968: 406) simply state that [U voice] is [- voice] in obstruents in all positions, cf. (1) above. It was suggested during the discussion of my paper at the conference that this is correct at best in nonintervocalic positions but that intervocalically, [U voice] is [+ voice]. Postal 1968 differs from both views. He admits the possibility that in languages without a Voice contrast ("a poorly understood limitation," p. 167n), intervocalic obstruents are in general voiced (p. 184), while "it is certainly not true in general that [U Voice] is [+ Voice] in consonants occurring between vowels" (p. 185).

Postal's interpretation, if it is correct, shows a weakness inherent in the proposal that considerations of naturalness (in the form of U's and possibly M's) should be incorporated in phonological rules; it is, indeed, the point Postal is making that "such a proposal would by no means be sufficient" (p. 184). This weakness is that a condition such as "in languages without a Voice contrast" cannot be incorporated in a phonological rule. The same is true of the non-merger specification in (15) and of all other conditions concerning the system in which a segment or a change functions. I believe that my proposal to separate interpretation from description throughout the grammar can remedy that deficiency, because there is no reason why systematic considerations should not enter into evaluational statements at the interpretive level.

In addition, Postal's interpretation, as well as the entire dispute, points out a weakness of the binary approach to problems of naturalness, i.e., the evaluation of feature specifications in terms of U and M (or 0 and 1). I consider it not only possible but very likely that none of the three interpretations above is correct. The distinction is probably much subtler than that between "natural" and "deviant from greatest naturalness." Chomsky and Halle (1968: 412-13) have pointed out one case in which probably neither feature specification is unmarked, namely the specification of Coronality in anterior oral stops: They decided to specify both /p/ and /t/ for Coronality in the lexicon,[19] which implies that both segments are evaluated as [M coronal]. The situation may in part be comparable in the case of Voice in intervocalic obstruents, although the uncertainty in the three interpretations above, as well as the suggested dependence on systematic factors, indicates that a more than binary differentiation along the naturalness scale is involved.

Furthermore, all three interpretations fail to consider whether the naturalness of Voice in intervocalic obstruents may depend on additional specifications. It seems to me that spirants are more susceptible to this process than stops. And even within the two series, further differentiations are relevant. While there may be disagreement about [f] and [ƀ], and [x] and [g], there can be little doubt that [s] is more natural than [z], and even less so that [ð] is more natural than [θ] in intervocalic position. Intervocalic [s] occurs in many languages, both those that do and those that do not possess a [z]. On the other hand, while [θ] is rare in general, it is even more so in intervocalic position. In particular, there seem to be few, if any, languages with intervocalic [θ] not supported by intervocalic [ð].

How can the difference in naturalness between intervocalic [s] and [z] on one hand and [θ] and [ð] on the other be captured by markedness theory? It has been suggested (Vennemann 1968a: 222n) that the marked value of Stridency in dental spirants depends on Voice in the following way:

(20)

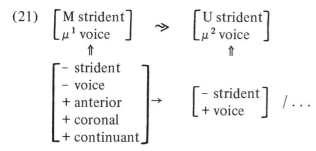

With a marking convention based on (20) (cf. Vennemann 1968a: 201), the change under consideration assumes the form (21).

(21)
$$\begin{bmatrix} \text{M strident} \\ \mu^1 \text{ voice} \end{bmatrix} \;\ni\; \begin{bmatrix} \text{U strident} \\ \mu^2 \text{ voice} \end{bmatrix}$$
$$\Uparrow \qquad\qquad\qquad \Uparrow$$
$$\begin{bmatrix} -\text{ strident} \\ -\text{ voice} \\ +\text{ anterior} \\ +\text{ coronal} \\ +\text{ continuant} \end{bmatrix} \rightarrow \begin{bmatrix} -\text{ strident} \\ +\text{ voice} \end{bmatrix} \; / \ldots$$

(21) explains why voicing of [θ] has a status different from that of other spirants: In the latter the question is one concerning Voice only, in the former voicing is actually a disguised unmarking of Stridency. Since Stridency is a higher feature in the hierarchy than Voice, the gain in Stridency naturalness makes (21) a D-rule independently of whether the change increases or decreases Voice naturalness.

I am now in a position to explain the Pre-OHG change of [ð] into [d]. Studied in the framework of the affected grammar, this change becomes a modification of the Proto-Germanic spirantization rule for voiced stops:

(22)
$$\begin{bmatrix} -\text{ sonorant} \\ +\text{ voiced} \end{bmatrix} \rightarrow [+\text{ continuant}] \; / \ldots$$

This rule is now restricted to non-coronal positions:

(23)
$$\begin{bmatrix} -\text{ sonorant} \\ -\text{ coronal} \\ +\text{ voiced} \end{bmatrix} \rightarrow [+\text{ continuant}] \; / \ldots$$

Although by no means certain (consider the extended substitution of [d] for [ð] in language acquisition, cf. Leopold 1947: 170), it is at least possible that (23) is a less natural rule than (22). The change from (22) to (23) is therefore in need of an explanation.

The D-rule nature of (21) provides this explanation: On the one hand, addition of (21) to the grammar would lead to a substantial merger of /θ/ and /d/; on the other, the positional unmarking of Stridency effected by (21) makes the addition of this rule highly desirable from the point of view of naturalness. The result is a compromise: (21) is added, but merger is prevented by a complication of (22). Although the modification of (22) is presupposed by the addition of (21), it is nevertheless a clear consequence of the latter.[20] We will later encounter a similar block of changes in which an entire rule is added to the grammar in order that a certain desirable change can take place without leading to merger, the reason being that the resulting grammar is more natural than the original one.

With the developments so far discussed, table (19) is transformed into (24), which is the phonetic obstruent system immediately before the specifically HG innovations began.

(24)

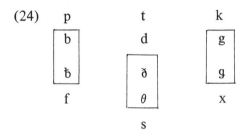

On the basis of this system, I will discuss the following consonantal developments of HG:

(25) (i) The High German Consonant Shift, i.e.:

> (a) The reflection of the Pre-OHG voiceless stops as geminate spirants postvocalically (single spirants in final position) but as affricates in initial, geminate, and postresonant positions (except for /t/ before /r/).
>
> (b) The reflection of Pre-OHG [b d g] as [p t k] and of [ƀ ǥ] as stops.

(ii) The change of Pre-OHG [θ ð] into [d].

(iii) The change of single Pre-OHG /s/ into [š] and [z] in complementary positions.

Nothing is known about the primum movens that caused these changes to take place. The literature trying to explain the HG CS is richer than that on any other problem of the history of German; it is, with its wealth of opposing views, self-defeating.[21] I abstain from a discussion of those attempts. Rather, I will make, without explanation, a minimal assumption which is, nevertheless, strong enough to derive the entire situation outlined in (25) by a series of assimilations and typological adjustments of D-rule nature.

The assumption made here is the affrication of the Pre-OHG voiceless stops.[22] It is minimal in the sense that it does not postulate intermediate stages such as gemination, aspiration, strengthening or weakening, or different causes for different environments. It also has the virtue of occurring as one step in a large number of otherwise quite different interpretations, ever since Braune (1874: 47–50) explained the geminate character of the resulting spirants through it. My assumption is not to imply that unconditioned affrication was at any time a rule of the grammar. I do not believe that a rule such as (26),

$$(26) \quad [\text{U delayed}] \quad \nrightarrow \quad [\text{M delayed}]$$
$$\Uparrow \qquad\qquad\qquad \Uparrow$$
$$\begin{bmatrix} - \text{ delayed} \\ - \text{ continuant} \\ - \text{ voice} \end{bmatrix} \rightarrow \begin{bmatrix} + \text{ delayed} \\ - \text{ continuant} \end{bmatrix}$$

which shifts an entire series—not counting some naturally exempted positions—can be part of a grammar,[23] just as I cannot accept the view that spirantization of all voiceless stops was ever a rule of Pre-Germanic. Since the affricates do not alternate with stops, there is no basis for deriving them from stops. Rather, they are represented as affricates in the lexicon. This follows from the principle that unless alternation requires a different analysis, the underlying representations of segments have to be identical with the phonetic representations (i.e., not counting certain low-level phonetic rules).[24] Wholesale affrication can at best have existed as a performance device of one generation (in the sense of Vennemann 1968b). A generation not exposed to the original stop articulation must do a lexical reanalysis of the new data perceived by them.

Assuming then that through some historical accident such affrication did occur, let us study the effects of this change on the system as a whole. According to principle (18), the change could not possibly occur without immediate consequences. Affrication alone would have resulted in a system in which the voiceless stops were represented solely in certain naturally neutralizing environments (in addition to the one sequence [tr]). The earliest documents from the dialect area where affrication was carried out in full generality already show spellings with *p t k* (or *c* for *k*) for Pre-OHG [b d g]. A series of voiced spirants presupposes both one of voiceless spirants and one of voiced stops. The unvoicing of the voiced stops, depriving the voiced spirants of one of their foundations, thus entails a further change, the interruption of the voiced spirants. The documents show *p k* for [ƀ ǥ] in Bavarian, *b g* in Alemannic (Braune/Mitzka 1967: § 88).

These changes, all of D-rule nature, are reflected in the resulting grammar not as added rules, but as modifications of lexical representations and of an existing rule: The underlying voiced stops became voiceless, and rule (23) was transformed into a stop voicing rule:

$$(27) \quad \begin{bmatrix} - \text{coronal} \\ - \text{delayed} \end{bmatrix} \rightarrow \quad [+ \text{voice}] \; / \ldots$$

In Bavarian it seems to have been given up altogether, probably after taking the form (27). It is likely, however, that the variability in the spelling only indicated slight positional differences in tenseness even for the time of the oldest documents (Braune/Mitzka 1967: § 88, note 3), which would mean that (23-27) was given up in all southern dialects. The uniform use of *pp tt kk* for Pre-OHG [bb dd gg], even after the spelling for nongeminate [p k] reverted to *b g* in all dialects, also points in the direction that degrees of tenseness, rather than a voiced: voiceless opposition, were indicated by the earlier differentiations.

A further argument in favor of the interpretation that surficial degrees of tenseness are the phonetic basis of the spelling fluctuations comes from a comparison of the representations in the different places of articulation. Even in the Bavarian documents, where *p* is used rather regularly for both Pre-OHG [b] and [ƀ], there is a preponderance of *k* (*c*) for Pre-OHG [g] above that for

Pre-OHG [g] . There is a plausible explanation to this observation. Certain isoglosses for shifted Pre-OHG /p/ reach considerably farther to the north than the corresponding ones for shifted /k/. This may indicate a temporal lag between /p/ affrication and /k/ affrication in certain positions even for a dialect area in which affrication has been carried out in full generality in both orders.[25] This would be no surprise. For although affrication is unnatural—a marked value—in both the velar and the labial order, it is even more so in the former than in the latter. This temporal lag would naturally entail a temporal lag also between the development of the labial voiced stops and spirants and that of the velar ones. This consequence is likely to have been reflected as a lag in tenseness adjustment, which in turn would then be responsible for the orthographical differences.

While the difference in spelling for the original voiced labials and velars thus seems to be one of degree rather than one in kind, the situation is much more severe for the dental order. Here we find no alternation between voiced and voiceless stops for original voiced stops and spirants in the documents of the southern dialects. Rather we find the spelling *t* throughout. Our first guess might be that this is the consequence of a more rapid spread of affrication in the dental order than in the other two. A more rapid spread of the dental affricate would be no surprise but rather a predictable development, because the voiceless dental affricate is considerably more natural than both the labial and velar ones, although all of them are segments marked for affrication and as such less natural in kind than the corresponding stops. The facts do indeed bear out our expectation: The dental affricate is found considerably farther north than both the labial and the velar ones.

However, I do not believe that this is a sufficient explanation of the uniform representation of Pre-OHG /d/ as *t* in the southern documents compared with the variability in the representations of /b/ and /g/. There must have been additional motivation to use the more consistent spelling for the new /t/ than for /p/ and /k/. Greater tenseness in the phonetic representation of /t/ would be such motivation. But why should there have been greater tenseness in the dental stop than in the others?

Table (24) shows that the dental segments in Pre-OHG were not only more numerous but also coordinated differently. The shifting of /b g/ did not create a situation in which further adjustments in their places of articulation could be predicted from general principles. In the dental place of articulation, on the other hand, there was at least one segment that was immediately affected by the change: [ð]. A phonological system containing /p t k/, and an [ð] independent of /t/, but no /b g/, no [ƀ ǥ], and no [d], is unknown to me. I doubt that it can exist: Principle (18) requires a series of voiced stops as a prerequisite for a series of voiced spirants, and this should also apply to the one-member series under consideration.

However, this situation is complicated by two factors. First, [ð] was, in Pre-OHG, in complementary distribution with [θ]. Secondly, [ð] occurred in positions where it could also be a variant of a /d/, as evidenced, for example, by Proto-Germanic, cf. (19), and Spanish. Clearly the system, containing [θ] and [ð] when it should really have a /d/, could not persist, but a change into [d] of [ð] alone was probably not a possible solution either.[26] Therefore, what is to be expected as the first step toward a solution is a voicing of [θ]. A general change of [θ] into [ð] is probably of D-nature, although this is less obvious than the case of the conditioned change (21).[27] However, even if it were not, there would be pressure enough in the system to bring about this change, because it made possible the tremendous decrease in complexity—entailing no mergers— which a total replacement of [θ] and [ð] by [d] represents.[28]

The documentary evidence supports this interpretation. The voicing of /θ/ in West Germanic had occurred only in medial position. But [d] replaces the earlier spirants first in final position (and after [n]), then in medial, and eventually in initial position (Braune/ Mitzka 1967: § 167, note 1). One document has đ throughout (§167, note 3), another has dh in all positions, with a number of d's occurring primarily in noninitial position (§167, note 4). The fact that usually th is employed to designate the spirant is no counterevidence. It is also used for the Old French voiced spirant (§167, note 4), and it occurs also medially, where voicing had taken place in Pre-OHG, not infrequently substituting for đ or dh (§167, notes 1-4).[29] In one document in which th and dh are used in a systematic way, the former occurs initially, the latter medially (§ 167, note 4). This need not indicate voiceless vs. voiced pronunciation, but may have been an attempt to capture orthographically the phonetic difference in tenseness which must have existed. It would thus parallel with the *p/b* and *k/g* spellings of Alemannic. Voicing of [θ], or lenition, or lenition in the south and voicing in the north, as an intermediate step during its change into /d/ is also generally accepted in the literature (e.g. Paul 1916: 107, Moulton 1954: 33, Hammerich 1955: 192, Braune/Mitzka 1967: § 166).

I am now in a position to explain why the new /t/ should have a more tense actualization than /p/ and /k/: When the older /d/ became voiceless as a consequence of the affrication of Pre-OHG /t/, it triggered the changes of [ð] and [θ] into [d] just described, which were well under way in the deepest south at the time of our earliest records. While /p/ and /k/ were the only phonological stops in their respective places of articulation, two distinct stops—one already established, the other just coming into existence as an allophonic variant of a spirant—had to be accommodated on the Voice-Tenseness scale.[30] Greater phonetic tenseness in the phonologically voiceless member is to be expected in this situation. It is also important that those positions where /p/ and /k/ had their laxer variants were among the first in which the new [d] developed. The variation in the labial and velar positions indicated by the *p/b* and *k/g* spellings could therefore not be paralleled in the dental region because this would have led to merger.[31]

I hope to have demonstrated that all the developments discussed so far are consequences of the initial change, affrication of the voiceless stops. They could be predicted on the grounds of principle (18) to happen in precisely the way that is evidenced in the records. Since there is, therefore, a causal nexus between all these changes, they must all have spread in the same direction. Most of them occurred in pre-documentary times, including even the general change of [θ] into [ð].[32] However, the last one, the change of [ð] into [d], developed in the full light of history, richly documented in all dialects: It spread from south to north. I conclude that the same is true of the entire CS.

This is indeed the generally accepted view.[33] However, the opposing view has also been proposed: first, implicitly, by Kluge (1909: 153-54), who doubts the southern origin of the HG CS because of certain problems posed by loan words (but cf. my note 25); by Kauffmann (1915), who assumes a northern origin of the postvocalic spirantization, and of the affrication of /t/ in all other positions, but a southern origin and northward spread of the labial and velar affricates (cf. in particular pp. 381-84, 386, 388-89); by Prokosch (1917), who assumes a spread of the CS from its "Ausgangspunkt im germanischen Stammlande zwischen Elbe und Oder . . . über das westliche und südliche Deutschland im Gleichschritt mit der deutschen Besiedlung dieses Landes . . . , überall bald nach der Germanisierung zum Stillstand kommend" (p. 4); and recently, with reference to Prokosch 1917, by Becker (1967: 61-64) and, based on Becker, by E. Bach (1968: 137-38) and in Emmon Bach and Robert T. Harms's contribution to this volume.

Becker's argument is based on the old concept of "sound change by rule change." Schuchardt, the discoverer of this mechanism, speaks of the "Metamorphose der Lautgesetze" (1885: 71). He does not specify whether such metamorphosis proceeds in the direction of specialization or generalization, although the examples he presents are cases of the latter (pp. 57, 71, 75) and are recognized by him as such ("Verallgemeinerung," p. 71). Kiparsky (1965 and 1968b), who introduced this concept into the generative model of phonological change, apparently without knowledge of Schuchardt's discovery, emphasizes the importance of generalization (i.e., rule simplification) but also allows for the possibility of specialization in the process of borrowing (1968b: 190).[34] Harms 1967: 172 says that one way in which sound change proceeds is through "the borrowing of rules (often in a more general form) from other related dialects."

Becker adopts this last view, which seems to settle the question about the direction in which the HG CS spread: It is more general in the south than in the north;[35] therefore, it must have spread from north to south. One must notice, however, that one of the three principles which Becker cites in support of the north-to-south hypothesis reads as follows: "Only under exceptional circumstances will a borrowed rule be less economical than the original rule upon which it is based" (Harms 1967: 173). Becker does not consider whether perhaps the circumstances are exceptional in the case of the HG CS. I believe that they are. The shift of the voiceless stops is of I-rule nature (cf. p. 240) above. Moreover, two of the resulting segments are among the rarest in the languages of the world: $[p^f]$ and $[k^x]$. It is hard to see why a rule shifting /p t k/ into [ff ss xx] postvocalically, and /t/ into $[t^s]$ in the remaining positions (these are the changes that cover the entire HG area), should generalize spontaneously as to produce these $[p^f \ k^x]$.[36] I have not studied this problem on a larger scale, but it seems to me that while it is generally true that rules tend to be simplified in the borrowing process, complication, i.e., specialization of a process, is possible in cases where the rule leads to highly marked segments.[37]

The situation becomes even more complicated if we consider that the HG CS, where it is carried out in full generality, was not a matter of an added rule at all but a remodeling of the segmental system, accompanied by changes in certain low-level rules. Little seems to be known about what happens when such a remodeled system and the unaltered one are in contact. Complete substitution of the new system for the old one appears least likely. One would rather expect the unshifted dialect to be infiltrated with shifted forms, the more natural substitutions being more easily accepted than less natural ones. All Pre-OHG dialects had segments to match the new affricates: [pf] for $[p^f]$, [ts] for $[t^s]$, [kx] for $[k^x]$. Medially after vowels, the two matching segments would be assigned to two different syllables. Here the borrowing process would begin, resulting first in a narrow rule. Paradigmatic alternation of bisyllabic with monosyllabic forms would be a basis for expanding the rule so as to cover all postvocalic voiceless stops. Next affrication in the remaining positions could be subsumed under the same rule, most easily in the dental region because $[t^s]$ is the least difficult of all the (nonpalatal) affricates, then with decreasing facility in the labial and velar regions. These rule generalizations were, in this interpretation, not spontaneous but occurred under the influence of the more strongly shifted neighboring dialects. The increasing degree of unnaturalness of the affricates in the three places of articulation explains the different extensions of the affrication areas. I leave this problem, but I should like to emphasize once more that the documented south-to-north movement of the change of [ð] (from [θ]) into [d] is the strongest theoretical support of the assumption that the entire CS spread in that direction.[38]

After the changes described so far, those dialects which had carried out the shift in full generality had the obstruent system (28), cf. (24) above.[39]

(28) p^f t^s k^x

p	t	k
(b)	d	(g)

    f   s   x

All these segments, except for the voiced ones, also occurred geminated.[40]

As already mentioned in (25ia), the reflexes of the shifted Pre-OHG voiceless stops in historic times are not simply affricates in all positions, but geminate spirants in postvocalic position and affricates elsewhere, i.e., in initial position, in post-resonant position, and in original geminate position; see table (29);

(29)

p				t				k			
#p	Rp	pp	Vp	#t	Rt	tt	Vt	#k	Rk	kk	Vk
p^f	p^f	pf	ff	t^s	t^s	ts	ss	k^x	k^x	kx	xx

The geminate character of the postvocalic spirants resulting from the shift follows from the fact that these spirants functioned like clusters in Middle High German, both in metrics, where they made a long syllable, and in the open syllable lengthening rule, where they kept short vowels short. The affricates deriving from geminate stops likewise kept short vowels short in the open syllable lengthening rule. This is the reason that I represent them as clusters in that position; see table (29). In the remaining positions the precise phonetic nature of the affricates is phonologically irrelevant. Therefore I represent them as affricates in those positions, although they may well be, or have been at one time, clusters there too.

I have mentioned earlier that following Braune (1874: 49—misrepresented in Braune/Mitzka 1967: §87, note 1), I interpret the bisegmental status of the new spirants, compared with the monosegmental status of the original voiceless stops, as a consequence of the substitution of, or development into, two heterosyllabic segments for each postvocalic affricate. In postvocalic position, geminates contrasted with single stops. This contrast was preserved when affrication and heterosyllabification took place. (The simultaneous existence of short and long affricates is postulated on documentary grounds in Steche 1939, especially pp. 141-43.)

Affricates are less natural than stops in the nonpalatal places of articulation.[41] Affricates are also less natural than spirants. This follows from Jakobson's typological and acquisitional universal of the unilateral foundation of the affricates on the spirants: The existence of affricates in a linguistic system presupposes the simultaneous existence of homorganic spirants in the same system.[42] The latter in turn presuppose homorganic stops (Jakobson 1941: 360-61). Every child acquiring German goes through a stage at which both affricates and spirants are reproduced as stops, and through a subsequent stage at which the affricates are reproduced as spirants. As a consequence, there have always been tendencies in German to alleviate the affricates by turning them into more natural sounds. Thus in some Swiss dialects we find initial [x] for older [k^x]. The change of initial [p^f] into [f] is widespread in the German dialects. In Northern German, the phonological contrast /t^s/:/s/ is frequently actualized as [s]:[z]. [p^f] was changed into [f] after liquids in OHG. There is no reason to believe that such tendencies are not as old as the HG CS itself.

In the case of the postvocalic affricates there was additional motivation to turn them into spirants: While affricates are unnatural per se, a length contrast in them is even more so. Thus the following two changes are well motivated:[43]

(30) (i) Spirantization

$$\begin{bmatrix} -\text{ continuant} \\ \alpha \text{ coronal} \\ \beta \text{ anterior} \\ -\text{ sonorant} \end{bmatrix} \rightarrow [+\text{continuant}] \;/\; V \underline{\hspace{1em}} \begin{bmatrix} \alpha \text{ coronal} \\ \beta \text{ anterior} \\ +\text{ continuant} \\ -\text{ sonorant} \end{bmatrix}$$

(ii) Affricate Alleviation

$$\begin{bmatrix} \alpha \text{ coronal} \\ \beta \text{ anterior} \\ -\text{ continuant} \\ -\text{ sonorant} \end{bmatrix} \quad \begin{bmatrix} \alpha \text{ coronal} \\ \beta \text{ anterior} \\ -\text{ continuant} \\ -\text{ sonorant} \end{bmatrix} \quad \begin{bmatrix} \alpha \text{ coronal} \\ \beta \text{ anterior} \\ +\text{ continuant} \\ -\text{ sonorant} \end{bmatrix}$$

$$\qquad 1 \qquad\qquad\qquad 1$$

Structure Change: 1 1 → 1

Both rules are D-rules. This is obvious for (30ii): Short consonants are more natural than long ones, and the change does not lead to merger. It is somewhat less direct in the case of (30i): Taken out of context, the change of a stop into a homorganic spirant is that of an unmarked value into a marked one. Within the given context, however, (30i) describes a case of assimilation resulting in a double spirant. We can assume that even a double (or long) spirant is more natural than an affricate. Therefore, we have for (30i) the following interpretation:

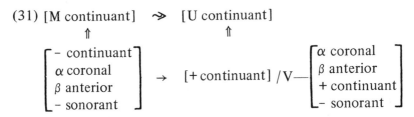

(31) [M continuant] ↝ [U continuant]

$$
\begin{bmatrix} - \text{continuant} \\ \alpha \text{ coronal} \\ \beta \text{ anterior} \\ - \text{sonorant} \end{bmatrix} \rightarrow [+ \text{continuant}] \, / \text{V}— \begin{bmatrix} \alpha \text{ coronal} \\ \beta \text{ anterior} \\ + \text{continuant} \\ - \text{sonorant} \end{bmatrix}
$$

The changes (30i, ii), as an A-rule and a T-rule (p. 240), are thus very plausible consequences of the affrication of the voiceless stops.

I turn now to the last problem connected with the HG CS, the development of the coronal spirants. Pre-OHG had both single and geminate *s*. These *s*-sounds did not merge with the new *s*-sound developing through the HG CS, neither where the new geminate *s* remained nor where it was simplified, as in final position and, later, after long vowels and diphthongs. Disregarding the change of *sk* into [š], which is not restricted to German, we find the following regular reflexes of Pre-OHG *s* and *ss* in the contemporary language (there is dialectal variation which I will ignore here):

(32) (i) *s* is [š] before consonants (in the Standard only initially), and usually after [r].

(ii) *s* is [z] elsewhere, except where general rules prohibit voice in obstruents, the obstruent cluster devoicing rule and the so-called final devoicing rule; in these positions *s* is [s].

(iii) *ss* is [s] (actually a case of (ii) because geminates are treated as clusters by the cluster devoicing rule and are simplified by a later general degemination rule).

Since [ss] from older /t/ and *ss* are kept distinct in the documents, and likewise single new [s] (occurring only after long vowels and in final position) and single old *s*, some qualitative difference between new and old *s*-sounds must have existed at the time when the new *s*-sound developed. Since the new [ss] is reflected as [s] throughout in the contemporary language while the old *s* has the development described in (32), it is safe to assume the contemporary (perhaps a slightly more dental) articulation for this new sound and a retracted point of articulation for *s*. A palatal, or semipalatal articulation is not only suggested by the positional development into [š] but also by transcriptions of foreign sibilants in OHG documents, cf. Braune/Mitzka 1967: §168: "palatal," "š-ähnlich," Schulze 1967: 1: "halbpalatal." Lessiak (1933: 77) writes: "Im Westgerm. wurde *s* vermutlich stark alveolar und mit weiterer Öffnung als unser nhd. *s* gebildet wie noch jetzt vorwiegend im Ndfrk., Nd. und Engl., was ihm akustisch ein mehr oder minder *š*-ähnliches Gepräge verleiht." The earlier view that *s* was voiced in OHG is rejected in the more recent literature. Moulton (1954: 37), "with an unhappy choice of symbol," writes /z/ for *s* but calls it a lenis spirant, qualitatively different from the new /ʒ/. He refers to Joos (1952), who distinguishes dorsal [s̲] (the new sibilant) from apical [ş] (the old sibilant), and compares them to the two non-palatal *s*-sounds of Basque (p. 373n). One may also think of retroflexion for *s*, which would essentially be in line with Joos's interpretation of *s* as apical. However, since none of the three reflexes of this segment is apical and since [š] is formed with wider contact than [s], it seems to me that both sibilants were dorsal (in Joos's sense) but that the difference was one of extent of contact: The inherited *s*-sound would be formed with extended contact, which would account both for its [š]-like quality and the dorsality of its reflexes. In the feature system of Chomsky and Halle 1968: 312–14 the new [s] would be [−distributed], the old *s* [+distributed].

I do not consider it necessary to assume the same pronunciation of the inherited *s* for Pre-OHG and for OHG, as in the quotation from Lessiak above. Pre-OHG had only one sibilant. It is, therefore, probable that some dialectal and positional variation existed. Such variation had, however, no function, and we must assume that phonologically *s* was an optimal obstruent, marked only for Continuance. Phonetically it cannot have differed greatly from optimal articulation either.

I assume that as the new [ss] developed, a slight allophonic difference became functional through the addition of rule (33).

(33)   [U distributed]   ⤳   [M distributed]

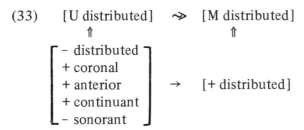

$$\begin{bmatrix} - \text{ distributed} \\ + \text{ coronal} \\ + \text{ anterior} \\ + \text{ continuant} \\ - \text{ sonorant} \end{bmatrix} \rightarrow \quad [+ \text{ distributed}]$$

(33) is an I-rule. I use the feature Distributed, but the I-rule nature of (33) would not change with any other feature substituting for this one. The important factor is that the underlying /s/ is changed from the most natural articulation to some less natural, and less stable, one. That the underlying status of /s/ did not change, i.e., that (33) remained a rule of the grammar, follows from two considerations: First, the new spirant remains phonologically an affricate; the phonetic contrast between *wissen* [visən], "know," and *Witz* [vitˢ], "wit," has remained the reflex of a phonological contrast between single and geminate affricate down to the contemporary language, while *weise* [vaizə], "wise," has phonological /s/ (even though in this particular case the /s/ may ultimately derive from the affricate of the other two words; cf. Vennemann 1968a: section I.2 and pp. 157-59). Secondly, the most natural coronal continuant is, to my knowledge, the dorsal dento-alveolar sibilant [s]. Since OHG did not have any other underlying coronal spirants, the old *s* must still have been /s/ phonologically, even though its phonetic actualization had changed.

The order of the spirantization rule (30i) and the I-rule (33) is, of course, that given in (34), where ṣ is an arbitrary symbol for the phonetic reflex of Pre-OHG /s/.

(34)   (i) Change of [s ss] into [ṣ ṣṣ] by (33).

(ii) Spirantization (30i), including the origin of new [ss], simplified to [s] in certain positions.

I believe nevertheless that the first rule is a consequence of the second, introduced to avoid merger of the old and new sibilants, which would otherwise come about as a consequence of the introduction of the spirantization rule.[44] The gain in system naturalness resulting from the spirantization of the affricates must have been greater than the loss resulting from the addition of rule (33). Phonological theory does not, to my knowledge, provide a formalism that would express such a close relationship between rules, called a rule block earlier in this paper. If it offered such a device— and there are indications that it should, because the instances presented in this paper are by no means singular cases—the concept of a D-rule could be extended so as to cover rule blocks. In particular, (34) would be interpreted as a D-block in this extended theory.

In Late Middle High German, the changing cluster /sk/ began to reach its present phonetic representation, [š] (Braune/Mitzka 1967: §146, Paul 1916: 347).[45] The language now had three strident coronal spirants, [s ṣ š], occurring in overlapping environments. All of them were voiceless, while a voice (or tenseness) contrast existed among the dental stops in all dialects, and in the central and northern HG dialects also in other places of articulation. The changes summarized in (32) and abbreviated in (35) are therefore not surprising.

(35) (i) $ṣ \rightarrow \check{s} / \ldots$

(ii) $ṣ \rightarrow z$

In certain positions, the voice change of (35ii) applied vacuously because voice was prohibited by overall principles. This applies to [ṣ] in clusters, including [ṣṣ], and in final position. Here [ṣ] simply merged with [s] from original /t/.

The positions where (35i) occurred and those where [š], from /sk/, already existed, are almost complementary; and [z] is a new segment in the language altogether. Furthermore, the unmarking of the feature Distributed was a greater gain in naturalness than the marking of new features was a loss, see (36).

Clearly both (36i) and (36ii) were changes of D-rule nature. They abolished a situation whose unnaturalness is indicated by the rareness of a twofold contrast among the strident coronal spirants in

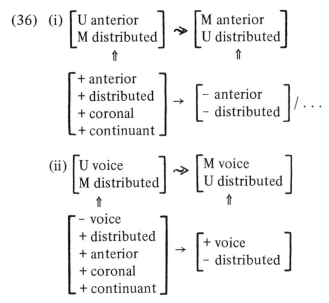

the languages of the world. The resulting grammar did not contain
(33) any longer, but had rules that changed /s/ directly into [š] and
[z], as is still the case in the contemporary language (cf. Vennemann 1968a: 111-31).

Summarizing this discussion of certain central consonantal developments of German, I have been able to explain a number of
dissimilar and apparently unrelated consonant changes as consequences of a single change of I-rule nature, affrication. Some of
the subsequent changes were recognized as dictated by linguistic
universals, while others could be shown in other ways to decrease
the phonological complexity of the system. This interpretation of
some central problems in historical German phonology was based
on the definition of segmental complexity in Chapter 9 of Chomsky and Halle 1968 with one modification: Whereas segmental
complexity in Chapter 9 is simply the *sum* of the marked values
of the segment, each M counting *one,* in my analysis it is the total
weight of the marked values. It seems obvious that a segment
marked for Murmur, Affrication, Glottalization, etc., is less natural
than one marked for Voice or Continuance. In other words, naturalness is a feature-dependent concept. This concept of "degree of
naturalness" or "weight complexity" is in part identical with the

hierarchy-of-features idea; in part it goes beyond it in that the weight complexity of a segment is to a great degree determined by its sequential environment and by the entire phonological system in which it functions. Since no metric for this concept of naturalness is at present available—even less so than a generally agreed upon feature hierarchy—this concept was used in an intuitive, non-formalized way: It was pointed out with references to the (scanty) literature on phonological universals or to common knowledge about phonological processes that the marking of certain given features under specified conditions weighed more than that of others under the same condition. The determination of an absolute metric remains an urgent task. In the framework of this theory I could elaborate a concept of rule plausibility: Given a phonological system, a D-rule is a change that decreases the weight complexity of the system without leading to unconditioned, or to excessive conditioned, merger. In simple cases, such a rule will change segments marked for a certain feature into the corresponding unmarked ones. However, more subtle examples of natural rules were discussed. E.g., the change of [θ] into [ð] was shown to be a change in Stridency at the interpretive level, disguised as a Voice change at the rule level; the unmarking of Stridency decreases the weight complexity of a system more than the marking of Voice increases it.

One assumption was implicitly made in this interpretation of consonantal developments in German: I-rules usually require an explanation by some external cause, usually borrowing. By contrast, both the assimilatory and the typological adjustment types of D-rules do not require any special explanation but are universally available for internal change. An example is the change of [θ] and [ð] into [d]. This was a D-change in HG, but not in Low German, where it led to merger with the inherited /d/. Characteristically, this change originated in HG and was borrowed by Low German.

Attention was drawn to one exception to this hypothesis about I-rules: A change functioning as a precondition for a certain D-change can originate system-internally if the two rules form a D-block, i.e., if the joint effect of the changes is a reduction of the weight complexity of the system.

It is tempting to propose hypotheses about the synchronic role of D-rules and I-rules, e.g., that only I-rules contribute to the complexity of a grammar, while D-rules do not add to (but perhaps subtract from) the complexity of a grammar. I will not follow this temptation, because much too little is known about the evaluation of grammars. However, I hope to have shown that some refined concept of segmental and sequential naturalness must play an important role in the evaluation of the phonological component of a grammar.

I would like to express my thanks for the valuable criticisms presented during the discussion of my paper at the conference, especially by Victoria Fromkin and Emmon Bach. These criticisms have led to a thorough revision of the original paper. I am cheerfully anticipating a second round of this stimulating disputation.

NOTES

1. Cf. Halle 1961 and, for application of this concept in various fields of phonological investigation, Halle 1964 (Introduction and Section I: definition of phonological simplicity; Sections II and VI: simplicity and the ordering of phonological rules; Section III: simplicity and lexical redundancy; Section IV: simplicity and lexical admissibility; Section VII: simplicity and the acquisition of phonology; Section VIII: simplicity and the addition of phonological rules; Section IX: simplicity and relative chronology of phonological changes; Section XI: simplicity and contrasting representations of phonetically identical segments). For recent discussion cf. Chomsky and Halle 1968 (see subject index s.v. "Evaluation procedure"), in particular the critique on pp. 400–402. For additional suggestions cf. E. Bach 1968. Cf. also the contributions to this volume by Emmon Bach and Robert T. Harms and by Sanford A. Schane.

2. Cf. Postal 1968 (Section 8 and the cross-references given there), Chomsky and Halle 1968 (Chapter nine). Kiparsky 1968b suggests the new concept of natural rule order ("marked and unmarked order," p. 200). Lakoff (1968) uses considerations of naturalness in his analysis of Grimm's Law. Lightner (1968a) analyzes a problem of Russian phonology in terms of markedness, and Lightner (1968b) the reduced final vowel of English (pp. 51–52) and consonant cluster and consonant onset and offset unvoicing (pp. 52–56). A brief introduction to the concept of markedness is given in Bierwisch 1967: 29-30. Schane (1968) demonstrates how the concept of markedness provides a basis for unique representations of segments of nonalternating forms in neutralization positions. For an application of markedness to the description of infant vocalization see Gruber 1966.

3. The most comprehensive collection of phonological universals known to me is in Jakobson 1939 and 1941. Jakobson's work is referred to in all three works mentioned in note 2. Some more recent studies of phonological universals not specifically cited in Postal 1968 or Chomsky and Halle 1968 are:

Jakobson 1958, 1962a (especially p. 655), Greenberg 1966b, Greenberg 1966c (parts of the memorandum and of Chapters 1-4, 9; cf. also the bibliography), Greenberg 1966a (Chapters 1, 2, 4), and a typological study using Jakobson 1941 as a frame of reference, Milewski 1953. The first application of Jakobson 1941 to a historical problem is Velten 1944.

4. Chomsky and Halle 1968: 402. The theory of phonological features is presented most fully in Jakobson, Fant, and Halle 1952, Jakobson and Halle 1956, and Chomsky and Halle 1968 (Chapter 7 and passim). The feature system of Chomsky and Halle 1968 is used in the present paper.

5. Since "blank" has no function in this system, either in description or in evaluation, it can be employed to indicate "unmarked." This notational convention is used for the purpose of optical clarity in Vennemann 1968a. It is implicit in the practice of omitting from descriptions all features that would otherwise occur only with the specification U (cf. Chomsky and Halle 1968: 403).

6. Cf. Jakobson 1941: 363-64, 368, Chomsky and Halle 1968: 407. This markedness relationship between [s] and [θ] is probably the same in all contexts. It is conceivable, however, that under certain assimilatory conditions, e.g., before [θ], the relationship is the opposite. In this case the example would have to be qualified accordingly.

7. Chomsky and Halle 1968: 419 leave nasals before stops unmarked for place of articulation. Like all unmarked nasals, such a nasal will then be specified as [n] by two of the marking conventions. A phonological rule finally assimilates such [n]'s to nondental stops where applicable. I am not sure that this interpretation of nasal assimilation is correct. It works for languages in which nasal assimilation occurs not only within morphemes but also across boundaries. It seems interesting in this connection that Chomsky and Halle develop their ideas about the naturalness of nasals from such examples as *concord* [káŋkərd] : *concordance* [kankɔ́rdəns]. However, take a language that has nasal assimilation only inside the morpheme. (Literary German is such a language, if we disregard certain lexical alternations of apparently marginal importance, e.g., the change in *Schande*, "disgrace," cf. *Scham*, "shame," and the idiosyncratic assimilation of [t] in the prefix *ent* into [p] before [f], which entails the expected nasal assimilation. Notice that pronunciations like [ha:bm] *haben*, "have," and [aŋkomm] *ankommen*, "arrive," belong to colloquial varieties of German.) The assumption of a language-specific nasal assimilation rule would clearly be wrong in the case of such a language. Rather I assume, deviating from Chomsky and Halle's conventions, that the place of articulation features of nasals before obstruents are interpreted in the lexicon *with reference to those of the obstruents* by universal rules, at no evaluational cost to the particular grammar. It seems to me that this was Chomsky and Halle's original idea when they compared the nasal assimilation rule with a less natural but "simpler" rule on p. 401. However, when their particular markedness formalism turned out not to be suited to account for rule naturalness, they abandoned their own well-put problems. I will return to the nasal assimilation rule directly.

8. Cf. Emmon Bach and Robert T. Harms's contribution to this volume for a number of further arguments against the mechanism of linking.

9. As always in discussions of naturalness, the argument behind this statement is in part circular, because the detail under consideration (here: final obstruent devoicing) is always among the evidence for the general principle quoted. Notice, however, that there is strong independent motivation to consider [-voice] as [U voice] in final obstruents: Languages without a voice contrast have the voiceless variants of obstruents in word final position, and children split their voiceless obstruents into pairs of voiceless and voiced members later in final position than anywhere else in the word.

10. Schacter says, "It is fairly easy to find *common* assimilatory processes not accounted for by the proposals made" and gives as an example point of articulation assimilation of nasals in pre-obstruent position (p. 27). It seems to me that a distinction between point of articulation and manner of articulation assimilation is important here. The former aims at identity of feature values, irrespective of whether they are + or −, M or U. The latter tends to specify both segments as + (with the notable exception of Voice in obstruent clusters), i.e., a certain manner of articulation property tends to spread rather than be given up. Notice that + is the marked value of manner of articulation features, though not in all contexts. Also a preferred direction principle plays an important role in both types of assimilation, but in the former more than in the latter: Properties tend to be anticipated in earlier segments more strongly than to be carried into following ones. (A notable exception: Murmur (cf. Ladefoged 1967: 9-10), which Chomsky and Halle (1968: 326) interpret as Heightened Subglottal Pressure combined with Voice and absence of Tenseness, spreads to the following segments; witness the absence of a murmur contrast in vowels after murmured consonants in Gujerati (Ladefoged 1967: 10) and Bartholomae's Law.) Some assimilation processes are in direct conflict with Schachter's universal (they may indeed be unnatural cases): E.g., nasals can become oral stops both before (Icelandic, Gordon 1962: 282-83) and after oral stops (Germanic, Prokosch 1939: 69-71). It seems to me that Schachter's convention is too complicated formally (with N and m rather than α and +) and at the same time not sufficiently differentiated materially.

11. Schachter 1969: 13 similarly suggests that N's in structural changes of rules not be counted.

12. At least this is true if the Chomsky-Hallean marking conventions are correct (pp. 404-407), which need only to be applied in the reverse order and from right to left in order to lead from (7) to (8). In the given order, they would develop a lexical item

$$+ \begin{bmatrix} \text{M segment} \\ \text{M anterior} \end{bmatrix} \begin{bmatrix} \text{M segment} \\ + \text{back} \end{bmatrix} +$$

into (7). (Chomsky and Halle consider both the back and the front vowels in the non-low range as marked.) More precisely speaking, the conventions would specify the /u/ as tense, because [U tense] in vowels is [+ tense] according to convention (XII), p. 405 (but cf. the authors' caveat on p. 409). It seems to me that convention (XII) applies only to languages without a distinctive tense-ness contrast in vowels, but that in languages with such a contrast, [U tense] is [– tense]. German does have such a contrast, even though it may be formal-ly preferable to describe it in terms of single vs. double vowels (cf. Venne-mann 1968a: 304n). My use of a feature Long in (7) and (8) is intended only to obviate a direct conflict with convention (XII).

13. Theodore Lightner reported such a change for Arabic at the conference.

14. Emmon Bach and Robert T. Harms's contribution to this volume shows that an increase of rule simplicity.*can* lead to a decrease of rule plausibility. Generally, however, rule simplification seems to be heavily controlled by con-ditions of naturalness. This applies to both segmental environments, as in the example above, and sequential environments: E.g., an unrestricted umlaut rule would be impossible. The following example shows that considerations of plausibility can prevent rule simplification in very subtle ways (cf. Venne-mann 1968a: 333-38, especially 334n). In German, a final /ə/ is lost in cer-tain grammatical classes, but only after segments without nonspontaneous voice, i.e., after sonorants and voiceless obstruents (cf. Chomsky and Halle 1968: 301 for the concept of nonspontaneous voice). After voiced obstruents, /ə/ is retained: compare *Gebüsch* [–š], "bushes," *Gewürm* [–m], "worms," with *Gebirge* [–gə], "mountain range." This rule has been transmitted unsim-plified by several generations. The only conceivable motivation prohibiting elimination of this apparently crazy condition seems to be that without it a root-final voice contrast would be neutralized in these categories through final devoicing. I have noted earlier that "fear of merger" seems to be a factor in the evaluation of rules.

15. I will discuss the difficulties of this interpretation in a different place. For a preliminary version of this discussion, cf. Vennemann 1969.

16. Postal (1968: 178-79) suggests the principle that if in any environment the marked value of a certain feature occurs in some morphemes, then there must occur morphemes in which the unmarked value of that feature occurs in the same environment—"unless there is a special rule to change the values." If care is taken that no rules are allowed in a grammar that shift an entire series from unmarked to marked status, this principle is in accordance with (18), i.e., it excludes all grammars that are ruled out by (18). It is, however, a stronger restriction than (18), because it excludes systems with U-holes not caused by rules. If such systems can be shown not to exist, the two principles become equivalent. (Proto-Indo-European /b/ seems to be a case in question. Judging from the merger of the so-called voiced aspirates with the voiced stops in a number of Indo-European languages, these two series are the marked and unmarked segments with respect to a certain feature. Now b^h was a fre-quent segment while b was very infrequent and possibly not represented at all at an early stage (Lehmann 1955: 109, 112). There is no evidence that /b/ existed at the lexical level and was changed by rule into a phonetically differ-ent segment.)

17. Braune/Mitzka 1967: §81. Where no other references are given, the date used in section 2 are taken from this book.

18. I cannot accept the "majority view" (Moulton 1954: 1, 38; cf. Lehmann 1962: 88, A. Bach 1965: §30) that at one stage in its development, Germanic had a phonetic series of voiced spirants (reflexes of the so-called voiced aspirates of Proto-Indo-European as well as of PIE /p t k/ under Verner's Law), but no voiced stops. According to principle (18), a series of voiced spirants presupposes both a series of voiced stops and a series of voiceless spirants. Therefore, voiced stops must have existed even among the earliest Germanic reflexes of the so-called voiced aspirates. Nor can I accept the view that the Germanic nonstrident voiced obstruents were structurally, or phonemically, a series of voiced spirants, with or without stop allophones (Lehmann 1953: 146, 1963: 233), because this view too is in conflict with principle (18). One of the arguments that have been proposed in support of the majority view, the positional merger of the reflexes of the PIE voiceless stops with those of the PIE so-called voiced aspirates (Moulton 1954: 38-39), is actually quite irrelevant to the question: Since both series of reflexes were voiced spirants in the positions susceptible to Verner's alternation at one time in history, they merged. This does not strengthen or weaken either of the two views. This merger assigned those [b̃ ð g̃] originating under Verner's Law which were not alternants of [f θ x] to the series /b d g/, because [b̃ ð g̃] were the unconditioned actualizations of /b d g/ in the sequential positions where Verner's Law operated. Therefore, after the merger, Verner's rule was restricted in its application to forms containing [b̃ ð g̃] that were paradigmatically related to such with [f θ x], and to forms with [z]. The only effects of the accent fixing were thus the changing of Verner's rule from a phonetically conditioned rule into a morphologically conditioned rule, and the changing into underlying segments of those [z]'s which were not paradigmatic alternants of /s/. (For a different view, cf. Lehmann 1961: 69-70, 74.)

19. Jakobson 1941: 391 compares the unilateral foundation of [f] on [s] with the ambilateral foundation of [p] and [t]: [f] presupposes [s], [p] and [t] presuppose each other. This difference is captured by Chomsky and Halle's markedness interpretation. Cf. Postal 1968: 174n for some discussion.

20. Moulton 1954: 21n considers this possibility for Pre-Old English but rejects it. He gives two reasons: "First, the change of [ð] to [d] presumably occurred before the Anglo-Saxon migration from the continent, since it is common to all the WGmc. dialects; whereas the voicing of medial voiceless spirants was apparently not completed at the time of our earliest OE documents . . . . Secondly, final [ð] became a stop just like medial [ð], even though final [þ] did not become voiced and thereby push [ð] into becoming a stop." Neither argument gives counterevidence to the assumption of modification of (22) plus addition of (21) also for Pre-Old English. First, there is no reason to believe that voicing occurred simultaneously in all Pre-Old English spirants; it is, on the contrary, more likely that voicing started in the segment for which the motivation to become voiced was the greatest, and that rule (21) was later

generalized in Old English (but not in OHG) so as to cover all spirants. Secondly, there is no reason to believe that the environment of the "push chain" have to coincide. The most straightforward way to prevent merger by addition of (21) was the change from (22) to (23); restriction of this modification to non-final position would only have resulted in a still more complicated rule.

21. Cf. Penzl 1964: 30-31 and passim for a brief presentation of some explanations of the HG CS, and Braune/Mitzka 1967: §§83-88 and especially A. Bach 1965: §§57-59 for discussion of a variety of views accompanied by a large number of references. The most likely interpretation within the model of phonological change proposed by Schuchardt (1885) and the generative grammarians would be that an original limited change, e.g., $t \rightarrow t^s$ in initial position, as in some varieties of Danish, was generalized to other positions and other stops until full generality was reached.

22. The so-called exceptions to this change (no affrication after spirants, no affrication of /t/ before /r/) are, of course, not exceptional at all. It would, on the contrary, be amazing if affrication had taken place in these cases.

23. For a different theoretical position cf. Vennemann 1968a: 206, 211.

24. This position has been convincingly advocated in Postal 1968: 53-77, and Kiparsky 1968a.

25. There is no direct evidence for any particular sequence in which affrication was carried out in the different places of articulation in pre-documentary times. In particular, there is no evidence from loan words. Earlier attempts to determine "Lautverschiebungsphasen" on this basis have been invalidated by more recent research (Cf. Penzl 1964: 34-36 and the references given there.)

26. The question of what the lexical representation of such a distribution could be is difficult to answer. /d/ would be optimal from the point of view of lexical economy, but a rule changing /d/ into [θ] in the positions where [θ] actually occurred would be a phonological monstrosity. A lexical /θ/, in the absence of both /ð/ and /d/, but with a positional variant [d], does not appear any more likely.

27. Strong support for the view that [ð] is more natural than [θ] in *all* positions comes from language acquisition. While [ð] occurs sporadically as early as the beginning of the third year and is usually used regularly early in the fourth, children acquiring English tend to have great difficulty with [θ] up to the age of five to seven years. Cf. Leopold 1947: 170 (especially the references in fn. 63).

28. The general voicing of [θ] would in this case be a *prelude* (in the sense in which Sanford A. Schane uses this word in his contribution to this volume) to the main objective of the development under consideration, the change of [ð] into [d]. Using a term introduced earlier in this paper and discussed further below, the two rules would form a block, specifically a D-block because the resulting grammar is more natural than the earlier one.

29. "Durch *dh* sowohl als *đ* wird zweifellos der Lenisspirant bezeichnet: diesen muss auch *th* ahd. wohl meist schon ausdrücken, da es unmittelbar durch *d* abgelöst wird" (Braune/Mitzka 1967: §166). Braune (1874: 55n) considered *th* as always representing a voiced sound.

30. The Voice-Aspiration scale has been studied in Lisker and Abramson 1964 and 1965 and Ladefoged 1967: 5-9, where (degree of) Voice and (degree of) Aspiration are interpreted as the timing of the onset of vocal cord vibration relative to the release of the stricture. I am not aware of similar experimental studies for Tenseness.

31. As a matter of fact, it is almost certain that the tenseness of /t/ was greater in noninitial than in initial position—just the opposite of the situation in the other two places of articulation. Those documents which indicate for older [θ] and [ð] a preponderance of spirant articulation in initial position but of stop articulation noninitially typically have a preponderance of *d* spellings for /t/ in initial position but of *t* spellings noninitially. (Cf. Braune/Mitzka 1967: §163.)

32. *"Wann* dies [the change of [θ] into [ð], T.V.] eintrat, kann nicht ergründet werden" (Braune/Mitzka 1967: §166). Moulton 1954: 33n correctly rejects Lessiak's view (1933: 24, 130) connecting the general voicing of [θ] with the (earlier and) later cases of spirant voicing. In particular, there is absolutely no basis for the statement made in Braune/Mitzka 1967: §102a that the change of [θ] into [ð] spread from north to south, beginning in the eighth century, even if it were correct that the lenition of /f/, etc., spread in this direction, which is not Lessiak's view. Notice that this statement is in conflict with the quotation at the beginning of this note.

33. There are interpretations which do not conceive of the HG CS in terms of spread at all. Heinertz 1957: 387-90 explains the gradation of the shifting as a consequence of differences in the density of a Celtic substratum population: "Je zahlreicher die Urbewohner, um so kräftiger die Veränderungen" (p. 390). Although I would not object to the hypothesis that the ultimate cause of affrication is a reinterpretation of part the Pre-OHG obstruent system on the basis of some non-Germanic language in a peripheral substratum area, I do not believe that there is any need for Heinertz' proportion hypothesis: Spreading of linguistic innovations is too common a phenomenon to justify such a strong assumption. Also Höfler 1955/56, 1957 does not believe in a spreading of the HG CS, or of any phonological innovation for that matter. Rather, he views phonological change as the effect of parallel developmental tendencies existing independently in related dialects. It is thus comparable to the onset of beard growth in a class of boys of identical age, where it would be equally misleading to speak of a spreading of this change from one student to the next (1955/56, 77: 33). Amazingly enough, this theory of sound change has found serious attention with a number of well-known scholars. (Cf. A. Bach 1965: §59d for discussion and references.)

34. Kiparsky's (1968b) footnote on p. 190 which says that Emmon Bach has pointed out to him the uncertainty of his examples (which include the HG CS) was not in the version of the paper to which Becker's criticism is addressed.

35. As a matter of fact, it is carried out in maximal generality in the south. This by itself should be puzzling to Becker: Why was complete generality of the shift reached precisely in the extreme south?

36. The language has been struggling to get rid of these unnatural sounds ever since they originated. Both $[p^f]$ and $[k^x]$ have been widely changed into spirants, a process which is evident already in OHG documents. $[k^x]$ has also given way to tense $[k]$ in its northern area (Braune/Mitzka 1967: §144, note 4; Lessiak 1933: 165-67; Prokosch 1917: 23). If one conceives of the CS as produced by rules even in the contemporary dialects, as Becker does, he must interpret the deaffrication of $[k^x]$ as a change of a rule environment from [+ obstruent, − continuant, + tense] to [+ obstruent, − continuant, + tense, − compact] (cf. Becker 1967: 59), i.e., as a case of rule complication, or specialization. Although this is not, properly speaking, a case of rule borrowing but rather of a spread of a rule complication, it is nevertheless problematic for Harms's and Becker's hypothesis.

37. So far, the fact that the umlaut rule, which also created more highly marked segments, was narrowed down in scope as it spread southward has never been challenged—except, of course, for Höfler 1955/56, who does not explain umlaut through rule borrowing at all, cf. my note 33. (Cf. Paul/Mitzka 1966: § 41.) (It has been and is being challenged, as I was to learn after the conference; cf. Antonsen 1969.)

38. The use of the terms south-to-north and north-to-south here and in the cited works must not be taken literally. What is meant is the spread from dialects with more extensive shifting to those with less extensive shifting, wherever the dialects were located at the time of the changes. Thus, the spread of the CS from Bavarian to Langobardic, where the shift was incomplete in documentary times (cf. Naumann and Betz 1962: 32-33), would be a south-to-north development. Note that the change of $[\theta]$ into $[ð]$ and ultimately $[d]$ could not spread to Langobardic because $[\theta]$ here was replaced by $[t]$, probably as a consequence of the progressive Romanization of the Lombards (Braune/Mitzka 1967: 167).

39. Except for [p b] and [k g], which have become independent segments (cf. Paul 1916: 261-76, 291-307) for the history of this split), (28) is the system used in Vennemann 1968a. Without the parentheses and boxes, it represents the underlying obstruent system of Contemporary Standard German.

40. The rare $[\theta\theta]$ had developed into [dd], together with $[\theta]$, and changed further into [tt] in OHG times, merging with [tt] from older [dd]. (Cf. Braune/Mitzka 1967: §167, note 10.)

41. The opposite is true in the palatal region, cf. Postal 1968: 191, Chomsky and Halle 1968: 406, 412.

42. Jakobson 1941: 360, 364. Cf. Postal 1968: 189-91.

43. If the geminate affricates are interpreted as bisegmental, rule (30ii) assumes the following shape:

$$\begin{bmatrix} \alpha \text{ coronal} \\ \beta \text{ anterior} \\ + \text{ delayed} \\ - \text{ sonorant} \end{bmatrix} \rightarrow [+ \text{ continuant}] \ / \ \begin{bmatrix} \alpha \text{ coronal} \\ \beta \text{ anterior} \\ - \text{ delayed} \\ - \text{ sonorant} \end{bmatrix} \underline{\quad\quad}$$

This rule too describes a case of affricate alleviation.

44. Inherited /ff/ and /xx/ are extremely rare (Braune/Mitzka 1967: §139, note 4 and §148, note 7). They simply merged with the new geminate spirants. In final position, a tenseness contrast must have existed between the old and new noncoronal spirants in the oldest period, as is still the case in very conservative dialects (Moulton 1954: 36n). Therefore, no special precautions were necessary in these two places of articulation as opposed to the dental one.

45. Phonologically, [š] has remained /sk/ in prevocalic positions down to the contemporary language (Vennemann 1968a: 117-31). This explains a phenomenon which had to remain a puzzle to Hermann Paul: "Auffallend aber ist, dass noch in Lehnwörtern jüngerer Zeit romanisches *sc* zu *sch* geworden ist: *Schachtel* aus it. *scatola, Scharmützel* aus it. *scaramuccio, Scharteke,* woneben anhd. *scarteke. Schöps* stammt aus tschechisch *skopec*" (1916: 352). The heard [sk]'s were simply subsumed under existing rules and actualized as [š]. (A similar origin can be assumed for the [ö] in *Schöps*.) Cf. Vennemann 1968a: 181n for a further example of segmental adaptation by means of phonological rules.

REFERENCES

Antonsen, Elmer H. 1969. Southern German forms without umlaut. Paper presented at the 22nd University of Kentucky Foreign Language Conference, Lexington, April 24-26.

Bach, Adolf. 1965. *Geschichte der deutschen Sprache,* 8th ed. Heidelberg: Quelle und Meyer.

Bach, Emmon. 1968. Two proposals concerning the simplicity metric in phonology. *Glossa* 2: 128-49.

Becker, Donald Allan. 1967. Generative phonology and dialect studies: an investigation of three Modern German dialects. University of Texas at Austin dissertation.

Bierwisch, Manfred. 1966. *Strukturalismus: Geschichte, Probleme und Methoden.* Kursbuch, no. 5. Hans Magnus Enzensberger, ed., pp. 77-152. Frankfurt am Main: Suhrkamp.

———. 1967. Skizze der generativen Phonologie. *Studia Grammatica VI: Phonologische Studien,* pp. 7-33. Berlin: Akademie-Verlag.

Braune, Wilhelm. 1874. Zur kenntnis des fränkischen und zur hochdeutschen Lautverschiebung. *Beiträge zur Geschichte der deutschen Sprache und Literatur* (Tübingen) 1: 1-56.

———. 1967. *Althochdeutsche Grammatik,* 12th ed. Walther Mitzka, ed. Sammlung kurzer Grammatiken germanischer Dialekte, A. Hauptreihe, 5. Tübingen: Max Niemeyer.

Chomsky, Noam. 1964. *Current Issues in Linguistic Theory.* Janua Linguarum, Series Minor, 38. The Hague: Mouton, 2nd printing, 1966.

———. 1965. *Aspects of the Theory of Syntax.* Cambridge: M.I.T. Press.

———. 1966. *Topics in the Theory of Generative Grammar.* Janua Linguarum, Series Minor, 56. The Hague: Mouton.

Chomsky, Noam, and Morris Halle. 1968. *The Sound Pattern of English*. New York: Harper and Row.

Gorden, E. V. 1962. *An Introduction to Old Norse,* 2nd ed. Revised by A. R. Taylor. Oxford: Clarendon Press.

Greenberg, Joseph H. 1966a. *Language Universals: With Special Reference to Feature Hierarchies.* Janua Linguarum, Series Minor, 59. The Hague: Mouton.

——. 1966b. Synchronic and diachronic universals in phonology. *Language* 42: 508-17.

——. 1966c. *Universals of Language,* 2nd ed. Report of a conference held at Dobbs Ferry, N.Y., April 13-15, 1961. Cambridge: M.I.T. Press.

Gruber, J. S. 1966. Playing with distinctive features in the babbling of infants. *Quarterly Progress Report* of the Research Laboratory of Electronics, M.I.T., no. 81, pp. 181-86.

Halle, Morris. 1961. On the role of simplicity in linguistic descriptions. *Structure of Language and Its Mathematical Aspects. Proceedings of Symposia in Applied Mathematics,* vol. XII, Roman Jakobson, ed., pp. 89-94. Providence, R.I.: American Mathematical Society.

——. 1964. Phonology in generative grammar. *The Structure of Language: Readings in the Philosophy of Language,* Jerry A. Fodor and Jerrold J. Katz, eds., pp. 334-52. Englewood Cliffs, N.J.: Prentice-Hall. Reprinted (with slight modifications mainly in the ninth section) from *Word* 18: 54-72 (1962).

Hammerich, L. L. 1955. Die germanische und die hochdeutsche Lautverschiebung. *Beiträge zur Geschichte der deutschen Sprache und Literatur* (Tübingen) 77: 1-29, 165-203.

Harms, Robert T. 1967. Split, shift and merger in the Permic vowels. *Ural-Altaische Jahrbücher* 39: 163-98.

Heinertz, N. Otto. 1957. Zwei Probleme der althochdeutschen Sprachgeschichte. *Moderna Språk* 51: 385-97.

Höfler, Otto. 1955/56. Stammbaumtheorie, Wellentheorie, Entfaltungstheorie. *Beiträge zur Geschichte der deutschen Sprache und Literatur* (Tübingen) 77: 30-66, 424-76; 78: 1-44.

——. 1957. Die Zweite Lautverschiebung bei Ostgermanen und Westgermanen. *Beiträge zur Geschichte der deutschen Sprache und Literatur* (Tübingen) 79: 161-350.

Jakobson, Roman. 1939. Les lois phoniques du langage enfantin et leur place dans la phonologie générale. In Jakobson 1962b, pp. 317-27.

——. 1941. Kindersprache, Aphasie und allgemeine Lautgesetze. In Jakobson 1962b, pp. 328-401. Page numbers refer to this edition. Translated as: *Child Language, Aphasia and Phonological Universals,* by Allan R. Keiler, Janua Linguarum, Series Minor, 72. The Hague: Mouton, 1968.

——. 1958. Typological studies and their contribution to historical comparative linguistics. In Jakobson 1962b, pp. 523-32.

——. 1962a. Retrospect. In Jakobson 1962b, pp. 631-58.

——. 1962b. *Selected Writings I: Phonological Studies.* The Hague: Mouton.

[Jakobson, Roman.] 1968. *Studies Presented to Professor Roman Jakobson by His Students.* Charles E. Gribble, ed. Cambridge, Mass.: Slavica Publishers.

Jakobson, Roman, C. Gunnar M. Fant, and Morris Halle. 1952. *Preliminaries to Speech Analysis: The Distinctive Features and Their Correlates.* Cambridge: M.I.T. Press.

Jakobson, Roman, and Morris Halle. 1956. *Fundamentals of Language.* Janua Linguarum, Series Minor, 1. The Hague: Mouton.

Joos, Martin. 1952. The medieval sibilants. *Language* 28: 222-31. Reprinted in *Readings in Linguistics,* Martin Joos, ed., 3rd ed., pp. 372-78. New York: American Council of Learned Societies, 1963. My page number refers to the reprint.

Kauffmann, Friedrich. 1915. Das Problem der hochdeutschen Lautverschiebung. *Zeitschrift für deutsche Philologie* 46: 333-93.

Kiparsky, Paul. 1965. Phonological change. M.I.T. dissertation.

———. 1968a. How abstract is phonology? M.I.T., dittoed.

———. 1968b. Linguistic universals and linguistic change. *Universals in Linguistic Theory,* Emmon Bach and Robert T. Harms, eds., pp. 170-202. New York: Holt, Rinehart and Winston.

Kluge, Friedrich. 1909. Gotische Lehnworte im Althochdeutschen. *Beiträge zur Geschichte der deutschen Sprache und Literatur* (Tübingen) 35: 124-60.

Ladefoged, Peter. 1967. Linguistic phonetics. *Working Papers in Phonetics,* 6. Phonetics Laboratory, University of California, Los Angeles.

Lakoff, George. 1968. Phonological restructuring and Grimm's Law. In Jakobson 1968, pp. 168-79.

Lehmann, Winfred P. 1953. The conservatism of Germanic phonology. *Journal of English and Germanic Philology* 52: 140-52.

———. 1955. *Proto-Indo-European Phonology.* Austin: The University of Texas Press.

———. 1961. A definition of Proto-Germanic: a study in the chronological delimitation of languages. *Language* 37: 67-74.

———. 1962. *Historical Linguistics: An Introduction.* New York: Holt, Rinehart and Winston.

———. 1963. Some phonological observations based on examination of the Germanic Consonant Shift. *Monatshefte* 55: 229-35.

Leopold, Werner F. 1947. *Speech Development of a Bilingual Child: A Linguist's Record.* Vol. II: *Sound-learning in the First Two Years.* Northwestern University Studies, 11. Evanston, Ill.: Northwestern University Press.

Lessiak, Primus. 1933. *Beiträge zur Geschichte des deutschen Konsonantismus.* Schriften der Philosophischen Fakultät der Deutschen Universität in Prag, 14. Brünn: Rudolf M. Rohrer.

Lightner, Theodore M. 1968a. An analysis of *akan'e* and *ikan'e* in Modern Russian using the notion of markedness. In Jakobson 1968, pp. 188-200.

———. 1968b. Review of Martin Joos, ed., *Readings in Linguistics. General Linguistics* 8: 44-61.

Lisker, Leigh, and Arthur S. Abramson. 1964. A cross-language study of voicing in initial stops: acoustical measurements. *Word* 20: 384-422.

———. 1965. Stop categorization and voice onset time. *Proceedings of the Fifth International Congress of Phonetic Sciences,* Eberhard Zwirner and Wolfgang Bethge, eds., pp. 389-91. Basel: S. Karger.

Milewski, Tadeusz. 1953. Phonological typology of American Indian Languages. *Lingua Posnaniensis* 4: 229-76.

Moulton, William G. 1954. The stops and spirants of Early Germanic. *Language* 30: 1-42.

Naumann, Hans, and Werner Betz. 1962. *Althochdeutsches Elementarbuch: Grammatik und Texte,* 3rd ed. Sammlung Göschen, 1111/1111a. Berlin: Walter de Gruyter.

Paul, Hermann. 1916. *Deutsche Grammatik,* vol. I. Halle a. S.: Max Niemeyer. Also photographic reprint, Tübingen, 1968.

———. 1966. *Mittelhochdeutsche Grammatik,* 19th ed., 2nd printing. Walther Mitzka, ed. Sammlung kurzer Grammatiken germanischer Dialekte, A. Hauptreihe, 2. Tübingen: Max Niemeyer.

Penzl, Herbert. 1964. Die Phasen der ahd. Lautverschiebung. *Taylor Starck Festschrift,* Werner Betz et al., eds., pp. 27-41. The Hague: Mouton.

Postal, Paul M. 1968. *Aspects of Phonological Theory.* New York: Harper and Row.

Prokosch, E. 1917. Die deutsche Lautverschiebung und die Völkerwanderung. *Journal of English and Germanic Philology* 16: 1-26.

———. 1939. *A Comparative Germanic Grammar.* Special Publications of the Linguistic Society of America, William Dwight Whitney Series. Philadelphia: Linguistic Society of America. Also photographic reprint, 1966.

Schachter, Paul. 1969. Natural assimilation rules in Akan. Xeroxed.

Schane, Sanford A. 1968. On the non-uniqueness of phonological representations. *Language* 44: 709-16.

Schuchardt, Hugo. 1885. Über die Lautgesetze. Gegen die Junggrammatiker. Berlin: Oppenheim. Reprinted (with omissions) in *Hugo Schuchardt-Brevier: Ein Vademecum der allgemeinen Sprachwissenschaft,* Leo Spitzer, ed., 2nd ed., pp. 51-87. Halle a. S.: Max Niemeyer, 1928. My page numbers refer to the reprint.

Schulze, Ursula. 1967. *Studien zur Orthographie und Lautung der Dentalspiranten s und z im späten 13. und frühen 14. Jahrhundert.* Hermaea, Germanistische Forschungen, Neue Folge, 19. Tübingen: Max Niemeyer.

Steche, Theodor. 1939. Die Entstehung der Spiranten in der hochdeutschen Lautverschiebung. *Zeitschrift für deutsche Philologie* 64: 125-48.

Velten, H. V. 1944. The order of the Pre-Germanic consonant changes. *Journal of English and Germanic Philology* 43: 42-48.

Vennemann, Theo. 1968a. German phonology. University of California, Los Angeles, dissertation. Available on microfilm from University Microfilms, Ann Arbor, Mich.

——. 1968b. Some informal remarks on phonological change. Department of Germanic Languages, University of California, Los Angeles, dittoed.

———. 1969. Historical German phonology and the theory of marking: Grimm's Law. Department of German and Russian, University of California, Irvine, mimeographed. Prepared for the conference documented in this volume, but not presented.

9.

Note on a Phonological Hierarchy in English

Arnold M. Zwicky,
The Ohio State University

1. Introduction[1]

A major point of contact between theoretical work in generative grammar and more traditional activities in historical linguistics is the search for conditions on the form and content of grammars. Such conditions function indirectly as predictions of the possibility of certain kinds of linguistic change; as a result, known changes can be used as a source of fruitful hypotheses about conditions in grammatical theory, and such changes can be inspected as sources of evidence for, or counterevidence to, particular systems of hypotheses. Much is concealed in my facile use of the phrases "conditions on the form and content of grammar" and "known changes," the latter in particular, for the pursuit of specific hypotheses normally entails a careful examination of accepted presentations of linguistic changes. But I shall not explore these issues here. Rather, I shall provide a few preliminary examples and then move to a consideration of some aspects of English phonology which supply evidence about the content of grammatical theory and thus, derivatively, about linguistic change.

1.1. PHONOLOGICAL HIERARCHIES

The following are some of the hypotheses which have been put forth about phonological theory:

(1) If a language has a rule dropping [b]² between vowels, that rule also drops [d] and [g]; and if a language has a rule dropping [d] between vowels, that rule also drops [g]. But the converse is not true in either case (see Foley's contribution to this volume). Put another way: a rule deleting intervocalic [b], or intervocalic [d], or both, is not a possible phonological rule.

(2) If a language has a rule lowering [i] to [æ], that rule must also lower [e] to [æ] (David Stampe, personal communication). Put another way: a rule lowering [e] to [æ] is not a possible phonological rule.

The form of such hypotheses is familiar from Jakobson's investigations of implicational universals:

(3) "If, in the languages of the world, or in child language, the fricative consonants are limited to a single phoneme, this phoneme is as a rule represented by s" (Jakobson 1968: 55).

(4) "The existence of back consonants in the languages of the world presupposes accordingly the existence of front consonants" (Jakobson 1968: 53).

All four hypotheses lead to specific predictions about possible historical changes, given the assumption (as in Halle 1962) that among the mechanisms of linguistic change are (a) moderate changes in existing rules and (b) the addition of new rules. We can conclude from hypothesis (3), for example, that an unconditioned replacement of [s] by [f] is an impossible phonological change, because it would yield a system in violation of (3). From hypothesis (1) we can conclude that a language with a rule deleting intervocalic [g] cannot change so as to generalize that rule to drop both [g] and [b] (but not [d]), and that the deletion of intervocalic [d] (without [g] also) or [b] (without [d] and [g] also) is an impossible phonological change, because all these changes would result in a system in violation of (1). Similar principles can be adduced in morphology—there is some predictability in case syncretisms, for example—and in syntax—some principles of word order imply others, for instance (cf. Greenberg 1963 and Ross 1967). Still more predictions can be made on the basis of additional specific assumptions about linguistic change itself, such as Kiparsky's (1968) hypotheses concerning the reordering of rules.

Hypotheses (1) through (4) all refer to hierarchical arrangements among the sounds of a language. Hypotheses (1) and (2), in par-

ticular, establish hierarchies with respect to individual rules (intervocalic deletion of voiced stops and lowering of vowels, respectively). It happens that both these hierarchies apply to the class of
segments affected by the rules in question. There is, however, no
reason to suppose that such orderings are limited in this way; similar hierarchies might appear in the environments of rules. Sections
2 through 7 of this paper will, in fact, describe hierarchies applicable to rule environments.

A discussion of hierarchies is significant only insofar as the same
or similar orderings (or their inverses) reappear at many points in
the grammars of many languages. That is, an argument that a particular hierarchy requires representation in phonological theory
will resemble arguments supporting particular choices of feature
systems or other notational conventions (see Chapters 7 and 8 of
Chomsky and Halle 1968, also Bach 1968). A ramified theory
would require an account of the relationships and interactions
among the various hierarchies, and to be completely satisfying,
the tenets of such a theory should have some external justification,
for example, in terms of phonetics. In the following sections, which
largely constitute a report on work still in progress, I pursue the
hypothesis that the hierarchy

(5) Vowels Glides [r] [l] [n] [m] [ŋ] Fricatives Stops

must be represented in phonological theory. I assume the rather
modest burden of illustrating the reappearance of this sequence
in English, without attempting to locate it within a ramified theory,
without attempting to produce external explanations for the membership and arrangement of this class, and without attempting
seriously to relate my remarks to current discussions of feature representations and markedness.

I use the features and notational conventions of Chomsky and
Halle (1968), except that to refer to subsets of (5) I occasionally
employ the ad hoc notations in (6).

(6) $[\pi \rightarrow \rho]$ to refer to the set of all elements in (5) beginning with π and
ending with ρ (regardless of whether π precedes or follows ρ in (5));
$[\pi]^{+}$ to refer to $[\pi \rightarrow \text{Stops}]$; $[\pi]^{-}$ to refer to $[\pi \rightarrow \text{Vowels}]$

Thus, [1 → Fricatives] denotes the class comprising [1], the nasals, and the fricatives, while [1 → Glides] denotes the class of liquids and glides; [1]⁺ refers to [1] together with all elements of (5) to the right of [1] (that is, to [1] and all true consonants), and [1]⁻ refers to [1] together with all elements of (5) to the left of [1] (that is, to liquids, glides, and vowels).

1.2. ALLEGRO VARIANTS

The rules under discussion are for the most part processes triggered in some fashion by speed of speech, style, fatigue, and the like. I have been obliged to make rather fine judgments about what is acceptable in "normal," "fast," and "very fast" speech. The difficulties of such an undertaking are obvious; in addition to having to judge the acceptability of many different versions of the same utterance at varying speeds and in varying styles, the investigator is required to judge whether unrelated processes are operative at the same speed and in the same style. Nevertheless, seeing no alternative to sensitive introspection and listening, I have attempted to make such judgments. I do not suppose that my decisions are entirely consistent. Certainly they will differ in many details from the decisions of other speakers.

The phenomena of fast speech merit much closer examination than they have received in the literature. The very richness of the data seems to have convinced many investigators that allegro variants are merely automatic consequences of faster speech, except for certain words that have idiosyncratic variants. However, the view that fast-speech forms have a direct explanation in phonetic terms presumes a coherent and detailed theory of linguistic phonetics, which cannot be said to be available yet, despite the work of Ladefoged 1967 and of Jakobson and Halle (notably Jakobson, Fant, and Halle 1961 and Chomsky and Halle 1968, Chapter 7). The view is nevertheless encouraged by a number of fast-speech processes, for example, the rule Pre-Stress Contraction discussed briefly in Section 2, and the transitional stop variation that is the subject of Section 5.

1.3. RULE EXTENSION

One notable characteristic of many allegro variants is that they involve extensions of (usually obligatory) rules of slow-speech phonology. Consider the rule Gliding, which shifts [i] to [y] oblig-atorily in such words as *pavilion, Pennsylvania,* and *invasion.* The process is extended in fast speech to *Lithuania, colonial, lithium, accordion, criterion* (to which Gliding does not apply in slow speech because no + boundary precedes the [i]), *spontaneous, permeate* (to which Gliding does not apply in slow speech because the vowel in question is [e], not [i]), *marsupial, oblivion, Kentuckian* (to which Gliding does not apply in slow speech because the conso-nant preceding the [i] is noncoronal), and *familiarity* and *pecu-liarity* (to which Gliding does not apply in slow speech because the vowel following the [i] has primary stress). The slow-speech re-strictions on Gliding are discussed in Chomsky and Halle (1968: 225-27).

More than simple generalization is taking place here, however. Chomsky and Halle (1968: 228) argue that the failure of Gliding to apply in the word *emaciate* (similarly, *propitiate, appreciate, initiate,* and many others) should be explained by the assumption that Gliding precedes the rule Alternating Stress, at least in those dialects (among them mine) in which Gliding is obligatory in words like *beneficiary* and *auxiliary*; if *emaciate* has final stress at the stage in its derivation when Gliding might apply, then Gliding will be blocked (as in *familiarity*), and a following application of Al-ternating Stress will shift the stress from the ultima to the ante-penult. But in fast speech the extended Gliding rule must apply to *emaciate* after Alternating Stress applies, for otherwise the allegro form *[əməšéyt] (instead of the correct [əméyšyèyt] or [əmêy-šèyt]) would be predicted.

It is tempting to suppose, in light of this example and the numer-ous situations in which allegro rules must be assumed to apply quite late in the sequence of rules, that all specifically fast-speech rules are ordered after all obligatory rules. S. Jay Keyser has suggested the following counterexample to me. There are English dialects in which the Flapping rule is obligatory in words like *writer* and *rider.* In these dialects, as in mine, words like *winter* do not have a flap in slow speech. But in faster speech the (specifically fast-speech) rule of Nasal Dropping (ordered after Nasalization of vowels) works to place the [t] of *winter* in the proper environment for Flapping, which then applies to yield [wĩDr]. Flapping is also called into play by the operation of the fast-speech rule Glide Deletion, which drops initial [h] (generally) and initial [w] (in a few words only) before unstressed vowels; phrases like *might have* [máyDə(v)] and *what would* [wáDəd] thus have flaps in fast speech. Another example is the rule Auxiliary Contraction, which (in conjunction with Glide Deletion) is responsible for the reduction of *is* and *has* to [z], *would* and *had* to [d], *have* to [v], *will* to [l], *am* to [m], and *are* to [r].[3] *Is* and *has* reduce to [z] after consonants as well as vowels, and if the preceding consonant is voiceless, the obligatory rule of Progressive Voicing Assimilation, familiar from its application to various formatives realized as [s, z, ɨz] or [t, d, ɨd], yields [s], as in *Chuck's not here* and *Pat's been sick.*

C.-J. Bailey has pointed out to me that a number of fast-speech phenomena can be explained as the result of a rule deleting boundaries in a variety of contexts. Although few of the phenomena discussed in this paper can be so explained (the applicability of Glide Deletion, Auxiliary Contraction, and Flapping in phrases containing unstressed auxiliaries or pronouns being the principal class of exceptions), it should be noted that this deletion must apply before a considerable number of obligatory slow-speech rules—among them, the Flapping rule already mentioned and the rules of Palatalization and Y Dropping, which apply in slow speech in the derivation of *actual, gradual, sensual,* and *visual* (Chomsky and Halle 1968: 230–32), and in fast speech to yield [dîǰə] for *did you,* [wôwčə] for *won't you,* and the like.

Also due to Bailey is the hypothesis that if the order of two rules with respect to each other changes in fast speech, it changes from the marked to the unmarked order (in the sense of Kiparsky 1968), never in the opposite direction. Let us examine the ordering of Gliding and Alternating Stress within this framework. In slow speech the order Gliding-Alternating Stress is marked, because if Alternating Stress were to apply first the domain of applicability of Gliding would be increased by the *emaciate* class, whereas the slow-speech form of Gliding neither decreases nor increases the domain of Alternating Stress. In fast speech this order remains marked, because the extended version of Gliding removes cases, the *emaciate* class again, from the domain of Alternating Stress, whereas Alternating Stress neither decreases nor increases the domain of the fast-speech version of Gliding. On Bailey's hypothesis, the reordering of Alternating Stress before Gliding is to be expected.

Bailey's hypothesis should be extended in some fashion to incorporate the observation that when specifically fast-speech rules are added, markedness in rule ordering tends to be minimized. This imprecise formulation of the principle is intended to cover such cases as the ordering of Nasalization before Nasal Dropping, Glide Deletion before Auxiliary Contraction, Nasal Dropping and Glide Deletion before Flapping, and Auxiliary Contraction before Progressive Voicing Assimilation.

Before turning to other matters, here is another example of rule extension in fast speech. Further instances are noted in the following sections.

The rule Nasal Assimilation, which assimilates the final [n] of the prefixes *con-, in-, syn-,* and *en-* to the position of any following obstruent except [f] (*conflation*), [v] (*convection*), [k] (*concussion*), or [g] *(congratulation)*, is extended in fast speech to apply (a) before [f v k g], (b) to final [n] of the prefixes *un-* and *non-* and of the first elements of compounds, which do not assimilate at all in slow speech, and (c) progressively, to nasals following obstruents, as in *eleven, bacon,* and *hypnotize.* I have specified that Nasal Assimilation applies generally before obstruents, and not merely before [p b], because I take this to be the same rule as the one specifying the nasal before [k g] within morphemes, as [ŋ] (*rink, ring*), and the nasal before [p b f] within morphemes, as [m] (*camp, amber, camphor*). That is, the obligatory (slow-speech) rule applies generally within morphemes and across the + boundary (the boundary in *comfort* and *congress,* which show assimilation in show speech—cf. *convent, concourse, infant*), but only before [p b] across the = boundary.[4]

It is natural to suppose that rather than the fast-speech rules being extensions or generalizations of normal (slow-speech) rules, the normal rules are restricted versions of the more general processes. I am indebted to David Stampe for the idea. The associated view of language acquisition is that the child embarks upon the task of language learning with innate knowledge of a set of quite general rules, and that what he must learn is (a) the way in which these rules are restricted in his language, plus (b) their order, insofar as it must be marked. The associated view of linguistic change is that the primary mechanism of change, aside from reordering, is the removal of restrictions on rules. What corresponds to "addition of a rule" within this framework is the removal of an absolute prohibition against the rule, so that it is to be expected that the earliest evidences of a rule will appear in considerably restricted environments (restricted in the class of segments affected, in the contexts in which the rule applies, and in the lexical items to which the rule applies). Some discussion of rule spread, in time and space, within similar conceptual frameworks, can be found in Bach (1968: 135-37) and in Labov's paper in the present volume. Foley's contribution to this volume puts forth a theory of linguistic change along similar lines.

Although this promising direction of investigation will not be pursued further here, it should be noted that not all phonological processes "extend" in the same fashion as Gliding and Nasal Assimilation. Thus, for example, the rule N+Resonant, which assimilates the final [n] of the prefixes *con-, in-, syn-,* and *en-* completely[5] to a following [r l m n], does not apply to a number of forms (e.g., *enrage, enlist, enmesh, inlay*). In fast speech the unassimilated clusters remain, and moreover the rule does not extend to [n] in *un-* and *non-*, nor to [n] at the end of first elements of compounds (*tin wrap,* as opposed to the Nasal Assimilation example *pinball*), nor to [n] before resonants in such names as *Conroy* and *Conlon.* Instead, in definitely fast speech Nasalization and Nasal Dropping apply to yield [əréyǰ] for *enrage,* [nãlíygl] for *nonlegal,* [kãròy] for *Conroy,* etc.

2. The Rule Slur

Let us begin with the following syncope rule:

(7)
$$\mathfrak{e} \rightarrow \emptyset \;/\; C \longrightarrow \left\{ \begin{matrix} r \\ l \\ n \end{matrix} \right\} \begin{bmatrix} - \text{cons} \\ + \text{voc} \\ - \text{stress} \end{bmatrix}$$

This rule applies in moderately fast or casual speech to delete the reduced unstressed vowels in examples like the following:

(8)(a) Before [r]: *hindering,*[6] *blunderer, puckering, elaborate* (adj.), *mackerel, amorous, doggerel, cadaverous, camera, every, laboratory, ephemeral, operative, separate, treasurer, reference, federal, impoverish, inaugural, lateral, directorate, dangerous, et cetera, temperature, Everest, Barbara*
(b) Before [1]: *pedaling, twinkling, suppler, awfully, respectfully, erratically, reciprocally, javelin, Emily, especially, excellent, equivalent, acidophilus, chocolate, easily, ambulatory, benevolent, desolate* (adj.), *leveling, channeling, Lancelot, Evelyn, chancellor*
(c) Before [n]: *happening, stiffening, opener, pardoning, seasonal, reasoning, reckoning, resonant, coordinate, personal, definite, infinite, arsenal, reasonably, gelatinous, effeminate, rational, larceny, traditional*

Slur applies obligatorily in *business*, and in my speech to a number of other words, e.g., *camera, every, celery, general, mystery, chocolate,* and *family*; most of these are instances of syncope before [r], although there are a few cases before [1].

I wish to emphasize that this rule is a general process, in contrast to many other English contraction rules, for example Auxiliary Contraction (see section 1.3), which is restricted to a small set of words and is restricted in a rather complex way by the phonological and syntactic environment of those words (see Zwicky 1969).

On the other hand, the deletion in Slur is not governed by any simple or obvious conditions on the "pronounceability" of the result, in contrast to the contraction rule Pre-stress Contraction

(9)
$$ \vartheta \rightarrow \emptyset \ / \ \# \ C \ \text{—} \ C \ \begin{bmatrix} - \text{ cons} \\ + \text{ voc} \\ + \text{ stress} \end{bmatrix} $$

which seems to have no relationship to the hierarchy in (5). Pre-stress Contraction manifests itself in quite fast speech in the dropping of the unstressed vowel in the first syllable of such words as

(10) *derivative, united,*[7] *development, galoshes, demonstrative, subordinate, senility, vicinity, ferocious, coordinate*

The rule does not apply in such words as *Decameron, revised, pedestrian,* and *deflation,* presumably for phonetic reasons.[8] Slur, in contrast, fails to apply in a great many cases in which the result would be easily pronounceable:

(11) Before syllables bearing stress: *degenerate* (vb.), *compensatory, imaginary, polarize, scandalize, hyphenate, Eucharist, vocalism, intellect, parallel*

(12) Before clusters: *development, honestly, graciously, earnestly*

(13) Before obstruents: *historical, relevant* (cf. *referent*), *divisible, voracity, Arabic, imperative, analogy*

(14) Before [m]:[9] *element, minimum, monogamy, astronomer, consummate* (adj.), *ultimate*

(15) Across strong (i.e., compound or word) boundaries: *counter-attraction, counterintelligence, inter-American, underexposed, castle adventure, button across*

Note also that the correct operation of Slur depends on the prior application of a number of other rules—vowel-reduction rules, because the rule applies only to unstressed vowels that have been reduced to [ə], and also an extended (fast-speech) version of Y Dropping (see sections 1.3 and 7), which eliminates the glide of [yə] (from careful speech [yuw]) in examples like *ambulatory* and *inaugural* and of [yə] in examples like *auxiliary,* because there is no trace of the [y] in the contracted forms of these words. Presumably, for speakers who do not obligatorily palatalize [ty dy] to [č ǰ] before unstressed vowels, an extension of Palatalization (and Y Dropping) precedes Slur in the derivation of such words as[10]

(16) *lecturer, cultural, congratulate, spatula, credulous, modular, fraudulent, fortunate*

all of which show palatals—e.g. [fórčnit] for *fortunate.*

In the notation of (6), Slur has the formulation

(17)
$$\mathrm{ə} \rightarrow \emptyset \ / \ C \ \text{---} \ [\mathrm{r} \rightarrow \mathrm{n}] \begin{bmatrix} -\text{ cons} \\ +\text{ voc} \\ -\text{ stress} \end{bmatrix}$$

which appears to be merely an unmotivated variant of

(18)
$$\mathfrak{e} \rightarrow \emptyset \ / \ C - \begin{bmatrix} + \text{cons} \\ - \text{obst} \\ + \text{cor} \end{bmatrix} \begin{bmatrix} - \text{cons} \\ + \text{voc} \\ - \text{stress} \end{bmatrix}$$

However, I shall argue that the exclusion of [m] from the environment of Slur is a relative rather than an absolute exclusion and that the acceptability of the output of Slur varies, being highest in position before [r], lowest before [n]. In fact, I shall argue that the hierarchy in (5) corresponds to a differential in the acceptability of the outputs of Slur, ranging from normally entirely acceptable before [r], to less acceptable before [n], to normally unacceptable before [m] and [ŋ], to entirely unacceptable before obstruents (as in (13)).

First, the contraction before [m] and [ŋ]. The Slurred versions of the examples in (14) strike me as unacceptable at the same rate of speech at which the examples in (8) are normal. But in faster speech they are not quite so bad, certainly much better than the Slurred versions of the obstruent examples in (13). A few words—*Quadrigesima, handsomer,* perhaps *unanimous*—are good even in only moderately fast speech. Examples of [ə] in the Slur environment before [ŋ] are not easy to find, but one such occurs in the proper name *Durringer* (when pronounced with simple [ŋ] rather than with [ŋg] or [ɲj̆]); Slur is inapplicable in this case.

Next, the exceptions to Slur. They are somewhat more numerous before [l] than before [r], and somewhat more numerous before [n] than before [l]. The exceptions before [r] are, so far as I have been able to determine, all of a single type: They are all cases of a failure of deletion before [riy]. My judgments on some words ending in [əriy] with respect to Slur in moderately fast speech are given in (19):

(19) (a) Slur applies: *discovery, menagerie, factory, summary, hosiery, misery, machinery, mastery, scenery, illusory, dispensary, shrubbery, bindery, every, nursery, cursory, robbery, slippery, hickory, memory, Bowery*
(b) ? Slur applies: *haberdashery, quackery, battery, chicory, napery, creamery, usury, surgery, perjury, feathery, periphery, sorcery, mockery, refinery, thievery, Calvary*
(c) Slur does not apply: *infirmary, nunnery, summery,*

> *lechery, perfumery, buttery, buggery, granary, cannery, gunnery, crockery, Hungary, plenary, greenery, notary, popery, snobbery, rotary, primary, rosary, rookery, deanery*

Note especially the *robbery-snobbery* and *summary-summery* contrasts. The classification of words in [əriy] according to the applicability of Slur seems to be largely arbitrary, although some generalizations can be made (e.g., adjectives in *-y*, "like," do not contract in moderately fast speech: *silvery, blustery, blistery, splintery, cindery, thundery, powdery, gingery, leathery, gossamery, summery, watery, papery, peppery, coppery, buttery*[11]). It is clear that Slur is being extended to new vocabulary items,[12] just as it is extended in very fast speech.

The exceptions to Slur before [l] are of two types. First, [ə] before the suffix *-ly* does not drop after a stressed syllable, with few exceptions (*easily, especially, finally*):

(20) (a) *-al-ly: mentally, eternally, morally, vocally, orally, totally, monumentally*
     (b) *-i-ly: readily, happily, prettily, jerkily, wheezily, chubbily, cloudily, stuffily, sunnily, drowsily*

(Cf. the words in *-ically*, which is always reducible to [ikliy]). The second class of exceptions contains most occurrences of [ə] derived from [yuw], except in *ambulatory*, perhaps in *particular*, and in the words in which the [y] of [yuw] has been absorbed by Palatalization and Y Dropping (e.g., *spatula*):

(21) *binocular, jocular, populous, popular, amulet, fistula, cumulus, truculence, circular, muscular, tabular*

Y Dropping, but not Slur, applies to these words in fast speech, so that *popular*, for example, has the variants [pápyuwlr̩], [pápyəlr̩], [pápəlr̩] in increasingly rapid speech.

The exceptions to Slur before [n] are diverse. The principal restrictions are against [mn] and [tn] clusters that would result from the operation of Slur. These restrictions must refer specifically to the rule Slur, for the clusters are not, in general, unacceptable in English (cf. the proper names *Hamnet, Simnall, Putney, Courtney*, and also *amnesia, insomnia*); moreover, the restrictions are not absolute, because there are some forms (e.g., *effeminate, scrutiny, gelatinous, fattening*) that reduce comfortably in fast speech, and because the domain of the rule is extended as the rate of speech increases. The following are some examples:

(22) (a) [mn]: *feminine, geminate* (adj.), *Gethsemane, stamina, phenomenal, nominal, abdominal, dominant, hominy, aluminum, voluminous, Germany, prominent*
(b) [tn] : *intestinal, Latinist, monotony, botany*

The reduction in *functional, inflectional,* and similar forms is relatively unacceptable, probably because of the complex [kšn] cluster created. I find the reduction of *traditional, emotional,* and the like quite natural, as opposed to the reduction of *confessional, processional,* and the like. And I find the contraction of *progeny, nitrogenous, misogyny,* etc. (to [ǰn]) less acceptable than the contraction of *fortunate* (to [čn]).

A final source of evidence for the ranking of the resonants in the environment of Slur consists of cases in which the rule could apply to either of two different resonants within the same word:

(23) (a) [ərəl] : *federally, generally, literally, laterally, cursorily, naturally, minerally, electorally*
(b) [ənəl] : *personally, subliminally, seasonally, conventionally, terminally, marginally, criminally*

In (23a) the contraction before [r] is clearly preferable to the contraction before [l] ; [ǰénrəliy], for example, is much better than [ǰénṛliy], although both forms can occur in fast or casual speech (for the latter form, see the next section). In (23b) the matter is not so clear; for some words (e.g., *personally*) I prefer the reduction before [l], in others (e.g., *criminally*) the reduction before [n]. The former cases provide some evidence for the dominance of [r] over [l], while the latter cases are neutral with respect to the question of the ordering of [l] and [n] —but this ordering is the one that is supported most strongly by the argument from exceptionality.

3. *The Rules Ruh-reduction and Ruh-lessness*

A number of words (e.g., *separable, preferable, cooperative, corroborative, tolerably*) have, in addition to the variants generated by

Slur, fast-speech forms that appear to show Slur in operation before obstruents: [séprbl̩], [préfr̩bl̩], etc.[13] But in fact, this reduction is dependent not on a resonant *following* the [ə], but rather on a resonant (more precisely, an [r]) *preceding* the [ə], as can be seen from the examples in (24), which exhibit a variation between normal speech [rə] and fast speech [r̩] in diverse positions.[14]

(24) *reciprocal, segregate, instrument, intricacy, introduction, hydroplane, profusion, pretend, professor, demonstrative, corporal, natural, pirate, hieroglyph, chiropractor, moral*

Clearly a rule distinct from Slur, moreover one that can apply to the output of Slur, is required. This rule, Ruh-reduction, is not conditioned by the stress on (or even the existence of) a neighboring syllable:

(25) rə → r̩ / [- word boundary] —— [- word boundary]

The context in (25) prohibits the rule from applying in initial position (*Ramona, reduction, risotto, romantic;* cf. *brassiere* and *professor,* which reduce) or in final position (*hydra, pellagra, Capra, Barbara;* cf. *apron* and *corporal,* which reduce). The formulation of the change itself requires some discussion. It does not seem possible to frame the rule as a straightforward [ə]-deletion rule (contracting the sequence CrəC to CrC, upon which the independently required rule Syllabication would operate to yield Cr̩C), because the reduction takes place after vowels (even lax vowels, as in *caraway*) as well as after nonsyllabics. Some speakers, as reported to me by David Stampe, have a clear intermediate stage [rr̩] between [rə] and [r̩], so that two rules are involved, the first an assimilation, the second a simplification of [rr̩] that is required in any event to account for the common pronunciation of *mirror* as [mír̩] (similarly, *horror, purer, pairer*):

(26) (a) ə → [+cor] / [- word boundary] r —— [- word boundary]
        (b) r → ∅ / —— r̩[15]

Because there is some independent evidence for (26b) and because the rules in (26) have a sort of internal motivation lacking in (25), I shall suppose that (26) is closer to the correct formulation of Ruh-reduction than (25), even though the intermediate stage [rr̩] is not prominent in my speech.

Ruh-reduction is applicable in definitely fast or casual speech (also in the speech of many children). Hence, forms like [préfṛbl̩] are less acceptable than forms like [préfrəbl̩]. In still faster speech some speakers eliminate the retroflex coloring of [ṛ], when unstressed and flanked by consonants, in many words. This rule, Ruh-lessness, is common in my speech in only a few forms (*surprise, governor, paraphernalia, thermometer,* and *particular*), for which dissimilatory influences are usually cited as the cause, as in Kenyon and Knott 1953: xlvi. Although the best examples of Ruh-lessness are in words with two [r]'s, the explanation in terms of dissimilation is not entirely convincing, because (a) some of the best examples would involve anticipatory dissimilation over long distances, e.g., three syllables in *particular* and *thermometer,* and (b) many speakers of otherwise [r]-ful dialects have [ə] for unstressed [ṛ] in allegro pronunciations of words lacking a second [r] (*instrument, profession, introduction, permission*). Nevertheless, Ruh-lessness is favored in dissimilatory environments, so that the reduction in *governor* is more acceptable than the reduction in *governess.*[16]

Ruh-reduction does not simplify [rə] only. It applies also, in a very restricted fashion, to [lə], [nə], and [mə]. These reductions are characteristic of quite fast or careless (for example, alcoholic) speech. I find the reduced [nə] and [mə] forms somewhat less acceptable than the reduced [lə] forms.

The generalized version of (26a) will assimilate some unstressed syllabics to some preceding resonants in the features *coronal, lateral,* and *nasal.* The details of the assimilations are not entirely clear to me. The generalized version of (26b) will then drop [r] before coronal vowels, [l] before lateral syllabics, and nasals before nasal syllabics. Without giving a concrete form to these revisions, I list here a few examples (many of which show, in addition to Ruh-reduction, assimilation rules not discussed here):

(27) (a) [lə] from Slur: *chocolate* [čákl̩ʔ], *ambulatory* [ǽbl̩-tòriy], *equivalent* [əkwívl̩ʔ]

(b) Other [lə]: *ablative* [ǽbl̩div], *complicate* [kǽpl̩kèyʔ], *Raglan* [rǽgl̩n], *restless* [résl̩s]

(c) [nə] from Slur: *coordinate* [kwórdn̩ʔ], *definite* [défn̩ʔ]

(d) Other [nə]: *abnegation* [ǽbn̩géyšn̩], *ignominious* [ìgm̩mínyəs], *sadness* [sǽdn̩s]

(e) (26b) applying to [n]: *kennel* [kḗ̃ḭ], *denim* [dḛ̃m̩],
linen [lḭ̃n], *canner* [kǽ̃ṛ]

(f) [mə]: *admonition* [æ̀dn̩míšn̩], *admiration* [æ̀d-
m̩réyšn̩]

(g) (26b) applying to [m]: *maximum* ⌊mǽksə̃m̩⌋, *camel*
[kǽ̃ḭ], *summon* [sʌ́m̩]

Note that my judgment is that [rə] is most likely to contract, then
[lə], then [nə] and [mə].

Ruh-lessness applies generally only to [r̩]. In extremely fast or
careless speech it may affect a few occurrences of [l] ([čákə ʔ] for
chocolate, [kǎpəkèyʔ] for *complicate*), but not the syllabic nasals.

4. *The Rule VVR*

Still another deletion of [ə] occurs, as in the case of Slur, before
resonants, but otherwise in an environment quite different from
the Slur contexts:

(28) $\mathrm{ə} \rightarrow \emptyset \ /\begin{bmatrix} - \text{cons} \\ + \text{voc} \end{bmatrix} \begin{bmatrix} - \text{cons} \\ - \text{voc} \end{bmatrix} - \begin{bmatrix} + \text{cons} \\ - \text{obst} \end{bmatrix}$

VVR applies to the words in (29) to reduce a sequence VGəR to
VGR:[17]

(29) (a) [r]: *dire, flower, diary, prior, theory, payer, fiery*
      (b) [l]: *jewel(er), dial, duel(ist), fuel(ing), royal(ly), con-
          strual, denial, real*
      (c) [n]: *Brian, Rowan, lion(ize), Zion(ist), Cohen*
      (d) [m]: *Noam, jeroboam, Hyams*
      (e) [ŋ]: *doing, sowing, saying, pawing, seeing*

The reduction before liquids is usual in fairly fast speech for me.
The reduction before the nasals is less normal;[18] some reductions are
impossible for me except in very fast speech:

(30) (a) [n]: *Malayan, Siouan, Korean, Samoan*
      (b) [m]: *museum, atheneum*

Also, I find the reductions before [ŋ] definitely less natural than
the other reductions, with the acceptability of the results correlated
to some extent with the degree of stress on the preceding syllable

(highest for the examples in (29), lower for *vetoing* and *tangoing*, and very low for *hulaing* and *subpoenaing*) and to some extent with the quality of the preceding vowel (highest for front vowels, especially [iy], as in *seeing* and *carrying*).

In summary, my judgment is that the contraction is most likely to take place before [r] and [l], then in the cases before [n] and [m] given in (29), then before [ŋ] and in the cases before [n] and [m] given in (30).

5. *Transitional Stops*

A variety of CCC clusters have CC variants in fast speech, with the middle C dropped. Conversely, a variety of CC clusters have variants with a transitional stop intervening between the two consonants. Thus, although some speakers of English have a distinction between [ns] in *prince* and [nts] in *prints* (in slow speech), in faster speech the two forms vary freely with each other. Some speakers do not appear to have the distinction at all. In general, the greater the number of feature distinctions between the first and last consonants, the more likely the variation. Without exploring in detail the principles of this variation, I provide first some examples with nasals (in conjunction with fricatives in (31) and (32), with stops in (33) and (34):

(31) *tenth, thousandth; prince, prints, answer, pencil, landscape; friendship, French, trench; warmth; Damson, damps; Canfield, panful, handful, grandfather; length; rinks; compunction, juncture; drumful, lumpful; Hampshire; ringful, tankful; gowns, grounds, lens, lends; strange, fringe; dams, damsel; rings, stirrings; Convair*

(32) *fishnet, rashness, rationing; casement, Westminster; Kastner, Flessner; Fishman, trashman; Hefner, roughness; business, Gesner*

(33) *dreamt, jumped; ranked; dreamed; ringed*

(34) *happening, raptness; weakening, weakness; Hickman*[19]

Now observe that [l] is involved in a similar variation. However, in contrast to the variation for the nasals, which is normal in fast speech for all speakers, and regular at all speeds for some, the variation for [l] is common only in definitely fast speech, and it is not

general (so far as I know) for any speakers. The following examples correspond to (31)-(34):

(35) *health; pulse, cults; Welsh, filch; shelf; balls, balds; valve*

(36) *Kessler,beastly, base line, mist line; Ashley, freshly; snaf-
fling, softly; dazzling, fuzzless; javelin, unraveling*

(37) *milepost, cold pan; welkin; callbox, coldbox; call girl,
Colgate; Colney, coldness*

(38) *rippling, capless; pickling, thickly, perfectly, exactly; rib-
less, stubbly; rugless, Raglan; landlady, inland, fondling*

The variant forms of the examples in (31)-(34), and of those in
(35)-(38), are by no means of a uniform degree of acceptability.
On the whole, however, the nasal cases are better than the [l]
cases.

[r] does not participate in this variation at all. I do not believe
that the variation is possible in such words as those in (39)-(42):

(39) *course, courts; turf, carful; harsh, lurch; cars, cards; curve*

(40) *mystery, mess room; mushroom; calf-rope, riff-raff, raft
race; misery; livery*

(41) *tarpon, cart pole; clerk, Perkins; carbon, card box; Car-
gill*

(42) *apron; Akron, Bactrian; rib roast, scabrous; vagrant*

6. *The Rule Dentdel*

The discussion of transitional stops in the previous section is complicated by the existence of a separate rule deleting [t] and [d]
preceding # (#C in moderately fast speech, but extended to apply
before vowels and in phrase-final position in faster speech) and
following [f s n l]. Thus, many examples of reduction of CCC to
CC, where the middle C is [t] or [d], can be taken either as examples of transitional stop variation or as examples of Dentdel:
Westminster, grandfather, lifts, handful, coldness. However, the
transitional stop variation (but not Dentdel) "expands" clusters
as well as reducing them, and it (but not Dentdel) eliminates labials
(*damped, damps*) and velars (*junked, junks*)[20] as well as alveolars,
while Dentdel (but not transitional stop variation) deletes [t] and
[d] in fast speech, even before words beginning with a vowel (e.g.,

past in *he went past a store* and *old* in *she gave me the same old answer.*

Dentdel applies after the continuant obstruents [f] and [s], but not [v z ž š]. This restriction follows from the fact that in most dialects the rule, even in fast speech, does not apply to [t] or [d] representing the past tense ending (thus, *coughed, sniffed,* and *tossed* cannot reduce, although *lift, past,* and *Christ* can[21]), in combination with the fact that the excluded continuants do not occur before [t] and [d] in morpheme-final position. An approximate statement of the rule is given in (43):

(43) $\left\{ \begin{matrix} t \\ d \end{matrix} \right\} \rightarrow \emptyset \ / \begin{bmatrix} + \text{cons} \\ + \text{cont} \end{bmatrix} \underline{\quad} \#$

In addition to the examples already given, some words subject to Dentdel are[22]

(44) *soft, excellent, test, must, shan't, won't, can't, don't, wouldn't; and, around, beyond, grand, land, friend; build, cold, hold*

Now notice that Dentdel does not apply to [t d] preceded by [r]. I find the reduction unacceptable in forms like *hard, heart, shirt, court, cord.*[23] This restriction can be incorporated into (43) by adding the condition that the segment preceding the deleted stop be either nonvocalic or anterior. Or, in the suggestive notation of (6):

(45) $\left\{ \begin{matrix} t \\ d \end{matrix} \right\} \rightarrow \emptyset \ / \ [1 \rightarrow \text{Fricatives}] \underline{\quad} \#$

7. Weak Cluster Conditions

According to Chomsky and Halle 1968: 241n., a distinction must be made in at least three obligatory rules of English phonology between a *strong cluster* (a [+ cons] segment followed by any [+ cons] segment except [r], or a cluster of three or more [+ cons] segments) and a *weak cluster* (a single [+ cons] segment, or one followed by [r] or [w]). The formula for a weak cluster—

(46) $[+ \text{cons}] \left(\begin{bmatrix} \alpha \ \text{voc} \\ \alpha \ \text{cons} \\ - \ \text{ant} \end{bmatrix} \right)$

must appear in the environment of these rules, the most notable of which is the part of the Main Stress rule that incorporates essentially the Classical Latin stress rule, by which *vertebra* is stressed on the antepenult but *umbrella* on the penult. In the nonce notation of (6) a weak cluster is represented as

(47) $[r]^+$ $([r]^-)$

Note that in this instance, as in the case of Dentdel and transitional stops, the problem to be solved is the exclusion of [r] (together with the glides) from a larger class to which [r] naturally belongs. Another example of this type may be the following restriction on the occurrence of [s] and [š] in initial position: Before [r], [š] but not [s] occurs; while before [l m n], [s] but not [š] occurs. Dialect variation in the treatment of [yuw] (when it bears some stress and follows a coronal nonsyllabic) might provide still another example. There are two extreme dialects with respect to Y Dropping (see section 1.3), one preserving the [y] in words like *tune, duty, assume, nuisance, lute,* and *ruin,* the other (mine) without a [y] in any of these words. I am aware of two intermediate dialects of interest in an examination of the hierarchy in (5). The first preserves the [y] in all cases except after [r l], the second in all cases except after [r] (*lute, Lucifer, illuminate,* and *lubricate* maintaining the [y], *ruin, ruby,* and *rule* lacking it).[24]

The processes in which [r] is excluded contrast with Slur, Ruh-reduction, Ruh-lessness, and VVR (perhaps also Syllabic Resonants —see note 9), in which the problem (aside from gradation in acceptability) is the exclusion of one or more of the nasals from a larger class to which they naturally belong.

8. *Prospectus*

Let us suppose, on the basis of the English rules discussed in sections 2 through 7, that the hierarchy in (5) requires representation in phonological theory. I shall not consider the question of how this representation is to be accomplished, but rather shall offer a few remarks on the relationship of the hierarchy to feature composition and to markedness, and then I shall approach (in a most tentative way) the question of the extent to which it can be predicted when the hierarchy is relevant to a given rule.

The hierarchy in (5)—vowels, then glides, then liquids, then nasals, then fricatives, then stops—corresponds to a gradation of sonority, from greatest to least. The sequence of the major classes is governed by the principles in (48), with (48a) applied before (48b):

(48) (a) (i) [- cons] precedes [+ cons]
          (ii) [- obst] precedes [+ obst]
      (b) (i) [+ voc] precedes [- voc]
          (ii) [+ cont] precedes [- cont]

By the principles in (48a) all vowels and glides precede all liquids, nasals, fricatives, and stops (i), and all vowels, glides, liquids, and nasals precede all fricatives and stops (ii). The result is a three-way division, with all vowels and glides preceding all liquids and nasals, which in turn precede all fricatives and stops. Principle (48bi) orders vowels before glides within their class, and liquids before nasals within their class (but does not affect fricatives and stops), while principle (48bii) orders liquids before nasals within their class, and fricatives before stops within their class (but does not affect vowels and glides).

Within the portion of the hierarchy of immediate interest to us, namely the liquids and nasals, the sequence is governed by the principles in (49):

(49) (a) (i) [- back] precedes [+ back]
          (ii) [+ cor] precedes [- cor]
      (b) [- ant] precedes [+ ant]

Principle (49a) orders [n m] before [ŋ] (i) and [n] before [m ŋ] (ii), without affecting the liquids. Principle (49b) orders [r] before [l] (and must be ordered after (49a) so as not to affect the nasals).

Note that the principles in (49) are applicable to oral consonants as well as to resonants; Jakobson's observations quoted earlier in (3) and (4) follow from (49a). In other words, the ordering of the nasals in (5) corresponds to the ordering with respect to markedness, from least to greatest, and not to the ordering with respect

to sonority, which is [ŋ n m].[25] On the other hand, the ordering of
[r] before [l] in (5) accords with the ordering by decreasing sonority, not with the ordering by increasing markedness, [r] being
marked in contrast to [l]. That is, the hierarchy in (5) is complex
with respect to the natural dimensions of sonority and markedness.

English contraction rules supply some evidence about other sub-
hierarchies of (5). For example, the rule Glide Deletion (recall section 1.3) drops initial [h] quite extensively, initial [w] in very restricted environments (only in the words *will, would*), and initial
[y] not at all. The rule is sensitive to factors of stress, speed, and
syntax in a complex way, but the sequence is not difficult to dis-
cern.[26]

Although it is impossible at present to predict when a hierarchy
will apply to a rule, or to predict which hierarchy (or hierarchies)
will apply and in which order (recall the contrast between transitional stop variation, Dentdel, and the weak cluster condition, on
the one hand, and Slur, Ruh-reduction, Ruh-lessness, and VVR, on
the other), some suggestive observations can be made.

Note first that all the rules discussed so far in which the hierarchy in (5) is applicable are rules in which the resonants appear
in the environment. In contrast, rules that change the major class
features of resonants are governed by principles cutting across
considerations of sonority and markedness. The relationships between [r] and [s], [z], [n], [l], [d], and [w], and similar relationships between [l] and various stops and glides, and between nasals
and sounds of other classes all appear to be quite independent of
the hierarchy in (5). Other processes that affect the resonants
directly, in particular the superimposition of secondary features
on the resonants, invoke the hierarchical principles. For example,
in Kolokuma Ịọ (Williamson 1965: 16) vowels and [w y r], but
not [l], are nasalized in the vicinity of nasals.

Although the characterization of the circumstances in which [r]
is favored, as opposed to those in which the nasals are favored, is
impossible on the basis of the tiny sample of rules considered
here, a rough conceptualization of the distinction is not out of the
question: [r] is favored when the strength of a syllabic nucleus is
reduced (by elimination of an initial resonant, as in (26b), or by

elimination of secondary articulations, as in Ruh-lessness, or by deletion, as in Slur and VVR) and when assimilations characteristic of vowels are operative (as in the first part of Ruh-reduction and the Ịjọ nasalization rule). In contrast, the nasals are favored when the "strength" of a consonant cluster is involved. Put very succinctly, the distinction is one between "vowel" rules and "consonant" rules. These excessively vague notions await much further investigation.

Finally, notice that other hierarchies interact with the one in (5). Thus, Dentdel is most likely when a consonant (especially an obstruent) follows the [t] or [d] to be deleted. Slur is normally inapplicable before stressed syllables, but in quite fast speech (and in some dialects) it extends to this position as well. The applicability of VVR is in part conditioned by the stress on and quality of the preceding syllable. The result is in each instance a complex pattern of acceptability, made still more elaborate when idiosyncratic lexical markings, rather than statable phonological or syntactic environments, contribute to the determination of acceptability, as in the case of Slur applying to [ə] before [riy].

A considerable amount of work will be required to sort out these processes and the restrictions on them—among other things, a survey of synchronic processes involving liquids and nasals, of historical changes involving these sounds, of principles of borrowing involving them, and of their treatment in language acquisition, all of these in a wide variety of language.[27] To this survey I offer the above observations as prolegomenon.

NOTES

1. I am indebted to Ann D. Zwicky for her many suggestions about the form and content of this paper. I have incorporated into the text a number of observations made by other participants in this conference. This is the version of February 16, 1969.

2. Throughout this paper I use italics to cite forms in conventional orthographies, surrounding brackets to cite transcriptions, which are to be taken as phonetic except where the context makes it clear that a more abstract representation is intended. My phonetic transcriptions are not uniform, being rather narrow for features under discussion, broad in other respects. In particular, I do not mark many distinctions of quality and quantity in vowels.

3. Auxiliary Contraction is related to the rule VVR discussed in Section 4 below, although the nature of the association is still unclear to me.

4. For discussion of the = boundary see Chomsky and Halle 1968. Names like *Canby* (with assimilation only in fast speech) must be treated as containing a # boundary associated with the formative *-by* (appearing also in *Whitby*, with failure of voicing assimilation, and in *Rugby*, with its unusual cluster of voiced obstruents.

5. I propose to demonstrate, on another occasion, that both this rule and the "assimilation" rule operative in words like *affect, support,* and *attest* are not rules of complete assimilation, but rather deletion rules, at least in my dialect.

6. In *hindering* and many similar examples the [ə] is first inserted by rule, then deleted optionally by another rule, in this case Slur. The underlying form of *hinder* does not have a vowel preceding the [r] because *hindrance* has two, not three, syllables in all dialects (compare *dangerous*). Schwa Insertion is required because in many dialects (mine among them) *hinder* and *hindering* have [ər], rather than [r̩], in slow speech.

7. The resultant [yn] cluster in *united* is pronounced [ɲ].

8. But note that there is no obvious phonetic explanation for the condition that the rule does not apply to initial [ə], as in *alembic, aroma, anemic,* and *amusing,* or to [ə] in syllables after the first, as in *Canaletto, paronymic, homiletic,* and *analytic.* However, some of the examples cited in note 13 below can be interpreted as undergoing medial applications of Pre-stress Contraction.

9. The exclusion of the environment before [m] (and [ŋ]) makes it unlikely that Slur is the same rule as Syllabic Resonants, which applies to the sequences [ər əl ən əm əŋ] to yield [r̩ l̩ n̩ m̩ ŋ̩] in such words as *pallor, pedal, bacon, ransom,* and *baking.* There does appear to be some gradation in the operation of Syllabic Resonants, at least to the extent that [ŋ̩] appears in faster speech than the other syllabic resonants, and perhaps that [m̩] appears in faster speech than [r̩ l̩ n̩]. I have not yet made a systematic investigation of these matters.

10. Kenyon and Knott (1953) give palatals for all of these words, but many speakers have clusters in fairly slow speech.

11. I know of but one exception, *wintry.*

12. In many British dialects Slur applies to the words in (19b) and (19c) as well as to those in (19a). These dialects also reduce (and subsequently delete) the penultimate vowel in words like *legendary, imaginary,* and *secondary,* which cannot have reduced vowels in my dialect, and in many of the words in (20) and (22) below.

13. The words *probably, mathematics,* and *vaudeville* are subject to an exceptional deletion of [ə], in the case of *probably* and *vaudeville* before an obstruent and in the case of *mathematics* before [m] followed by a stressed vowel. Note that the corresponding reduction of *probable* is unacceptable. C.-J. Bailey has pointed out to me that various dialects syncopate [ə] *following* [r l], in words like *America, orange, Carolina, guarantee, caramel, Phila-*

delphia, skeleton, Europe (the relevant examples differ from dialect to dialect), none of which are reducible in my speech except at high speeds.

14. The word *iron* has no form with nonsyllabic [r] in my speech. Thus, in slow speech I have a contrast between *irony*, "like iron," [áyṛniy] and the figure of speech *irony* [áyrəniy] (although the contrast is eliminated in fast speech by the application of Ruh-reduction to the latter form). *Iron* then requires either the obligatory application of Ruh-reduction or else the unusual underlying representation /īVrn/.

15. For the appearance of the feature *coronal* in (26a), see Chomsky and Halle 1968: 304. The reduction of *mirror* and similar forms indicates that (26b) is not restricted by occurrences of # in the way that (26a) is. Note that the rule Syllabic Resonants mentioned in note 9 might be treated essentially as the mirror image of (26).

16. In a few cases the second [r] is deleted instead of the first, as in *interpret* [intṛpit], where the first [r] is stressed and the second unstressed.

17. In examples like *burial, Albanian, criterion, geranium,* and *linoleum,* VVR does not apply, because the extension of Gliding applies first, changing [iyə] to [yə].

18. Except in a few words like *diamond* and *diaper,* where VVR is obligatory for me.

19. Words like *tentful* and *Pitman* (also *saltpeter,* with [l], and *cartful,* with [r]) do not have acceptable variants without a medial stop, in my speech. What happens is that a Glottalization rule replaces [t] by [ʔ] in these words, yielding [tẽʔfl̩] and [píʔmm̩]. Glottalization (which also applies to [t] in *mountain* and *mutton* and to [p] in *popbottle*) must therefore precede the processes of variation with transitional stops, if the latter are to be blocked. Glottalization is much more extensive in some dialects, Scots English for one, than it is in mine.

20. An extension of Glottalization applies to *damp* and *junk* in very fast speech, even before vowels and in phrase-final position, to yield [dæ̃ʔ] and [jÃʔ], which cannot be further reduced. Glottalization applies to [t] as well as [p k]: note [kæ̃ʔ] for *can't* in fast speech. The reduced versions of words like *went* [wen] cannot be considered as resulting from Glottalization followed by a [ʔ]-deletion rule, for two reasons: (a) [d] drops in the same environments as [t], but has no intermediate form [ʔ], and (b) after the operation of Glottalization, original [p t k] have fallen together as [ʔ] and cannot be distinguished in the operation of a putative [ʔ]-deletion rule, which nevertheless would have to drop [ʔ] from original [t] but not from [k p].

21. William Labov has pointed out that in some Black English dialects the rule is extended to the past tense ending as well.

22. Dentdel, or a rule having a similar effect, is obligatory in words like *fasten, soften, hasten,* and *moisten.*

23. Final [d] remains, and final [t] is replaced by [ʔ] in very fast speech (see notes 19 and 20 above).

24. In my wife's dialect the [y] is preserved except after [s r l]. This treatment of the [y] involves a principle separate from the hierarchy in (5),

namely the functioning of [s] with [r] as continuants, in opposition to the stops, both oral and nasal.

25. Also [g d b]. Foley's hierarchy in (1) is ordered by sonority, presumably on the basis that the most sonorous stops, the voiced velars, are most likely to drop when surrounded by the maximally sonorous segments, vowels (especially stressed vowels). Note Fletcher's values for "phonetic power" cited by Jakobson, Fant, and Halle 1961: 28).

26. A complicating factor is the treatment of initial [ð], which is affected by Glide Deletion in approximately the same way as [w].

27. Hans Hock has called my attention to a number of difficult cases in the development of various Indo-European languages. The common feature of Hock's examples is the exclusion of one nasal from a larger class containing the other nasal and the liquids. Presumably, principles other than the one discussed in this paper are to be invoked, although these matters are by no means clear. An apparent, rather than real, difficulty is the Latin rule assimilating the [n] of con- to a following resonant, a rule sometimes said (as in Hale and Buck 1966: 25) to apply before nasals and [r] but not before [l]; as Eric Hamp and C.-J. Bailey have pointed out to me, what appears to be the case is that new formations with con-, with no assimilation only at first (regardless of whether [r] or [l] followed), were made at different periods in the history of Latin.

REFERENCES

Bach, Emmon. 1968. Two proposals concerning the simplicity metric in phonology. *Glossa* 2: 128-49.

Chomsky, Noam, and Morris Halle. 1968. *The Sound Pattern of English.* New York: Harper and Row.

Greenberg, Joseph H. 1963. Some universals of grammar with particular reference to the order of meaningful elements. *Universals of Language,* Joseph H. Greenberg, ed., pp. 58-90. Cambridge: M.I.T. Press.

Hale, William G., and Carl D. Buck. 1966. *A Latin Grammar.* University, Ala.: University of Alabama Press. Reprint of 1903 edition.

Halle, Morris. 1962. Phonology in generative grammar. *Word* 18: 54-72.

Jakobson, Roman. 1968. *Child Language, Aphasia and Phonological Universals.* The Hague: Mouton. Translation by Allan R. Keiler of *Kindersprache, Aphasie und allgemeine Lautgesetze,* 1941.

Jakobson, Roman, C. Gunnar M. Fant, and Morris Halle. 1961. *Preliminaries to Speech Analysis,* 4th printing. Cambridge: M.I.T. Press.

Kenyon, John S., and Thomas A. Knott. 1953. *A Pronouncing Dictionary of American English,* 4th ed. Springfield, Mass.: G. & C. Merriam.

Kiparsky, Paul. 1968. Linguistic universals and linguistic change. *Universals in Linguistic Theory,* Emmon Bach and Robert T. Harms, eds., pp. 170-202. New York: Holt, Rinehart and Winston.

Ladefoged, Peter. 1967. Linguistic phonetics. *Working papers in phonetics, 6.* Phonetics Laboratory, University of California, Los Angeles.

Ross, John Robert, 1967. Gapping and the order of constituents. Paper presented at the 10th International Congress of Linguists, Bucharest.

Williamson, Kay. 1965. *A Grammar of the Kolokuma Dialect of Ịjọ.* West African language monographs, 2. Cambridge: Cambridge University Press.

Zwicky, Arnold. 1969. English contractions: interactions between syntax and phonology. The Ohio State University. Dittoed.